DOLL READER

Make & Dress

Volume III

Edited by Virginia Ann Heyerdahl

Article Reprints

Published By Hobby House Press Cumberland, Maryland 21502

Additional copies of this book may be purchased at $14.95
from
HOBBY HOUSE PRESS, INC.
900 Frederick Street
Cumberland, Maryland 21502-1298
or from your favorite bookstore or dealer.
Please add $3.30 per copy for postage.

Doll Reader® **Make and Dress, Volume III,** is a compendium of articles which have been previously published in **Doll Reader** magazine. The research and publication of this book was not sponsored in any way by the manufacturers of the dolls, doll costumes or accessories mentioned in the articles.
© 1991 by Hobby House Press, Inc.

Introduction

Following the success of **Volumes I** and **II** of **Doll Reader**®
Make and Dress, Hobby House Press, Inc., is pleased to publish
Doll Reader Make and Dress, Volume III, a compilation of
outstanding making and dressing articles appearing in previous
issues of **Doll Reader**® magazine. We feel these articles will
prove to be invaluable aids to both the doll maker and the doll
costumer.

This volume is divided into two main chapters: Doll Dressing and Doll Making. In the first chapter, Doll Dressing, there
are four sections containing 24 articles which include patterns
for costuming both your antique and modern dolls. There are
patterns for outfits to fit china dolls, Schoenhuts, cloth, babies,
bisque and fashions dolls as well as others. The Costuming Aids
section will provide designing, sewing and other tips to enable
you to more easily and professionally complete your projects. A
frilly bonnet pattern is given in the Bonnets and Hats section
and the Accessories section provides instructions on making
doll jewelry and socks as well as other items of interest.

The second chapter, on Doll Making, is divided into four
sections containing a total 14 articles to assist you in all phases
of making dolls. The Porcelain Dolls section guides you in
cleaning your greenware to sculpting original portrait dolls and
making the mold of your portrait head. The Cloth Dolls section
includes six patterns for making dolls out of cloth while a Pantin
paper doll project comes under the Other Media section. Finally there are patterns for a variety of doll bodies in the Doll
Bodies section.

We feel that the variety of making and dressing articles
presented here will appeal to all segments of the doll costuming
and doll making population. We hope you will continue to
enjoy the doll making and costuming articles that appear in
Doll Reader magazine and if you do not already subscribe, we
invite you to do so in order to further your enjoyment of making
and dressing your dolls.

Virginia Ann Heyerdahl
Editor — April 1991

Gary R. Ruddell
Publisher — April 1991

TABLE OF CONTENTS

DOLL DRESSING:

SEWING FOR YOUR DOLLS:

Popular Textile Prints 1770 to 1790

by **Kathleen Songal**

Many dollers love to execute doll dresses reminiscent of the Marie Antoinette, Martha Washington and Thomas Gainsborough time period. Fortunately, today, many fine authentic looking doll patterns are commercially available in these styles. However, in order to achieve a completely accurate costume, it is important that the selected fabric be researched as carefully as the dress pattern itself.

This study will concern itself with printed cotton fabrics that were commonly used for dresses between the years 1770 to 1790. Although silks were definitely worn during this period, cotton fabrics gained particular popularity during the latter quarter of the 18th century and, therefore, deserve a special detailed presentation all their own.

Both the wealthy and the average working class wore dresses made of **calico. Calico** was the broad term when used to describe all woven cotton fabrics (often with a mixture of linen) that were printed, sometimes painted, in colorful designs. After studying many books on the subject,[1] it became apparent that calico designs fell into a number of distinct categories, ranging from very simple designs used for dress linings and servants' wear to expensive patterns that were intricately detailed. Only the single common denominator of color linked all of these designs. This fact became increasingly obvious after viewing numerous orignial printed and painted fabric samples. Color as produced in the available madder colors of the day were unmistakable, and must be one of the chief considerations used when selecting fabric.

If the colors are not right, even if the design is suitable, the fabric should not be used.

Illustration 1. French fashion plate from the *Galerie des Modes,* 1780, illustrating a caraco a la poloñaise with a **vermicelli** pattern on calico.

6

Due to the dying technology then in use, colors used in 18th century textile printing were restricted to a limited number of hues. (See *Illustration 2.*) Lighter and darker values of these same hues helped broaden the spectrum, as did the addition of black and brown. Green was produced by the time-consuming method of hand painting (penciling) blue over yellow. The simplest prints, of course, were monotones. At the other end of the scale, the most elaborate polychromes consisted of three reds, two purples, blue and yellow; these colors were further blended to produce green, crimson, orange, buff, olive and chocolate.

The next important consideration in selecting an appropriate dress fabric is pattern design. Some of the most common categories were:

1. **Trailing Florals** were represented by twisting meandering vines, usually of a fine line, that produced flowers, berries, fruit and leaves. The simplest of these designs were executed in one color. The more elaborate patterns were printed with a red and/or black outline and filled in with additional colors. (See *Illustration 3,* Figures 1 and 8.)

2. **Scattered Bouquets** consisted of all sizes and types of flowers from forget-me-nots to roses of a natural size. (See *Illustration 3,* Figure 2.)

3. **Vertical Stripes** were of equal or varying widths having their spaces filled in with (a) solid colors, (b) serpentining foliage, (c) twisting ribbons or (d) geometric shapes. (See *Illustration 3,* Figure 3.)

4. **Geometric Prints** included polka dots, diamonds and other assorted figures. These figures could appear either (a) in color on a white background or (b) in white on a colored background (resist dying). (See *Illustration 3.* Figure 4.)

5. **Stylized Objects** were arranged in rows often having (a) a vertically striped background, (b) a geometric frame about the object or (c) a plain background. (See *Illustration 3,* Figure 5.)

6. **Toile Prints** depicted scenes of people that told a story. Greek mythology, significant historical events and pastoral scenes were popular motifs. Most toiles were produced in monotones of sepia, blue, purple or red and were of

Illustration 2. These colors duplicate as closely as possible some of the most popular color hues used on original 18th century calicoes.

OPPOSITE PAGE: Illustration 3. These contemporary fabric swatches have all been recently purchased from local fabric stores. They have been chosen for their appropriate scale, authentic looking colors and for pattern designs that most closely resemble original 18th century prints. Please note that the bold names given these fabric patterns are of the author's creation and not the manufacturer's.
Figure 1. **Trailing Florals** by Cranston Print Works Co. Figure 2. **Scattered Bouquets** by Cranston Print Works Co. Figure 3. **Vertical Stripes** by Ameritex. Figure 4. **Geometric Prints** by R. J. R. Figure 5. **Stylized Objects** by Beachwood. Figure 6. **Toile Prints** by Marcus Brothers. Figure 7. **Tracery** by (unknown). Figure 8. **Fine Pin Dots** by R. J. R. (Color added with felt tip pens.) Figure 9. **Vermicelli** by Concord for Joan Kessler.

very high craftsmanship. (See *Illustration 3.* Figure 6.)

Finally the backgrounds, themselves, for these designs often varied. While white and natural colored backgrounds were the most popular choice, dark grounds of black, dark red and brown were not unusual. Still other fancy backgrounds consisted of tracery, fine pin dots and vermicelli.

7. **Tracery** resembled fine threadlike vines. Most often **Trailing Florals** and **Scattered Bouquets** were executed over this backdrop. (See *Illustration 3,* Figure 7.)

8. **Fine Pin Dots,** also called sable or sanded background, were another popular choice. (See *Illustration 3,* Figure 8.)

9. **Vermicelli** patterns were characterized by bumpy worm-like shapes arranged in swirling patterns. (See *Illustration 3,* Figure 9 and *Illustration 1.)*

Of course, the story of pattern design and color used on 18th century calicoes cannot be entirely capsulated into just one short discourse, but it is

hoped that these basic guidelines will help the doll dressmaker develop a better degree of discrimination when selecting a printed fabric to be used on a circa 1770 to 1790 dress. □

[1]Books consulted:
British Textile Design in the Victoria and Albert Museum. Tokyo: Gakken, 1980. *Vol. II, Rococo to Victorian (1750-1850).*

Clouzot, Henri, and Morris, Frances. *Painted and Printed Fabrics.* New York: Metropolitan Museum of Art, 1927.

Little, Francis. *Early American Textiles,* New York: Century, 1931.

Montgomery, Florence. *Printed Textiles: English and American Cottons and Linens, 1700-1850.* New York: Viking, 1970.

Nylander, Jane C. *Fabrics for Historic Buildings.* Washington, D.C.: The Preservation Press, 1983.

Pettit, Florence H. *America's Printed and Painted Fabrics, 1600-1900.* New York: Hastings House, 1970.

Body Shapes -- or -- Why Doesn't That Pattern Fit?

by **Joan Chiara**

Have you ever purchased a lovely pattern to costume your doll, only to find that when the gown was completed, it did not fit the doll you intended it for? Your doll may be 12in (30.5cm) tall with a lady's figure; and you purchased a pattern for a 12in (30.5cm) doll with a lady figure. Why doesn't it fit? Is your doll like one of these sketches in *Illustrations 3, 4, 5* or *6*? The pattern may have been originally designed for a doll shown in *Illustration 5*, and you may have wanted it to fit a doll as shown in *Illustration 3*.

Normally, commercial pattern companies of the past 40 or so odd years have given a fair amount of detail on their pattern envelopes, along with pictures of the dolls wearing the outfits. Their patterns will state, "This pattern will fit all 11½ inch teen fashion dolls such as *Barbie, Christie, Cher* and *Candi*" (or whatever particular dolls they are meant for). If they do not mention the specific trade name of the doll you plan to dress, you can judge from the pictures on the pattern envelope if the figure is the same or similar to your doll; or if you can make adjustments easily.

When buying doll costume patterns by mail, finished professional pictures of the specific doll in the outfit are not always available. The primary concern of doll costume designers such as myself, is in giving the customer as detailed a picture of the costume itself, as possible. In this instance, one must rely on a knowledge of doll figures and sizes, and the description given in the catalog or list from which you are ordering, to enable you to decide on the proper pattern for your doll.

The sketches (*Illustrations 1* through *12*) show a variety of body shapes in four sizes. If you ordered a pattern for any of these four doll heights, the pattern may only fit one of the body shapes shown in that particular size group.

Perhaps these illustrations along with the suggestions below will help doll seamstresses check out the patterns purchased in the future.

If patterns are not specifically identified (other than the doll's height), follow these five simple suggestions in ordering and sewing:

1. If you see a pattern that you think will fit your doll, but you are unsure -- ask the person who designed the pattern for the name and shape of the doll she made that specific pattern to fit. If necessary, request measurements of the chest (or bust), waist and hips.

2. If you are unsure of the type of patterns or the size range that they cover, write the designer a brief description of the doll you want to dress and give specific details and measurements of your doll, such as: 20in (50.8cm) china head doll with a straw-like stuffed muslin body in a lady figure. Her body measurements are (give bust, waist and hip dimensions), and she has china lower arms and lower legs; however, they are exceptionally thin for her proportions. She also has a protruding derriere.

Notice that any unusual features in the doll's shape are mentioned, because

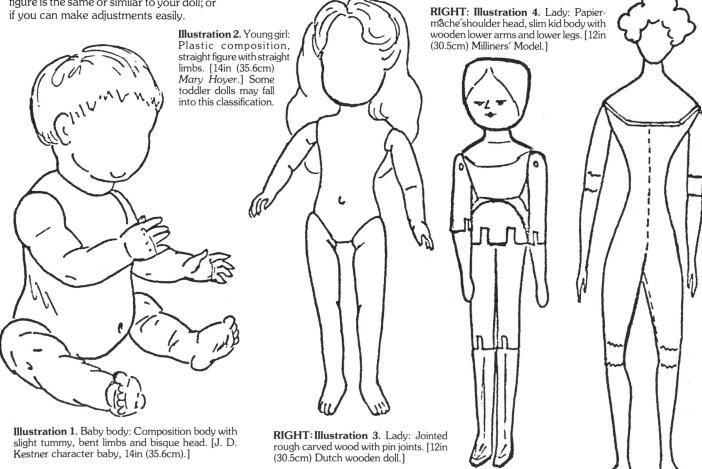

Illustration 2. Young girl: Plastic composition, straight figure with straight limbs. [14in (35.6cm) *Mary Hoyer.*] Some toddler dolls may fall into this classification.

RIGHT: Illustration 4. Lady: Papier-mâché shoulder head, slim kid body with wooden lower arms and lower legs. [12in (30.5cm) Milliners' Model.]

Illustration 1. Baby body: Composition body with slight tummy, bent limbs and bisque head. [J. D. Kestner character baby, 14in (35.6cm).]

RIGHT: Illustration 3. Lady: Jointed rough carved wood with pin joints. [12in (30.5cm) Dutch wooden doll.]

this could mean quite a big difference in the way one pattern will fit this china doll in comparison to another pattern. It could also determine if specific pieces on the pattern can be easily altered to fit the unusually shaped body parts; or if it should necessitate moving up or down one size, or to a completely different style. To be even more accurate, I would give the designer the exact measurements of the extra thin limbs, for her convenience in locating the proper pattern.

Most designers of period costumes are familiar with the style each particular type of doll should wear. However, if you want to specify the year of your doll, it could be most helpful.

Before cutting into your good fabric, use an old bed sheet, muslin or other worn non-raveling fabric, and cut the pattern from it. Baste the pieces together and fit on your doll. It is easier to adjust from this, if adjustments are needed, than to ruin (or run out of) the good fabric as a result of re-cutting pieces that do not fit properly.

Use your muslin pieces for your finished pattern (but be sure not to stretch them out of shape).

4. After cutting your good fabric, always baste the garment together first. Then fit it on your doll and adjust any darts or seams where necessary. Many times even a perfect fitting pattern will need adjusting as a result of extra fine or too bulky fabrics.

5. When fitting the garments on your doll, always fit the outer garments over the underwear that the doll will be wearing with that particular outfit. Remember: on dolls, the smallest gather, seam, dart or trim is extra bulk and adds to the measurements.

Here are a few suggestions for identifying costume patterns. These examples immediately identify the maker,

size and shape of the specific doll for which the pattern is intended to fit.

"To fit: 19in (48.3cm) to 21in (53.3cm) jointed kid body, child figure, with derriere, bisque shoulder plate, bisque head, and bisque lower limbs. Originally made for a 20in (50.8cm) Bru Jne." (See *Illustration 11*.)

"To fit the 11½in (29.2cm) *Barbie** size dolls. Most 11½in (29.2cm) to 12in (30.5cm) lady figure dolls made today can wear the *Barbie** size clothes." Figure measurements are similar, with ⅛in (.31cm) to ⅝in (1.6cm) variance in circumferences; and an occasional extra ½in (1.3cm) in height. (See *Illustration 6*.)

Barbie is a copyrighted trademark of Mattel, Inc.

Illustration 6. Lady: Hard or soft vinyl or plastic, or combinations of both. [11½in (29.2cm) to 12in (30.5cm) contemporary fashion dolls such as teen model *Barbie* types.] Although these dolls have a full lady figure, they are referred to as "teen" fashion dolls by the manufacturers.

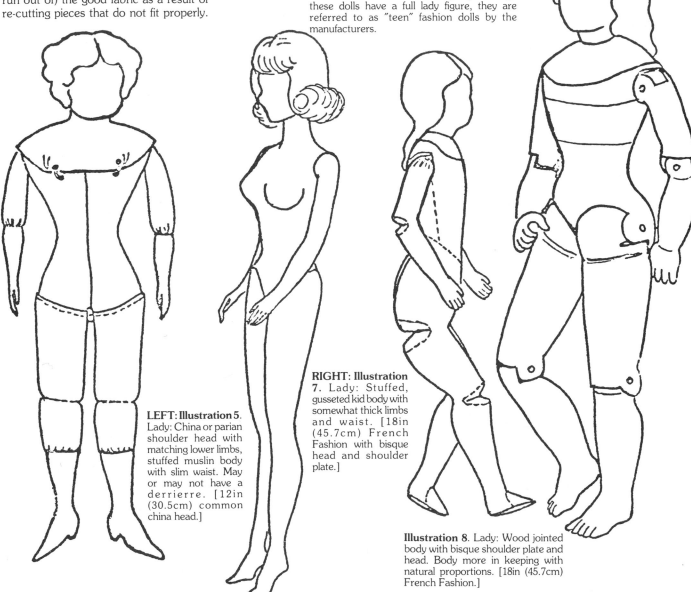

LEFT: Illustration 5. Lady: China or parian shoulder head with matching lower limbs, stuffed muslin body with slim waist. May or may not have a derrierre. [12in (30.5cm) common china head.]

RIGHT: Illustration 7. Lady: Stuffed, gusseted kid body with somewhat thick limbs and waist. [18in (45.7cm) French Fashion with bisque head and shoulder plate.]

Illustration 8. Lady: Wood jointed body with bisque shoulder plate and head. Body more in keeping with natural proportions. [18in (45.7cm) French Fashion.]

Illustration 9. Lady: Hard or soft vinyl or plastic body and head. [18in (45.7cm) Madame Alexander *Cissy*.]

BELOW: Illustration 11. Child: Gusseted kid stuffed body with bisque or wooden lower limbs, and bisque shoulder plate and head. Slimmer French figure of a child. [22in (55.9cm) French *Bru*.]

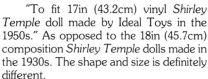

"To fit 17in (43.2cm) vinyl *Shirley Temple* doll made by Ideal Toys in the 1950s." As opposed to the 18in (45.7cm) composition *Shirley Temple* dolls made in the 1930s. The shape and size is definitely different.

"To fit a slim lady figure doll kit with bisque shoulder head, muslin body and bisque lower arms and lower legs. Originally designed to fit the *Miss Detroit* doll by Diana Crosby from the 1970 United Federation of Doll Clubs (UFDC) National Convention." Although this was meant for the *Miss Detroit* doll specifically, it would also fit a reproduction doll kit of similar size and shape, and may, with slight alterations, fit the doll in *Illustration 4*.

"To fit 13in (33.0cm) to 15in (38.1cm) composition body baby doll with bent limbs and bisque head. Originally designed for a 14in (35.6cm) J. D. Kestner character baby doll." (See *Illustration 1*.)

"To fit a 21in (53.3cm) to 23in (58.4cm) child figure ball-jointed German composition body with bisque head. Originally designed to fit a 22in (55.9cm) Heinrich Handwerck doll." (See *Illustration 12*.)

When I have designed a new pattern for a specific doll, and I am aware that, although this doll falls into one of the illustrated categories shown, it may be over-stuffed to a fat appearance, or it may have exceptionally thin arms and legs, I mention this in the pattern description. This notifies the prospective buyer that there is a deviation from the expected standard measurements.

There are many excellent costume pattern designers for dolls today, and although they do not follow the same pattern description procedures as mentioned in this article, it does not mean that their patterns will not fit your dolls. It may mean, however, a bit of correspondence between customer and designer prior to purchasing, in order to clarify measurements and other details. Please, in doing so, be sure to send the designer a self-addressed stamped envelope with all inquiries. For those designers who mail out lists or catalogs, perhaps identifying a specific doll name and measurements in your pattern descriptions will help the potential customer find that perfect fit for her doll.

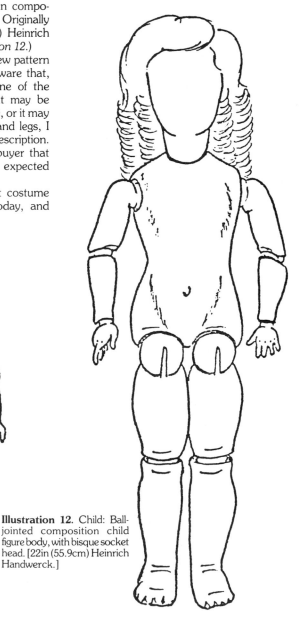

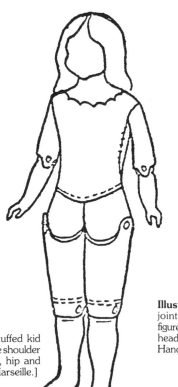

Illustration 10. Child: Pin-jointed stuffed kid body, with bisque lower limbs and bisque shoulder head. Somewhat thick at the elbow, hip and knee joints. [22in (55.9cm) Armand Marseille.]

Illustration 12. Child: Ball-jointed composition child figure body, with bisque socket head. [22in (55.9cm) Heinrich Handwerck.]

Diminutive Dressmaking:
Tips on Sewing for Dolls
by **Marguerite Lyons**

Illustration 1. A Grace Corry Rockwell doll shown wearing an original design by Carol J. Tribble. The pattern and instructions for this dress are included in this article. The dress is made of cotton dotted swiss. The undergarments are of cotton batiste. The ribbon is satin and the lace is cotton. Directions are also included for the bloomers.

Illustration 2. Back view of the Grace Corry Rockwell doll wearing the original design dress as seen in *Illustration 1.*

Editor's Note: The opinions expressed are not commerical endorsements of the Doll Reader™.

It may not take a lot of fabric to make a doll dress, but it does require a heap of patience and talent, keen eyesight and a love of itty-bitty sleeves, teeny-tiny ruffles and itsy-bitsy seams and darts.

Someone who has these talents in great quantity and produces exquisite doll fashions as proof is Carol J. Tribble of upstate New York. A seamstress most of her life, Carol seriously began creating doll clothes only a few years ago. Today a whole upstairs bedroom in her contemporary home is devoted to her diminutive dressmaking. There, tucked neatly away

in dresser drawers and a closet, are the makings of beautiful miniature fashions — fabrics, trims, laces, ribbons and buttons. Shelves also are lined with doll dressmaking books and boxes hold her many doll fashion patterns. And, of course, there is a collection of antique and reproduction bisque dolls modeling Carol's dresses. It is in this setting that Carol creates her highly prized clothes for New England doll artisans.

Each sewing project begins with careful research. Many volumes on doll dressmaking are consulted to determine the correct style, fabrics, trims and colors that would most accurately capture the proper historical nature of the doll she is about to dress.

Carol also gets ideas for dressmaking at museums, doll conventions and auctions. She records what she sees with a camera so ideas can be used later.

Carol, who sews for all kinds of antique, reproduction and new dolls, uses commercial patterns and also creates her own designs. Quite often, she explained, the commercial doll dress patterns are copies of the clothing originally worn by particular dolls. Other patterns offer clothing designs suitable for dolls made during a stated era, or just for baby dolls or lady dolls and little girl and boy dolls.

It should be noted that patterns from any of the commerical companies might have to be altered depending on the size of the doll's body. "A 12in (30.5cm) doll," she explained, "could be a chubby baby doll, a slimmer little girl doll or a shapely thin fashion doll. In addition, the body size for a particular type of doll will vary. For instance, one baby doll will be chunkier than another one, so alterations of the pattern might be necessary."

"If I think I might have to make alterations in the pattern I am using, I trace the pieces onto pattern tracing cloth so the original pieces will still be whole and I can use them later with another doll. I always check around neck and armholes to make sure the dress will fit. If I have to make changes I do it with the traced pieces," she explained. If Carol cannot achieve the look she wants with commercial patterns, she designs her own which she finds very rewarding.

"Materials you use are just as important as patterns," Carol noted. "I always try to use natural fabrics — cottons, fine wools, silks, very fine linens, fine cotton batiste, fine wool challis and fine cotton organdy. The only synthetics I use are the old ones, rayon and acetate. I try very hard to avoid polyester and polyester blends."

She also believes all seams should be 1/4in (.65cm) to avoid jamming the fabric on the sewing machine. "You can always trim the seams to 1/8in (.31cm) when you are finished. Be sure and finish off all seams. I usually zigzag mine or use French seams. I also line clothes a lot so seams do not show at all. I even line sleeves. Use a lightweight fabric for linings."

A fine sewing machine needle should be used when working with the thin delicate fabrics that are needed for doll clothing.

Other tips from Carol included using very thin straight pins for holding material to minimize making holes in the fine fabrics.

Also, it is important that all laces, rosettes, ribbons, bows and so forth be of the right scale for the doll. "Trims, like prints in fabric, must be scaled to match the doll," Carol cautioned. "I use all types of ribbons — rayon, acetate, grosgrain and so forth. I also use nylon laces, cotton laces, even polyester if the look is right. I especially like Swiss and French cotton laces. Much of the new lace is much heavier than the older ones so I prefer using old trims and laces when possible."

Carol uses lots of snaps as closures for her fashions. "They were invented a long time ago and I use them unless I make handmade buttonholes. Machine buttonholes are fine if your machine can make really good ones. I'd rather use the snaps and then sew tiny pearl buttons on the outside. It looks like the dress is really buttoned. Mail order companies offer small buttons," she added.

Finally if the dress is not going together right, put it aside for a while. "Pick it up when things are better," she advised.

Frequently, Carol, who is a certified public accountant by profession, spends up to 80 hours making a complete costume for a doll. But it is worth it because she said, "The clothes bring out the doll's personality. They make her look just right." □

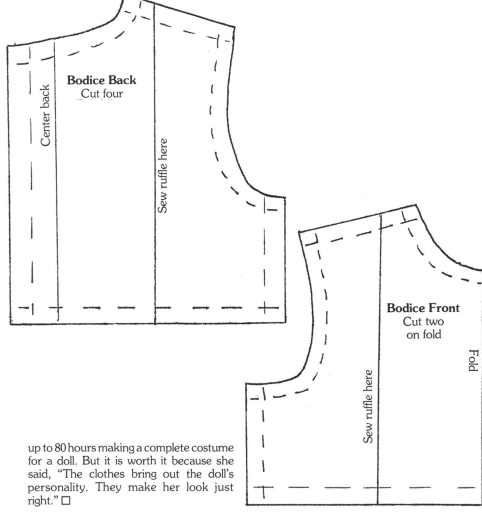

13

13in (33cm) Doll Dress
(9in [22.9cm] French toddler body)
Dress, Slip and Bloomers
by Carol Tribble

Doll measurements:

Head circumference: 9½in (25.2cm) to 10in (25.4cm)

Chest: 7¾in (19.8cm) to 8¼in (21cm)

Waist: 7in (17.8cm) to 7½in (19.1cm)

Hips: 7½in (19.1cm) to 8in (20.3cm)

Crotch depth: Fits up to 7in (17.8cm)

Materials Required

3/8yd (.33m) of fine batiste, dotted swiss, voile, or other for dress

1/4yd (.23m) of fine batiste or nainsook or underwear

20in (50.8cm) of 1in (2.5cm) to 1½in (3.8cm) cotton lace for shoulder ruffles (optional, may use self-fabric ruffles instead)

2yd (1.82m) of 1/2in (1.3cm) cotton lace

24in (61cm) of 1/2in (1.3cm) to 3/4in (2cm) double-faced satin ribbon

2yd (1.82cm) of 1/4in (.65cm) single or double-faced satin ribbon

8 snaps or buttons

1/2yd (.46m) of 1/4in (.65cm) elastic

1/2yd (.46m) of 1/8in (.31cm) elastic

General Instructions

Trim and overcast all raw seam edges or make French seams. Press seams as you go.

Bloomers

Sew center front seam. Sew narrow lace on stitching line on each leg. Turn up fabric on stitching line and press. Lace now extends beyond fabric edge. Turn raw edge under again and stitch close to edge to form casing for 1/4in (.65cm) elastic. Thread elastic through casing to fit doll's leg and secure ends.

Make casings on waistline edge by turning fabric under twice as marked on pattern and stitching close to edge. Thread 1/4in (.65cm) elastic through casing, fit to doll's waist and secure ends.

Sew center back seam and then crotch seams.

Slip

Two of the four pieces cut will be the lining. Sew slip front and back together on side seams. Repeat for lining. Slide lining inside the slip, so right sides are facing each other, matching neckline and armhole edges and seam lines. Stitch around neckline, shoulders and armholes. (NOTE: You may want to use featherweight pellon in shoulders as reinforcement for snaps or buttons.) Trim seam and clip curves, turn and press. Side seams for slip and lining should not be showing and you have a nicely finished edge around the top.

Zigzag bottom edge of slip and lining together. Trim any loose threads of fabric. Turn up narrow hem towards OUTSIDE of slip and press. Cover raw edge with slightly gathered narrow lace and 1/4in (.65cm) ribbon. Lap shoulder edges to fit doll and sew a snap on each shoulder.

Dress

One bodice front and two bodice backs are the lining. Sew shoulder seams. Repeat for lining. Cut 20in (50.8cm) piece of lace into two 10in (25.4cm) pieces. For optional fabric ruffles: Cut two piece of fabric 2½in (6.4cm) wide and 10in (25.4cm) long. Fold each piece of fabric in half lengthwise, WRONG SIDE OUT. Make a narrow seam on long edge, turn and press. Gather and sew to bodice as marked on pattern. By hand, tack narrow ribbon over gathering.

With right sides together sew bodice and lining together on back and neckline edges. (NOTE: You may want to use pellon interfacing on back edges.) Trim seam and clip curves. Turn and press. By hand, whipstitch gathered narrow lace to neckline edge.

Sew lace on sleeve edges as marked on

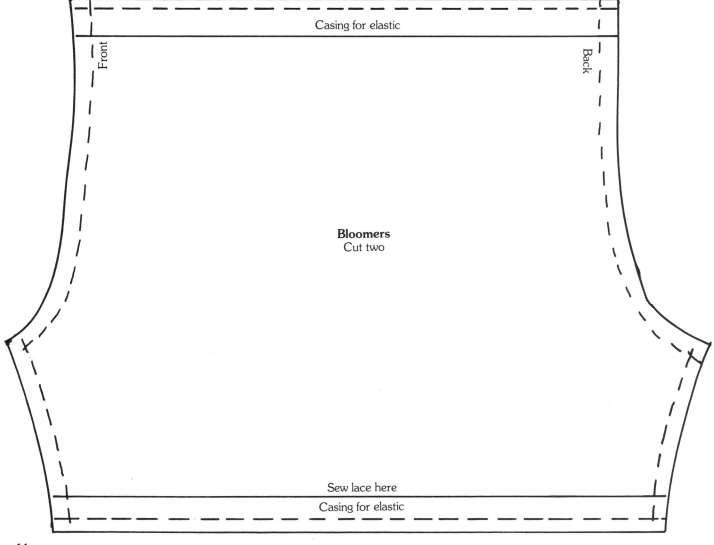

Casing for elastic

Front

Back

Bloomers
Cut two

Sew lace here

Casing for elastic

pattern. Turn up narrow hem, folding fabric twice so that raw edge does not show, but lace extends beyond fabric edge. Press. Using 1/8in (.31cm) elastic, tack at one side of sleeve at stitching line. Zigzag OVER elastic on inside of fabric, stretching it slighlty as you sew (this makes it narrower). You now have formed a casing for the elastic with the zigzag stitching. Pull up elastic to fit doll's upper arm, but allow enough to fit sleeve over doll's hand easily. Secure end. Gather top edge of sleeve to fit armhole. Sew sleeve into armhole of bodice (lining should be left free). Sew underarm and sleeve seam in one continuous seam.

Staystitch around lining armholes. Clip curves and turn raw edge under on stitching line. Sew underarm seam. On BODICE press sleeve-armhole seam allowance towards bodice. Matching bodice armhole seam with folded edge of lining armhole, whipstitch together by hand. Be sure no stitches show on the outside. You now should have no raw edges on the inside of the bodice, except the waistline edge.

To make the skirt, cut one piece of dress fabric 24in (61cm) by 6in (15.2cm). On bottom (along one long edge) and back opening (two short edges) of skirt turn up 1/4in (.65cm) and stitch. Fold back opening edges under again 1/2in (1.3cm) and PRESS. Turn up 1in (2.5cm) hem along bottom edge and blindstitch by hand. Gather top of skirt to fit bodice and stitch — lining should be left loose. Fold lining edge towards inside of bodice, match seam lines and stitch by hand — raw edges of waistline seam allowances are all hidden.

Sew three snaps to bodice back and three on skirt. Tie wide satin ribbon sash in a bow in back. Tack small bows on sleeves.

Hair Ribbons

For headband, cut about an 8in (20.3cm) piece of narrow ribbon to fit over top of doll's head from earlobe to earlobe. Make two puffy bows with 12 to 15 loops of ribbon — it helps if you use a straight pin as the center and make the loops over it. Tack loops together in center and remove pin. Tack bows approximately 3in (7.6cm) apart on the headband.

Dress Skirt: One 24in (61cm) by 6in (15.2cm) piece of fabric.
Optional, fabric ruffles: two 2½in (6.4cm) by 10in (25.4cm) pieces of fabric.

A

Fold

Slip Front and Back
Cut four on fold

Sew lace here

B

A

B

Φ

Gather to fit armhole

Sleeve
Cut two

Sew elastic here

← Sew lace here →

"...And Set on a Bow..." — All About Bows

by **Sylvia Mac Neil**

Drawings by **author**

Photographs by **Richard Cahoon**

Illustration 1. *18in (46cm) unmarked Huret-type fashion doll; wood body with metal hands and joints; pale bisque with an unusual face; replacement wig; blue-gray paperweight eyes, pierced ears; wears an original fawn-colored barège dress lavishly trimmed with rows of pleats, braid and rust taffeta bows.*

Costumes worn by fashion dolls of the mid to late 19th century were ornamented with tucks, insertions, ruches and lace, folds of satin and loops of velvet, rows of poufs and box plaited flounces, festooned by fancy jeweled ornaments and garnished with evanescent little fripperies. One such frippery which found favor with doll couturiers was the bow. These were formed from satin, taffeta or grosgrain ribbon, either tied simply, or constructed with various numbers and lengths of loops and ends. Other bows were made from fabric which matched the dress, or the contrast fabric used for trim. They may have been made by cutting lengths of material, leaving the edges unfinished, then slightly raveling them to give a decorative effect. Some were folded with no raw edges visible, and others were finished with a bias trim.

In reading *The Age of Dolls* by Evelyn, Elizabeth and Dorothy Coleman, the use of bows as a garniture was mentioned often. "The trimming for the apron over-skirt consists of folds, puffs, ruffles, and bows of grosgrain ribbon." "Bind the cloak narrow, and set on a bow of black velvet." "...dressed in an elegant ball costume trimmed with lace and bows of grosgrain ribbon." "Trim the skirt with ruffles and gathered strips of cashmere and on the joining seams set silk ribbons which are tied in a bow behind." "...a rich costume of dotted swiss, trimmed throughout with bands and bows of colored satin and lace edging." "The slashed sleeves are trimmed with folds, bows and lace, and are finished by tulle and lace undersleeves." "The overskirt is caught together in the back with a bow made of mohair and bound with brown satin." "Trim the over-skirt with lace and set a bow of blue satin ribbon on the front." "...sleeves are fin-

Illustration 2. Rust-colored taffeta bows cascade splendidly down the back of this fawn-colored promenade costume.

Illustration 3. The trained skirt flares gracefully as "Solonge" strolls along.

ished with two plaitings and a band and bow of the fancy goods." "The skirt with long train is trimmed in front with ruffles, rolls, and bows of the material." "Cuffs are of a simple shape, merely corded on the edge and decorated with a bow." "Trim the waist with black lace, ruches and bows." "...pockets placed on plain long basques...gathered like old-fashioned reticules, and have a bow for ornament." "...and set on bows of narrow satin ribbon as shown in the illustration."

These bows, viewed more than a century later, having been pressed, crushed and wrinkled, with corners folded back and edges worn, take on an interesting and different look. They no longer resemble the neat and perfect little bows that they started out to be. In order to reproduce these popular trims, let us take a look at some bows which garnish original dresses. The illustrations shown here were made from antique dresses worn by fashion dolls produced in France from 1870 through

the 1880s. Some drawings were made from dolls in the author's collection; others were drawn while visiting museums and expositions, as well as private collections in Europe and America.

The drawings illustrate an entire range of bows which were thoughtfully placed on the costumes. Each bow was carefully designed and executed — none was quickly tied and tacked on haphazardly, merely as a last-minute effort to complete the outfit. Shown are bows used to decorate sleeves and cuffs, necklines, skirts and bustles and trains. Some march jauntily down the front of a costume, while others, such as those in *Illustration 2*, cascade splendidly along the length of a trained skirt.

Thirteen bows of five different types decorate this spectacular costume, as can be seen in *Illustrations 2* and *3*. They are important to the overall trim used on the gown. An unmarked Huret-type fashion doll measuring 18in (46cm) wears this promenade dress of

semi-transparent fabric of wool and silk was originally made in Barèges, France, in the French Pyrenées in the 1850s. It is sometimes printed with floral designs and referred to as Barège de Pyrenées.

"Solange," the fashion doll, wears some interesting accessories which are shown in *Illustration 1*. A small hat of fawn-colored barège. This gauze-like pinky-beige taffeta trimmed with pink feathers, ribbons and a frill of frothy lace peeking out from under the brim, is perched on her head. Earbobs of gold beads and a pearly opalescent bead dangle prettily from her ears, and a gilt and "diamond" pendant hangs from a chain around her neck. She carries a brass mesh purse with a watch set in the mesh, and leans on a brown taffeta parasol with a turned wooden handle. On yes, we can see a couple of bows decorating the hat, and another bow on the parasol handle, but we will save those bows decorating other than dresses for another time.

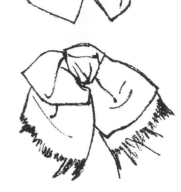

Illustration 4. *Bow of rust-colored taffeta ribbon set on the jacket waistline.*

Illustration 5. *Taffeta bows such as this decorate the side pleats on the train.*

Illustration 6. *These two different bows are on the overskirt.*

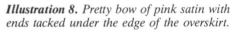

Illustration 8. *Pretty bow of pink satin with ends tacked under the edge of the overskirt.*

Illustration 7. *Three bows like these are set on the train. Note the opposite placement of loops and ends.*

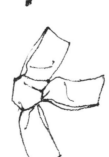

Illustration 9. *These two bows of ivory satin trim draping on a skirt.*

Eleven of the 13 bows found on the barège dress are on the back. The first is on the jacket, three are set on the overskirt and another three on the center pleat of the train. Four other bows are set at a slight angle on the side pleats of the train. Bows 12 and 13 are on the sleeve trim. Strangely enough, not one bow is to be found on the front of the costume! This is surely unimportant, and we can easily forgive the modiste for this omission when the back view is so wonderful.

All of the bows on this barège costume are constructed of rust-colored taffeta ribbon in two different widths and tacked together in back with tiny stitches, rather than tied. The first bow, shown in *Illustration 4*, is the one placed at the center of the waistline of the jacket. It has two loops on the left, and two ends cut at an angle, pointing out at the right side.

The bow shown in *Illustration 5* is a classic bow with two loops and two ends cut at an angle. Four such bows, set at a slight angle as shown, are placed at the side pleats of the train, on the top of a row of pleated trim.

Two bows are set on the pleated trim on the sleeves. They are similar to the bow in *Illustration 5*, except the ends are cut quite short.

The top two bows on the overskirt are different. They have only two loops — and no ends. The third bow has two

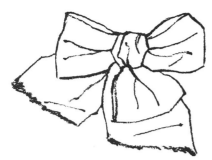

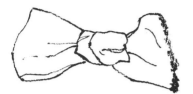

Illustration 10. *Pink taffeta bow with three loops and ends pointing upward.*

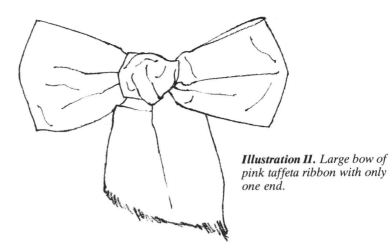

Illustration 11. *Large bow of pink taffeta ribbon with only one end.*

Illustration 12. *Bow with only one loop and one end pointing upward.*

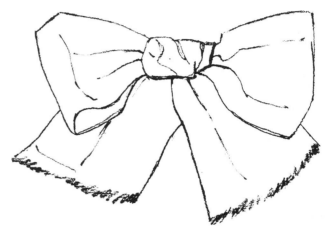

Illustration 13. *Large classic bow of pink taffeta ribbon.*

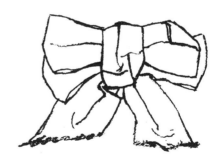

Illustration 14. *Bow of aqua taffeta ribbon with double loops and two long ends.*

Illustration 15. *Similar to bow in* Illustration 14 *but with short ends.*

---

loops, two ends, with the loop on the left being quite short. See *Illustration 6.*

Illustration 7 shows the last type of bow used on this dress, which decorates the train. Each bow has one loop and one end on each side. The top bow in the illustration shows a loop on the left with a longer end underneath. The right side of the bow is made just the opposite — the end is short on the top, and a longer loop is underneath.

The second bow in this illustration shows the same kind of bow, but the placement of the loops and ends is the exact opposite. A third bow, like the bow at the top, is placed near the hemline. Leave it to the Parisian dressmakers! However, it is details such as these unique bows which give that distinctive touch.

The bow in *Illustration 8* is made from pale pink satin ribbon and decorates the overskirt of a soft rose taffeta dress. Bias strips of the same shade of pink satin trim the costume. One bias band edges the overskirt which dips up at each side and is accented by the delightful bow shown here. It is constructed, not tied. There are two loops

on each side with two long ends hanging down. The bow is placed on the overskirt, close to the bottom edge. The two ends, bottom edges cut at a sharp angle, are tacked underneath the overskirt and fall prettily from behind the lace, lending a different and charming touch.

The next two bows, shown in *Illustration 9*, are found on a lavishly trimmed gown of pale pink brocade. These two bows, both constructed from ivory satin ribbon, are the only bows on the outfit. The one on the left has two short loops which face up, while two

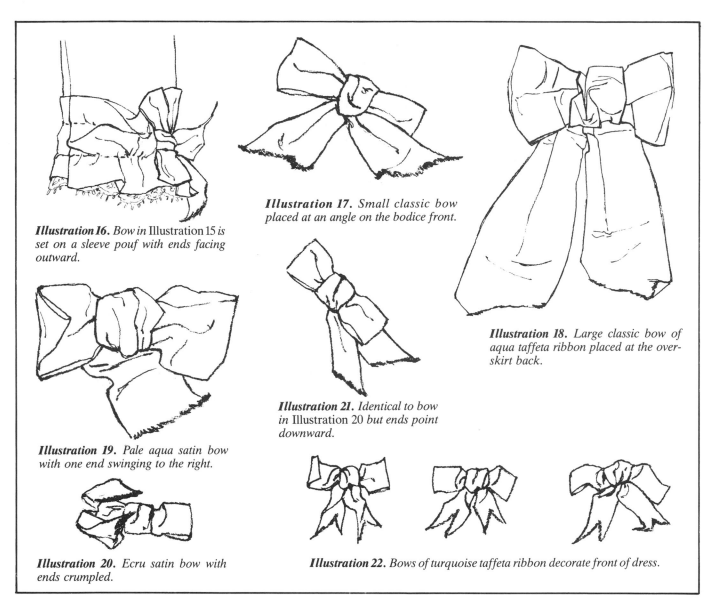

Illustration 16. *Bow in* Illustration 15 *is set on a sleeve pouf with ends facing outward.*

Illustration 17. *Small classic bow placed at an angle on the bodice front.*

Illustration 18. *Large classic bow of aqua taffeta ribbon placed at the over-skirt back.*

Illustration 19. *Pale aqua satin bow with one end swinging to the right.*

Illustration 21. *Identical to bow in* Illustration 20 *but ends point downward.*

Illustration 20. *Ecru satin bow with ends crumpled.*

Illustration 22. *Bows of turquoise taffeta ribbon decorate front of dress.*

longer loops and two ends hang down. The edges of the long ends are cut at an angle and both face the same direction. This bow is placed on the left side of the front skirt panel, at the edge of a bias skirt draping which is higher on this side, dropping down low on the right side, to a skirt ruffle which trims the hemline. The bow on the right in the illustration, formed by three loops facing up and to the left, is set at the point where the bottom of the draping meets the ruffle.

Illustrations 10, 11, 12 and *13* show an assortment of pink taffeta bows which are carefully placed on an outfit made from a sheer white cotton organdy. Three different widths of the same type of ribbon were used. Each bow is constructed and tacked together. The first drawing, *Illustration 10*, is of a pretty little bow made of three loops, the third of which points upward, as do the two ends, which are cut at a gentle angle. Three of these bows decorate the front bodice closure. One is placed at

the neckline, one at the midriff and the last is slightly below the waist. Two identical bows are set on the lace edging at the bottom of the three-quarter-length sleeves. The ends of these two bows face downward, rather than up as the other bows. The large bow in *Illustration 11* is placed at the bottom edge of the bodice, directly beneath the three smaller bows. It has two large loops, each facing to the side, and only one end, cut on a gentle angle, falling downward.

The bows in *Illustrations 12* and *13* trim the skirt. *Illustration 13* shows a rather simple bow, classic in style. It is formed of two loops and two ends, both facing down. This bow is the largest of all ten bows decorating the dress. Two such bows are set on the train, one low on the hipline and the other below this on the small fan-shaped section of the train which flares out behind. Two last bows, made as shown in *Illustration 12*, are placed on the seam line of the skirt back and side back sections. Set on top

of lace that heads a hemline ruffle, they have one loop and one end, pointing upwards as shown in the drawing. A simple dress could be made into a stunning outfit by utilizing the variety and number of bows shown in these illustrations.

The bows shown in the next four illustrations are made from aqua taffeta ribbon and decorate a costume made from aqua and creme striped cotton. Each bow is constructed from separate pieces of ribbon tacked onto a scrap of buckram, forming the loops, knot and the ends. *Illustration 14* shows the bow which is placed at the neckline. It has two loops on each side; two very long ends fall down the front, one slightly longer than the other, both cut at sharp angles pointed in the same direction. The bow in *Illustration 15* is virtually the same bow with short ends. It is placed vertically on the ruching at the sleeve edge, ends facing out, as shown in *Illustration 16*. A very similar bow is shown in *Illustration 17*, but this bow

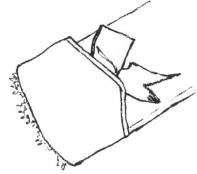

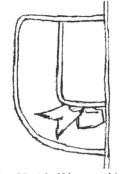

Illustration 23. *This bow decorates a box pleat at the back.*

Illustration 24. *A half-bow tucked under the cuff.*

Illustration 25. *A half-bow peeking out from a pocket.*

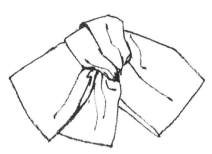

Illustration 26. *Ivory satin bow with one loop and one end facing downward.*

Illustration 27. *Different placement of bows which are identical to bow in* Illustration 26.

Illustration 28. *Bow with only two long loops falling gracefully downward.*

Illustration 29. *Six bows like these garnish the front of a princess dress.*

---

has only two loops, one on each side. This bow is placed at an angle on the bodice front at the waistline on the right side. A second bow, facing left, is placed on the left side. The last bow in this group is the very large bow in *Illustration 18*, which is placed on the center of the overskirt in back. The long ends fall gently over the folds of the skirt, adding a simple but effective touch.

The bow in *Illustration 19* is made from a very pale aqua satin ribbon. Two such bows are placed in the center, one above the other, on the front skirt section of a costume made from pale aqua taffeta. It is constructed of two loops and one end only, which swings to the right side. *Illustration 20* shows a bow made from ecru satin ribbon, found on the same outfit. This bow has two loops and two ends, both pointing up. One bow is placed at the bottom edge of each sleeve. It is set perfectly straight up and down, and the ends and top loop have folded and crumpled somewhat. The next bow, shown in *Illustration 21*,

shows an identical bow, but the two ends point downward on this one. This bow is set at a slight angle, as indicated in the drawing, and is placed at the neckline. The use of bows is somewhat unusual on this costume, since they are made from two different colors of ribbon — pale aqua on the skirt and ecru on the bodice.

Three kinds of bows made from turquoise taffeta ribbon garnish a child fashion's dress of dark blue velveteen, and are seen in *Illustrations 22* through *25*. Five bows like the ones in *Illustration 22* are placed down the center front closure — the first is at the neckline and the last one is at the edge of a row of kilt pleats at the hemline. Each bow is tied, unlike all the previous bows shown which are constructed and tacked together. The bow is classic in design, with two loops and two ends which are cut in two long points. *Illustration 23* shows another tied bow, decorating a box pleat at the back of the dress. *Illustrations 24* and *25* show yet another

type of bow — a half-bow, actually, which is set under the cuff and at the bottom edge of a pocket. These bows have only one loop and one end, and create a different treatment for trimming a pocket and a cuff.

The next three illustrations show two different bows made from ivory satin ribbon which are found on a princess style dress of creme lightweight wool. The bow in *Illustration 26* is constructed of one loop and one end, both of which face down. Four of these bows decorate the front closure and, as on the previous dress, the top one is at the neckline, and the bottom one is near the hemline. *Illustration 27* shows two identical bows, but placed at a different angle with the ends pointing to the right and to the left. Two of these bows are placed at each side back panel, on the seam line of the side back and back sections. The bow shown in *Illustration 28* is placed near the hemline of the demi-train, just above a ruffle. This bow is constructed of two long

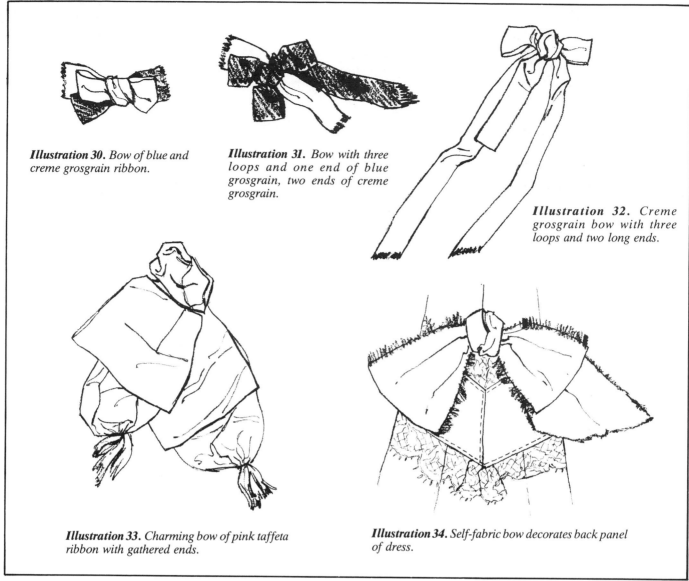

Illustration 30. Bow of blue and creme grosgrain ribbon.

Illustration 31. Bow with three loops and one end of blue grosgrain, two ends of creme grosgrain.

Illustration 32. Creme grosgrain bow with three loops and two long ends.

Illustration 33. Charming bow of pink taffeta ribbon with gathered ends.

Illustration 34. Self-fabric bow decorates back panel of dress.

loops falling gracefully downward from the knot. Both types of bows on this dress are quite simple, but so very effective when used in the quantity and placement described.

The bows in *Illustration 29* decorate the front of a princess style gown made from lime green taffeta. The bows are constructed of the same green taffeta fabric, cut on the bias and folded to form a tube with the seam on one of the folded edges. Each bow has three loops facing down from the knot. Six bows are positioned from the neckline to the hemline of the front closure.

Illustrations 30 and *31* show two bows which are found on another princess style dress. This dress is made from a medium blue lightweight wool and is trimmed with bows constructed of creme and blue grosgrain ribbons. The bow in *Illustration 30* has two loops and one end, cut straight on the edge, of the creme ribbon, and one loop and one shorter end, also cut straight, of the blue ribbon. Three of these bows are

set on the front panel of the dress. The first is midway between the lace-trimmed neckline and the waist, the next is at the waistline, and the third bow is placed just below the hips and above three rows of lace which edge the hemline. *Illustration 31* shows another bow of the two ribbons. This bow has three loops and one long end of the blue grosgrain, and two ends, one medium length and one short, of the creme ribbon. The edges of these ends are also cut straight. One of these bows is placed on the bottom of the lace-trimmed three-quarter-length sleeves. The combination of the two colors, and the rather long ends, add a nice touch to the simple sleeves.

The blue princess dress also has a matching circular cape with a hood. It is trimmed with feather stitching along all the edges and lace at the neckline. The bow shown in *Illustration 32* is made of creme grosgrain and is placed at the point of the hood. It consists of three loops, one which is quite long, and two

long ends, both cut at a sharp angle and both facing the same direction. This bow hangs prettily down the back of the cape.

The remainder of the drawings show various large bows which decorate the back of a dress. Some are made from self-fabric, others from ribbon. Each is different, and each is effective.

A very charming bow is shown in *Illustration 33*. It is placed on the hipline at the back of a princess style dress made of white dotted swiss. This bow is constructed of pink taffeta ribbon with two loops and two ends, all hanging down. The bottom edge of each end is fringed, then tied tightly together to form a tassel, a unique touch to the only bow on this costume.

The bow in *Illustration 34* is found on a princess style dress for a fashion doll representing a young lady. The dress is made from a blue-green taffeta, and the bow is of the same material. A strip of fabric was cut on the straight of the goods, with the edges raveled. The

Illustration 35. Simple bow of ivory satin ribbon with loops and ends falling downward.

Illustration 36. Self-fabric bow with one loop and two wide ends.

two loops — one a bit shorter than the other, and the end are made from one strip of fabric. The center is folded and pinched, then tacked onto a piece of buckram. The knot is separate and tacked on top. The entire bow droops downward slightly. It is placed just above a pretty V-shaped decoration at the hipline of the center back seam.

The ivory satin bow in *Illustration 35* is quite simple. It is set at the back draping of an overskirt on a costume of plum-colored taffeta. It is a bow which

has been tied, with two long loops and two long ends, the edges cut at a sharp angle and both face the same direction. The loops and ends are tacked together just under the knot, to make them fall downward gracefully.

The next bow, shown in *Illustration 36*, is set at the back of the waistline of an overskirt. The costume is made of turquoise taffeta, trimmed with bias bands of white satin. The bow is made of self-fabric, cut on the straight. It is then folded in half and stitched, the

seam being at one of the folded edges. This bow is constructed of separate pieces, all tacked together at the back. It consists of one loop and two ends, cut straight across and raveled slightly, and of course, a large knot at the top.

The bow shown in *Illustration 37* is placed at the waistline of an overskirt, with the bottom edge of the jacket just covering the top of the bow. The outfit is a lovely dark turquoise faille, trimmed with garnitures of self-fabric — rows of kilt-pleated ruffles with

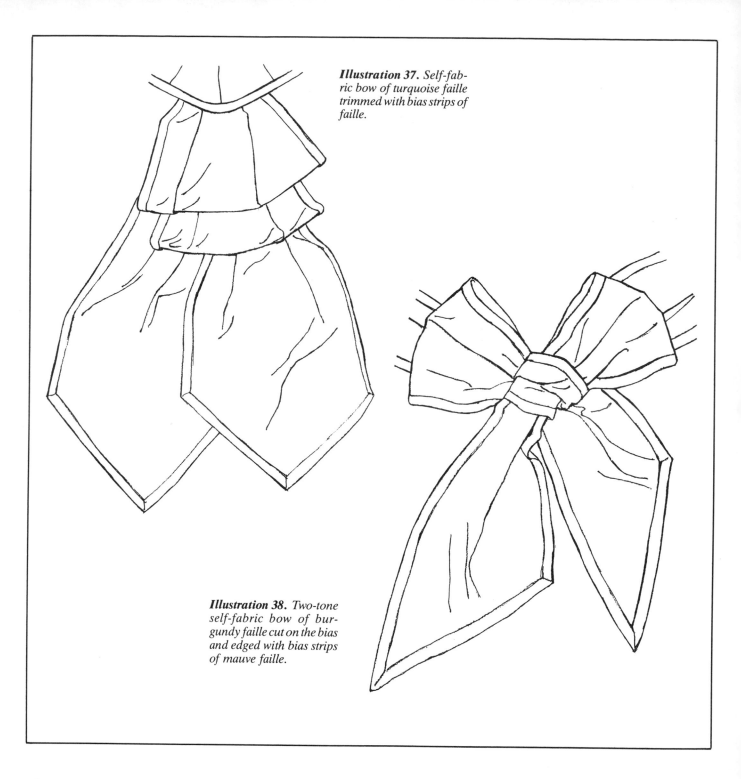

Illustration 37. Self-fabric bow of turquoise faille trimmed with bias strips of faille.

Illustration 38. Two-tone self-fabric bow of burgundy faille cut on the bias and edged with bias strips of mauve faille.

edges raveled, and this large bow. The fabric is cut on the straight with all edges bound with bias strips of the faille. The bow has two large wide loops, and two long ends, cut in points on the bottom. Again, this bow is made of separate parts, tacked together at the top. It is the focal point of the back of the costume.

Another self-fabric bow is seen in the last drawing, *Illustration 38.* The outfit which is adorned by this bow is made of burgundy and mauve faille. It is trimmed with ruffles and ruching and bias strips of the mauve fabric. The ties forming this bow are tacked under the sides of an apron over-skirt. Two long pieces of burgundy, cut on the bias and edged with mauve bias strips, form the bow. The fabric is tucked and looped and tacked to form the knot, two loops and two ends. The two long ends, cut at a sharp angle, fall nicely over a ruffle at the hemline.

As we can see, the variety of bows and combination of loops and ends is limitless. Attractive bows can be created with a little thought and planning, being mindful of the importance of the overall proportion of the length and number and position of loops and ends. Use these drawings as inspiration and a guide for dressing a fashion doll or refurbishing an original costume — when a bow or two will provide that oh, so special finishing touch! □

Designing Doll Clothes To Fit Your Dolls

by **Pat Nelson**
Photographs by **Author**

Clothes for dolls are as varied as clothes for people: no one pattern fits all bodies, regardless of size. The most common error is to buy a pattern for a doll by height, without taking measurements or knowing body type. Since the shape of the body is the factor in well-fitted clothes, long lean bodies or short fat bodies take a different size. Also, bodies of cloth differ from those of composition or porcelain. Some are ball-jointed while others have a straight figure, and widths or circumferences of arms and legs are also to be considered. To fit your dolls with quality clothes, become familiar with BODY TYPES. (See illustrations on a variety of bodies.)

How many of you have purchased a pattern by height of doll, cut and sewed a dress for your doll, then found out it did not fit? It may have been too tight, too loose or in need of other adjustments. This experience possibly soured you in sewing for your dolls, making you "fear" trying again by saying, "I'll only ruin it again." "Fear" is a negative attitude that can close the door to your creativity in becoming a doll's dressmaker. We will open your door and show you how to fit your dolls by making your own basic pattern, a pattern that can be modified in many ways for a variety of clothes. Patterns are made by body types with my easy method.

First, take some time and undress a few of your dolls with different body types, or carefully study the illustrations given to be knowledgeable how they do differ. Baby and toddler bodies are more plump, German bodies are also wider in most cases when compared to French bodies. Fashion dolls are especially noted, for the hourglass figures must be fitted to show the figure to its utmost beauty. Bosoms also add to the figure and patterns to fit must have darts in the right places. On

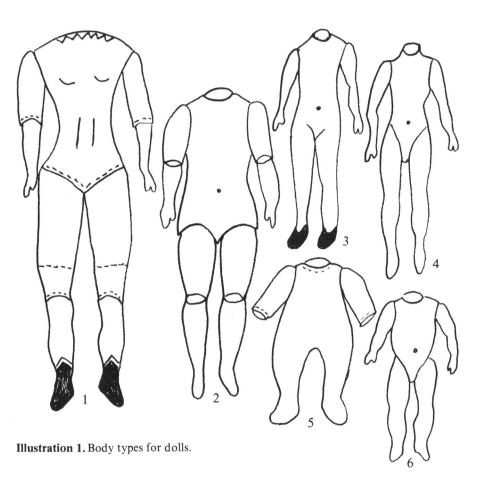

Illustration 1. Body types for dolls.

BODY TYPES ARE (left to right):

1. Cloth body used with china heads, limbs, some stout or thin (adult).
2. Antique jointed composition body (adult).
3. Straight leg child's body.
4. Young girl's body, one-piece arms and legs.
5. Infant cloth body as used for *Bye-Lo* or sleeping baby.
6. Toddler hard plastic body, one-piece arms and legs.

cloth dolls, the body may change with the doll maker making adjustments to a pattern to give her the height or width of the body to suit her needs. My original dolls have a cloth body I especially designed for them, and they vary from child, man or woman. This also applies to doll manufacturers;

therefore, patterns must be made to fit those particular dolls. Once you have made up a good fitting pattern for one doll, you will try another. That is the purpose of this article, to fit your own particular dolls, regardless of make, using body types.

Another factor in dressing your

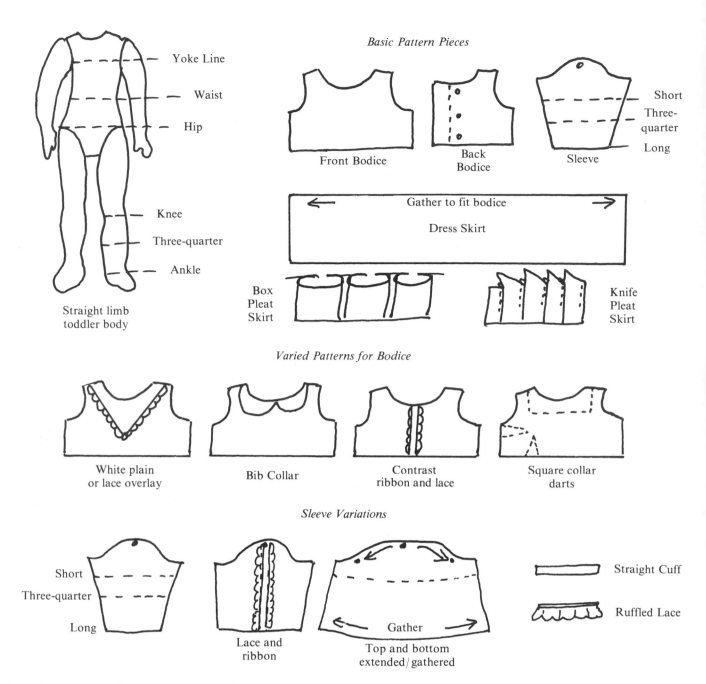

Illustration 2. Basic body and pattern illustrations.

dolls authentically, is to identify the doll by year, for time period determines fashion. Modern dolls are easy, for we are familiar with styles of our time, but with dolls of the 1800s and early 1900s, it is wise to research styles. Note the fabrics used for that time period, also popular colors, and what accessories were used and types of trims and sashes or bows used to accent clothes. Using modern fabrics on vintage dolls is not done; yet we can find old materials at a thrift store if costs are limited or order materials from special stores who make these available by special order. Look-alike fabrics can be used carefully, and with the age of cotton now popular, we

are able to buy them at reasonable prices. Handmade laces can also help on vintage dolls, so buy some at garage sales. Matching fabrics weight to size of doll is most important; also, limit floral or checked fabrics for smaller dolls.

Before beginning our pattern making, make sure the doll has been repaired, cleaned or painted and the paint dry. Handling of the doll with wet paint can mar the finish. Prepare a clean work area, and read all instructions before starting. This gives you time to understand each step taken, and to assemble all needs for making your basic pattern.

Place your doll on a doll stand, so measurements can be taken, and noted on paper with pencil. Each part of the body and limbs should be measured with a measuring tape, and measurements jotted down on paper to aid you in making a correct pattern. You will also need a piece of sturdy cotton cord, to tie at the waistline, a file card to make permanent record, quality paper towels; straight pins, scissors, pencil and paper, sewing needle and thread for basting.

TAKING BODY MEASUREMENTS:
On a sheet of paper, identify the doll,

Illustration 3. *Charleston Flapper*, a doll in an original pattern designed by Pat Nelson.

Illustration 4. *Betsy Ross*, a doll in an original pattern designed by Pat Nelson.

indicate body type, year of make, and height. Indicate if toddler, baby or adult.

1. Head circumference:_____in.
2. Neck:_____in.
3. Bust:_____ in. (if any)
4. Waist:_____in.
5. Length of arms:_____ in.
6. Bodice front:_____in.
7. Bodice back:_____in.
8. Skirt length:_____ in.
    a. Length to knee:_____ in.
    b. Length to ankle:_____ in.
    c. Mid-calf:_____in.
Baby Clothes: Full dress:_____in.
Yoke:_____ in.
Dress bottom:_____in.
If doll is ball-jointed, note measurements on arms and legs as follows:
Arms (shoulder to elbow):_____in.
Elbow to wrist:_____in.
Legs (hip to knee):_____in.
Knee to ankle:_____ in.

When taking measurements, have the doll in a standing position so you can turn and measure the doll as needed. Tie a cord around the doll's waist for waistline, so bodice can be measured. Measure bodice front from center front neck to cord at waistline, and back neck center to cord for front and back bodice. If a yoke pattern is desired, as used in baby clothes, tie another cord around the body close to underarms. Yoke dresses require longer skirts, and are to have separate measurements. Measure the same as for front and back bodice, but use the underarm cord for length of yoke, plus 1/2in (1.3cm) for seam allowance around pattern.

Once all measurements are made, record them on a file card and file.

MAKING A BASIC PAPER TOWEL PATTERN (Illustrations are given to vary pattern pieces).

Paper towels are ideal for basting and making a try-on dress from the measurements taken. Adjustments can be made by cutting and adding as needed for sure fit.

1. *Front and Back Bodice:* Lay the doll in an outstretched lying position, then drape the doll's body with a paper towel long enough to reach the waist, and wide enough to reach from side to side of the body. Hold towel firmly with one hand, and with a pencil in hand, outline neck, then armholes, sides of body and waistline. It should look like a bodice. Repeat the same procedure for back, then cut back pattern 1in (2.5cm) wider from center back line, and discard other piece. Now cut another paper towel the same as the three-quarter one, as this will be a folded opening for center back. Fold under and overlap one over the other piece, secure with a straight pin at bottom to hold. Folded bodice should match front bodice in width, adjust accordingly, then remove bottom pin, but keep it folded. Baste front and back bodice at shoulders only, and lay outstretched so we can make a sleeve pattern.

2. *Sleeves:* (Sleeves can be widened for puff). Place another paper towel *under* the outstretched bodice pattern, and pencil the shape of the armhole. Measure length of sleeve desired and mark on pattern. With pencil, draw a line from top to bottom of sleeve on each side, tapering to wrist for long sleeve. This is a fitted sleeve, adjustable if desired, see samples. Add 1/2in (1.3cm) seams around pattern shape, and cut. Baste sleeve to armholes (cut two), then fit on doll. Make any adjustments if needed. Fit should allow bending or movements.

3. *Dress Skirt:* Since this is a basic pattern, we will make a gathered skirt. Using waist measurements, we multiply by three, and cut paper toweling that length. We then measure from waistline to length desired on skirt, and cut accordingly. Gather skirt and baste to bodice, allowing a fold at back opening to be the same as bodice back. When back seam is sewn, leave 2in (5.1cm) open at waist, so doll's body can be dressed easily. Fold up hemline and tack with straight pins to hold.

4. *Neckline:* Ruffled lace can be added to the neckline and finished with a facing or bias tape. Collars can be added over the basic pattern or sewn to the neckline. Cuffs: same as collar. (Samples of collars are illustrated.)

Each body type requires its own pattern, but the pattern can be varied by making a change to sleeves, collars, bodice inserts, fitted or gored skirts, and more. Expansion of pattern pieces is easy, but do know where, then make another pattern with your changes. For additional information, review any sewing book, for it has many visual aids that can help you. Like people, clothes for dolls vary, but the sewing techniques are the same.

When the paper pattern has been proofed to the doll for fit, you can choose fabrics to suit your doll. Bulky materials can be used on larger dolls, avoid them on smaller ones, along with bold prints and plaids. Avoid materials that shed threads when cut. Pinking shears must be used, or make a fine line on the edges of cut material with clear nail polish to hold threads in tact. Neat sewing and pressing of the garment makes a quality dress. □

Here Comes The Bride!
What Is She Wearing?

by **John R. Burbidge**

Illustration 1. Queen Victoria.

Illustration 2. Queen Alexandra.

". . .she walked very slowly, giving enough time for all the spectators to gratify their curiosity, and certainly she was never before more earnestly scrutinized."[1]

Thus did the young Queen Victoria enter the Chapel Royal in the Palace of St. James on the tenth of February 1840 to be married to Albert, Prince of Saxe-Coburg-Gotha. This description of her progress down the aisle is attributed to one of her bridesmaids, Lady Wilhelmina Stanhope, and could easily describe any bridal procession, royal or otherwise, since time immemorial. It also points out that the curiosity surrounding the bride's dress is as old as the marriage ceremony itself.

This summer that curiosity must be gratified when Miss Sarah Ferguson becomes the bride of Prince Andrew the great-great-great-grandson of Queen Victoria.

Between Sarah and Andrew there are four royal brides, four Queens of England, (Alexandra, Mary, Elizabeth [The Queen Mother] and Elizabeth II) who link him in direct line to the great Victoria. Like Sarah, they too were most earnestly scrutinized and their

---

[1](Victoria R.I. Her Life and Empire, by the Duke of Argyl, 1901)

---

bridal finery duly noted, for no matter how grand the pageantry or sacred the marriage ceremony, what the bride wears will always dominate the proceedings.

QUEEN VICTORIA

Even in Victoria's day the mystery of the dress and especially the lace that adorned it had the press scurrying about playing guessing games. The account of the royal wedding sold 30,000 copies of the Times on the following day.

Her wedding gown was in the simple cut and style of the day. The bodice was tightly fitted with an off the shoulder neckline framed with a beautiful lace bertha collar. The sleeves were a double puff and finished with a flounce of matching lace.

The skirt was approximately four yards in circumference and, in the fashion of the period, made up of straight panels of material pleated into the waistline. The fabric was silk satin lined in silk as was the separate court train which was edged with clusters of orange blossoms. According to Lady Stanhope it was six yards long.

The main feature of the dress was the twenty-four inch deep lace flounce which was attached flat to the pleated skirt. This particular lace along with the matching pieces on the bodice and the veil (which was attached to a wreath of orange blossoms) was the subject of much discussion and speculation at the time. (Evidently, Victoria did not have a weight problem so the press dwelt on her lace instead.)

It was called Honiton and was British made. The lace industry in England was at a low ebb, partially to a preference for Brussels Point by the bride's of the period. It was said that Victoria was persuaded to use Honiton in order to stimulate the industry proving that even Queens on occasion must bow to the practical.

Whatever the reasons, it proved to be a fine choice as the pattern was quite magnificent and at the completion of the work all of the designs were destroyed to insure that it would be unique.

Later the lace was to be removed from the wedding dress and worn by the Queen on several important family occasions. It's last wearing was in 1893 at the marriage of her grandson, the Duke of York, to Mary Princess of Teck, who were to become George V and the incomparable Queen Mary.

(It is interesting to note that both the dress and the lace have survived and are displayed from time to time in the Museum of London.)

QUEEN ALEXANDRA

In 1863, the marriage of the Prince of Wales to the Danish Princess Alexandra took place in St. George's Chapel, at Windsor Castle. This was an arranged marriage set in motion by Prince Albert before his sudden death in 1861 of typhoid fever. The Queen, whose sole contribution to fashion was the fashion for mourning, had submerged herself in widowhood, and every decision she made as far as her family was concerned was "as dear Albert would have wished it."

Of her son and heir, Edward, she constantly despaired; for he was the complete opposite of that paragon of virtue, "that angel," his father. Whereas Albert had been a humorless intellectual, Edward had great personal charm but a decided "appreciation" for life's pleasures — especially the worldly variety.

It was because of these "pleasures" that the Queen refused to share any of the sovereign's duties with her son (although Victoria's possessive attitude concerning her royal prerogatives may have been closer to the truth). Of course once his irresponsible ways were rectified it would be "different," and naturally marriage to the right girl would solve this tiresome problem.

The candidate for this delicate and quite impossible mission, who was culled from a long list of eligible Princesses, was Alexandra of Denmark.

Considered one of the most beautiful women of her time, she was charming, dignified, and extremely elegant. She captivated the Queen (who at the time was unaware that the Princess would one day become one of the glittering lights of the Edwardian Era). She also enchanted her Prince for awhile, but he was a born "bon vivant" and the most perfect Princess in the world could not have held him for long — as neither did his score of mistresses.

Alexandra's wedding gown was originally to have been a magnificent dress of Belgian lace, a gift of King Leopold of the Belgians (was he trying to stimulate the Belgian Lace trade?). However, politics once again reared its head and it was decided that, as the bride of the Prince of Wales, she should wear a wedding gown of English origin.

It had the wide dramatic sweep of the crinoline period and was of silver tissue festooned with Honiton lace, cascades of satin ribbon, and the ubiquitous trimming of wax orange blossoms which no 19th century wedding gown could seem to escape. She wore a lace veil and a wreath of orange blossoms.

In 1901, Edward ascended the throne and the beautiful Danish Princess became Queen Alexandra. Never noted for her intellectual prowess she was, during her reign, a dazzling and much loved figure on the throne, and the last Royal Fashion leader. It is interesting to note that as time past Edward the Seventh became a paunchy old man, while Alexandra's beauty and ravishing figure never altered, and in the photographs of the period they appear to be grandfather and granddaughter!

QUEEN MARY

Queen Victoria reigned for sixty-four years and Edward the Prince of Wales remained on "heir-in-waiting" well into middle age. Denied any active role in government by his mother he and Alexandra ruled over the glittering social world of London and set the tone of what would become known as the Edwardian Era — the opulent Belle Epoque.

In the meantime their eldest son,

Prince Albert Victor, was the heir presumptive and in 1892 the marriage wheels began to turn.

Secluded as she was, nothing escaped the old Queen's attention, especially matchmaking, and the royal blessing was given in favor of Princess Mary of Teck as being suitable Queen Consort material. She was the daughter of Victoria's cousin Princess Mary Adelaide, Duchess of Teck, a flamboyant and personable lady known for her rather expansive figure (she weighed 238 pounds).

The match was not made in heaven. It was simply an arrangement between two professional royals. In fact, Prince Albert Victor was a bit of a problem being extremely lacking intellectually and noted for his "dissipations," which made him a very unhappy prospect for the throne. Fortunately, all this was resolved by typhoid fever to which he suddenly succumbed in the middle of the wedding preparations.

This was a most inconvenient turn of events especially as the bride's very expensive trousseau had been completed. Nothing could be done about this (it simply disappeared), but there was no sense in letting an eligible bride be lost. The Queen, who was quite fond of "dear Mary," decided that it would be perfectly suitable for her to marry Prince George, the new heir presumptive and brother of the deceased.

Mary was brought up to obey royal commands. Despite her "bereavement" she was well aware that the opportunity to sit on the throne of England does not come every day (let alone twice in one year), and furthermore her second "choice" was far more to her taste than the first. (The cost of an entire new trousseau was, or course, incidental.)

Fashion in the early 1890s was well suited to the figure of Princess Mary. It was the age of the tall, voluptuous woman, well corseted with a defined waistline and beautifully rounded shoulders, not to mention a "maternal" bosom.

There is at Buckingham Palace a lovely painting by Tuxen of the wedding ceremony showing the Princess kneeling with her long train spread out behind her. There is also an official photograph of the wedding party which shows off Mary's wonderful figure against the rather glum background of her sisters-in-law who she found intellectually inferior.

The gown was rather simple (for

Illustration 3. Queen Mary.

Illustration 4. Lady Elizabeth Bowes-Lyons, Queen Elizabeth.

the period) but quite elegant. It was made from a silver and white brocade woven at the English Spitalfield mills. The bodice was comprised of a flattering off-the-shoulder neckline draped in lace, and short sleeves. The narrow skirt front shows flounces of lace and features a polonaise drape ending in a long train. Of course, there is a liberal display of wax orange blossoms which also appeared tucked here and there about her diamond head piece.

Illustration 5. Elizabeth II.

In later years, as Queen Mary, she would develop a style of dress uniquely hers. An imposing figure at any time, she was especially striking in evening clothes ablaze with millions of dollars worth of diamonds and pearls, every inch the Queen.

QUEEN ELIZABETH, THE QUEEN MOTHER

In 1923, Lady Elizabeth Bowes-Lyons became the bride of Albert, Duke of York, the second eldest son of George V and Queen Mary.

Mary may have been the image of the perfect Queen but she was part of an age that believed in children being seen and not heard, and her royal brood of six were raised in a manner that bordered more on the ceremonial than the affectionate.

The young Duke of York (Bertie) was shy, a poor student, afflicted with a stammer, and completely in awe of his formidable mother. But fortune smiled on him in the form of the lovely, gay, and charming Elizabeth Bowes-Lyons, daughter of the Earl of Strathmore. Theirs was to be a love match rather than an affair of state, and their wedding in Westminister Abbey was the first of the son of a reigning monarch since 1269.

The shy Duke and his "smiling Duchess" would have two children — the Princesses Margaret and Elizabeth (the future Elizabeth II). In 1937 the Duke's brother David (Edward VII) would abdicate the throne for the American divorcee Wallis Warfield Simpson in the scandal of the century, and overnight the Duke and Duchess of York would become George VI and Queen Elizabeth the Queen Consort, Emperor and Empress of India.

Perhaps the greatest tribute to the charming Elizabeth Bowes-Lyons is that she is now affectionately known as Britain's "Queen MUM."

Fashion in the twenties was not in one of it's most flattering moods. Corsets were out and "straight" was in. To be told that you were flat as a board was considered a compliment. The diminutive Elizabeth's gown was of chiffon and lace, and embroidered in a sort of "medieval" look in silver and pearls. To offset the rather shapeless cut it had a train and veil of rare lace on tulle, the lace loaned to the bride from her royal mother-in-law's collection.

(In one of the official photographs of the ceremony, Queen Mary appears magnificent and totally regal, splendidly dressed in her own distinctive style (which ignores the current fashion), wearing one of her famous toques as if it were the imperial crown.)

QUEEN ELIZABETH II

The reign of George VI was to be a difficult one. The King was a man that had never been meant to occupy the throne and had grown up in the shadow of his highly visible and romantic brother David. A shy man encumbered with a speech impediment, the crown for him was an incredibly heavy burden, and as a further test of courage he saw England engulfed in the tragedy of World War II.

But despite all this he and his enchanting consort were perfect for the period. With their two daughters, Elizabeth and Margaret Rose (with the majestic Mary always in view) they represented the stability that is the keystone of the English monarchy and which had been so shaken by the abdication of Edward VII.

The British public along with the world's "royal" watchers doted on the vivacious Queen in her romantic crinoline evening gowns, and followed the growing up of the little Princesses with "soap opera" intensity.

And finally (just like in the fairy tales) the Princess Elizabeth met her Prince and the whole world stood still for a royal wedding — and not just another royal wedding — for this was the wedding of the heiress to the throne, the first since Queen Victoria.

It was 1947, the war just over, and the world was ready for a good dose of old fashioned splendor. After years of clothes rationing, the prospect of a royal wedding gown sent the fashion press and most of the world's female population into a tizzy.

The gown was more ceremonial than fashionable but rich in tradition and certainly most suitable for the setting and the future Queen. The style followed the trend of the times featuring square shoulders, long fitted sleeves, sweatheart neckline, fitted bodice, and circular cut skirt. Basic in line, it was completely exclusive in the magnificence of its jeweled embroidery. Garlands of roses, star flowers, wheat, and orange blossoms bloomed all over the rich Ivory duchesse satin and tulle court train 15 feet long. A double tulle veil fell from a diamond tiara. It was a gown fit for a royal Princess - and a royal budget!

The dress was designed by the late Sir Norman Hartnell (the only man I ever knew of that was knighted for being handy with a needle). He contributed much to the Queen's wardrobe over the years but unfortunately her wedding gown was perhaps the last dress to shake the fashion world. She soon acquired the image of a safely and correctly dressed wealthy matron with what must be the world's largest collection of handbags.

HRH PRINCESS ANDREW, Duchess of York, Countess of Inverness, and Baroness of Killyleagh, nee Sarah Ferguson

As Victoria was "earnestly scrutinized" so was Sarah. Of course in Victoria's case it was only a select few who had the opportunity to view "the gown" and to pass judgment. However, anyone in the world with access to a television set could attend the entire wedding of Sarah and her Prince, and dissect her choice of bridal wear between sips of their morning coffee.

Having been for thirty-eight years a designer of bridal dresses I dutifully arose at five-thirty in the morning, switched on the VCR and the television, cleaned my glasses, made a cup of coffee, and waited to see if Sarah would rock the bridal business to its satin foundations.

Sarah's Royal Gown

Illustration 6. Sarah, Duchess of York (Full Length).

Illustration 7. Sarah, Duchess of York (Close up Bodice Detail).

When first asked to do this article, I had had all kinds of material available concerning the other royal brides, but Sarah was a complete unknown to me. So I called an English friend who resides on the Isle of Wight. Celia is an ardent royalist and I felt she might provide me with some insight. I was informed that the lady in question had "been about," was a bit on the dowdy side, and had a weight problem but was trying to "scale down." The family was anxious to have Andrew settled, and that Sarah was fond of horses which should please the Queen. In addition to these tidbits she sent me a copy of the Royal Wedding Official Souvenir, filled with color photographs of Andrew and Sarah from infancy on up.

Out of these pages I saw the face of "the girl next door" save for one glamour photograph taken at Buckingham Palace. Here was the look of the English lady, the swept up hair, the off the shoulder formal ballgown, diamonds sapphires, captured momentarily against the glitter of a drawing room — but only momentarily.

It was the girl next door that stepped from the glass coach in a girl-next-door gown — providing next door was very rich, and marrying a Prince!

Fashionwise her dress was in keeping with the prevailing wedding gown styles. Its difference lay in the long court train (which echoed that of Princess Diana's, though this designer seemed to have a better grasp of suitable train lengths) and the symbolic embroidery pattern that formed the decoration.

Much had been made of Sarah's weight problem, but as my British source said she had either "scaled down" or her designer had made use of a bit of fashion Trompe L'oeil" (deceive the eye). The bodice of the gown was very well fitted and ended in a V below the waist. The neckline was pleasantly rounded (always flattering to ladies who have been blessed) and the sleeves of a medium size leg-of-mutton style gave width to the shoulder line. Thus, one's eyes traveled from the broad shoulder line down to the V waist, and this was further accented by the V design of the embroidery which creates a very nice figure line regardless of what that figure might be in reality.

The full gathered and flared skirt nicely disguised any hip problem and billowed romantically as she moved through the Abbey. The train was most likely a separate piece attached to the dress by a series of hooks. Called a court train after those worn at court presentations and attached either at the waist or shoulders, they are usually made from very elegant fabrics and are often a sort of display piece for the embroiderer's art. Sarah's was attached discreetly to the dress under a large draped bow and this could be considered a fashion plus as bows are "in." The fabric was pure silk satin — a classic wedding gown choice — and was most likely specially woven in Britain. One newspaper claimed it came from Italy but historically royal English brides buy their materials close to home for obvious reasons.

What sets this dress apart, other than the new-found fame of its wearer, is the individuality of the embroidery details. According to the press reports what appeared as glitter and sparkle was a bee and thistle motif taken from her coat of arms (provided for her by the College of Arms) and "hearts, anchors, and waves" representing Andrew's naval career (I hope not from a tatoo), plus the couple's initials. These details alone should insure against mass copying.

The veil, which covered the entire train, was of silk tulle and edged with a fine lace pattern featuring tiny bows. It was attached to a wreath of flowers which I felt was too large and sat too low on the forehead, which made it necessary to bring the veil from the front of her head and over the back which is difficult to control and does not give a graceful appearance when viewed from the back. She had elected to wear her hair long, whereas hair either done up or pulled back provides a better background for bridal headpieces and veils. It was interesting to note that after the ceremony she laid aside the floral headpiece and wore a diamond tiara befitting her new rank — Her Royal Highness The Duchess of York.

All this adds up to a rather basic wedding gown style, but flattering to the wearer and suitable for a young lady who is more interested in marrying her Prince than making fashion history.

The trumpets are now stilled, the flowers withered, the guests departed, and the bridal couple who afforded us this spectacle have become a part of royal wedding history. Whether Sarah's choice of bridal gown pleased us or not is really irrelevant for it is every bride's right to please herself and her groom.

One of the most delightful and touching moments during the solemnity and splendor of the occasion was the look of joy on Andrew's face when he caught his first glimpse of his bride. It was obvious at that moment that, regardless of all the fashion critics in the world, Sarah had made the right choice. □

Early Dolls' Clothes Patterns from McCall's

by **Shirlee Funk**

It was in 1863 that the paper pattern industry began. The very first patterns were cut and folded by family members of Ebenezer Butterick at their home in Massachusetts. These first patterns were for men's and boys' clothing and it was not until 1875 that the Butterick Company, in its magazine *The Delineator*, began publishing a series of dolls' clothing patterns.

Other companies joined in making the paper pattern business very successful, and the names of McCall's and Butterick patterns are as well-known to today's home sewers as they were generations ago. Illustrations of McCall's patterns were published in *McCall's Magazine*. Four of these illustrations of patterns for dolls' clothes are reproduced here.

Although none of these clippings is dated, the scrapbook in which they are

McCall Pattern No. 2380
Cut in 4 sizes, 18, 20, 22 and 24 inches long.

No. 2380—**Dolls' Dress, Coat and Bonnet**, requires for 20-inch size, for dress, 1 yd. material either 22 or 27 ins. wide, or ⅝ yd. 36 ins. wide; for coat, 1 yd. material either 22 or 27 ins. wide, or ⅝ yd. 36 ins. wide; for bonnet, ¼ yd. material either 22, 27 or 36 ins. wide. ***Price, 10 cents.***

McCall Pattern No. 1780
Cut in 4 sizes, 18, 20, 22 and 24 inches long.

No. 1780—**Girl Dolls' Jumper Dress and Coat**, requires for 22 and 24 inch size, for dress, 1½ yds. material 24 ins. wide, 1⅜ yds. 27 ins. wide, or ⅞ yd. 44 ins. wide; for coat, 1⅜ yds. material 24 ins. wide, 1¼ yds. 27 ins. wide, or ⅞ yd. 44 ins. wide. For guimpe, ½ yd. material either 24 or 27 ins. wide, or ⅜ yd. 44 ins. wide. ***Price, 10 cents.***

Illustration 1. Four patterns for dolls' clothes cut from the pages of McCall's Magazine in 1907 to 1908. All are offered for dolls sized 18in (46cm) to 24in (61cm). Three are for child dolls and one is for lady dolls. Patterns today cost about 50 times the prices listed here!

contained holds other material all dated 1907 or 1908. Pattern No. 9271 is illustrated in Colemans' *The Collector's Book of Dolls' Clothes, Costumes in Miniature: 1700-1929*. The Colemans date it to the December 1905 *McCall's Magazine*. It is likely that it was available for a number of years. Colemans also include the suggested fabrics for this pattern: "Flannel, serge, mohair, or almost any sort of cloth can be used to make the coat while the natty little suit is very pretty of blue woolen with a collar of pique or embroidery and a tie of red silk" (page 432).

Pattern No. 1830 is described as a "'Fluffy Ruffles' Dolls' Suit." Apparently it was intended for the lady doll called *Fluffy Ruffles* advertised by Samstag & Hilder Bros. in 1908. The pattern features a coat, a kilt pleated skirt and a "waist" or blouse with a snugly banded neckline.

The other two patterns were intended for girl dolls and mirror the little doll owner's own wardrobe of everyday dresses and coats. Other clippings in the same scrapbook feature very similar styles in children's sizes. □

McCall Pattern No. 1830
Cut in 4 sizes, 18, 20, 22 and 24 inches long.
No. 1830—**"Fluffy Ruffles" Dolls' Suit**, requires for 20-inch size, for coat, ¾ yd. material 22 ins. wide, ⅝ yd. 27 ins. wide, or ⅜ yd. 36 ins. wide; for waist and skirt, 1⅞ yds. material 22 ins. wide, 1⅜ yds. 27 ins. wide, or 1 yd. 36 ins. wide.
Price, 10 cents.

McCall Pattern No. 9271
Cut in 4 sizes, 18, 20, 22 and 24 inches long.
No. 9271—**Girl Dolls' Coat** (in Three-Quarter or Reefer Length, and Sailor Dress having Two Styles of Collars and Kilt-Pleated Skirt), requires for 22-inch size, for coat, ⅞ yd. material 27 ins. wide, ⅝ yd. 36 ins. wide, or ½ yd. 44 ins.
Price, 10 cents.

Fabrics Past and Present

by **Lyn Alexander & Owanah Wick**

You are always faced with choosing appropriate materials when you costume an antique doll. True antique fabrics are difficult to find, and often too fragile to sew. New natural-fiber fabrics are available, but are you sure which new fabrics substitute effectively for the old ones?

To make it easy to bridge the gap between fabrics of the past and present we have compiled this concise condensed listing. Keep it in your costuming file, and use it when you shop for material.

NOTE: The new fabrics described here are sold in some specialty stores, or by mail from firms advertising in this and other doll magazines.

COTTON

OLD

NAME: Batiste
DESCRIPTION: Semi-sheer soft lightweight cotton in plain weave. Mercerization gives it a slight sheen.
USES: Christening dresses, baby clothes, shirts, underwear and summer dresses.

NEW

NAME: Batiste
DESCRIPTION: Today's Swiss batiste is available in several weights. Fine is the most sheer. Medium is less sheer but still has sheen. Dress weight has a high thread count and most closely resembles the fabric used in many old undergarments.
NOTES: The finest quality batiste is Swiss 100 percent cotton. American batiste has a small percentage of synthetic fibers, is less expensive and less sheer. Costume purists prefer all-natural fiber fabrics for antique dolls.

OLD

NAME: Cambric
DESCRIPTION: Fine somewhat stiff cotton with some gloss. It has slightly heavier threads and a looser weave than batiste.
USES: Underwear, also outerwear for German dolls.

NEW

NAME: Cambric
DESCRIPTION: Still made today, but usually in linen of handkerchief weight. Good quality cambric is hard to find.
NOTES: Used often on antique German dolls. Old handkerchiefs are a good source for doll clothes.

OLD

NAME: Chambray
DESCRIPTION: High thread count yarn-dyed cotton, with colored warp and white filling. Has a silky iridescent appearance.
USES: Everyday summer dresses, shirts and play wear. Excellent for larger dolls over 16in (41cm).

NEW

NAME: Chambray
DESCRIPTION: Chambray today still has colored warp and white filling. The most common combinations are blue/white, red/white, gray/white. Modern chambray is not as iridescent as the old.
NOTES: Easy to find. Superior quality chambrays are being manufactured in England and Switzerland.

OLD

NAME: Dimity
DESCRIPTION: A fine soft sheer cotton with stripes or crossbars of heavier cords.
USES: Summer dresses, shirts and underwear.

NEW

NAME: Dimity
DESCRIPTION: Difficult to find. Lawn or medium weight batiste can be substituted, but they do not have a corded effect.
NOTES: Has the feel of organdy when it is starched.

OLD

NAME: Lawn
DESCRIPTION: Thin lightweight somewhat stiff plain weave cotton.
USES: Excellent for underwear.

NEW

NAME: Lawn
DESCRIPTION: Slightly heavier and tighter weave than batiste, yet soft enough for dolls. Available in white, colors and prints. The finest quality is Swiss lawn, but Japanese lawn is very good quality also.
NOTES: Lawn was used for handkerchiefs, and they are good for doll clothes. Was woven in Laon, France.

OLD

NAME: Muslin
DESCRIPTION: A plain-weave cotton that was available in many weights from coarse sheeting to fine sheer dress fabric. It came in white, colors and prints.
USES: Sturdy muslin was commonly worn by the working class. Used for dresses, blouses, aprons, shirts and underwear.

NEW

NAME: Muslin
DESCRIPTION: Can be bleached or unbleached, and is available in a variety of weights. Modern muslin is not like the old. Lightweight percale resembles some old muslin.
NOTES: Because unbleached muslin is inexpensive, easy to work with and keeps its shape, it is used for making trial garments to check fit.

OLD

NAME: Nainsook
DESCRIPTION: Soft lightweight plain-weave cotton that was a little heavier than batiste. Mercerizing gave it a slightly glossy finish.
USES: Used by the working class for dresses and underwear. Also used for baby clothes.

NEW

NAME: Nainsook
DESCRIPTION: Today's nainsook is a sheer gauzy fabric that is very inexpensive. The best quality is made in Switzerland.
NOTES: Excellent for German doll costuming and underwear.

<table>
<tr><td>**OLD**</td><td>**NAME:** Organdy
DESCRIPTION: Very sheer flat open-weave fabric of high quality with permanent crispness.
USES: Aprons, bonnets, linings or underlinings of suits, coats or dresses, and stiff petticoats.</td></tr>
<tr><td>**NEW**</td><td>**NAME:** Organdy
DESCRIPTION: Today's organdy is stiffer, but otherwise not much different from old fabric. Silk organza is softer than all-cotton organdy.
NOTES: Came in white and colors and was sometimes embroidered.</td></tr>
</table>

<table>
<tr><td>**OLD**</td><td>**NAME:** Cotton velvet
DESCRIPTION: Soft cotton woven with pile like velvet, but the backing was not a twill weave like today's velveteen.
USES: Coats, jackets, trim and bonnets.</td></tr>
<tr><td>**NEW**</td><td>**NAME:** Cotton velvet
DESCRIPTION: Today's cotton velvet is heavier than the antique kind. A good substitute is lightweight cotton velveteen.
NOTES: Good quality velvet is available today in a variety of colors through specialty stores or mail order.</td></tr>
</table>

LINEN

<table>
<tr><td>**OLD**</td><td>**NAME:** Linen
DESCRIPTION: Linen is harsher than cotton or silk, and feels cold and smooth. Wrinkles easily. Can be of tight or loose weave, in various weights from heavy to sheer. Pleats well, and can be pressed into sharp creases.
USES: Warm weather dresses, blouses, shirts, baby clothes and underwear.</td></tr>
<tr><td>**NEW**</td><td>**NAME:** Linen
DESCRIPTION: Has changed little from ancient to modern times.
USES: Linen is spun from flax and is one of the oldest garment fibers we know.</td></tr>
</table>

<table>
<tr><td>**OLD**</td><td>**NAME:** Handkerchief linen
DESCRIPTION: Lightweight, thin and smooth. Wrinkles easily.
USES: Summer dresses, blouses, shirts and fine underwear. Drapes and gathers well.</td></tr>
<tr><td>**NEW**</td><td>**NAME:** Handkerchief linen
DESCRIPTION: About the same as the old fabric. Modern mercerizing methods make it softer than old linen.
NOTES: Large old linen handkerchiefs are in great demand for costuming dolls.</td></tr>
</table>

OLD   **NAME: China silk**
DESCRIPTION: Soft-textured silk fabric in plain weave that ravels easily. There may be slight imperfections in the weave.
USES: Very versatile, can be used for child or adult dresses, ladies' elegant underwear, linings and christening gowns.

NEW   **NAME: China silk**
DESCRIPTION: Available in several weights. The best for doll costuming are 6mm — the most sheer, similar to mull, but difficult to find in colors. 8mm — still sheer enough for small dolls, but more crisp than 6mm. Comes in many colors. 10mm — has more body than 8mm but not often in colors. Is very crisp. 12mm — is the heaviest doll costumers should use. Limited suitable colors. Best for larger dolls.
NOTES: Produced in China as early as 1200 B.C. Wide range of colors and an easy fabric to dye.

OLD   **NAME: Crepe de Chine**
DESCRIPTION: Fine lightweight silk fabric with creped or twisted filling yarns, giving it a pebbly surface.
USES: Children's party dresses. Ladies' dresses with drapery or clinging lines, underwear and nightwear. Crepe is often chosen as the foundation for beading because it is strong enough to bear the weight of the beads.

NEW   **NAME: Crepe de Chine**
DESCRIPTION: Today's Crepe de Chine is similar to the antique kinds. Usually of silk, but sometimes made of rayon.
NOTES: Has wonderful draping qualities. Was woven in both France and China.

OLD   **NAME: Mousseline de soie**
DESCRIPTION: Very sheer lightweight silk with a stiff finish, but softer than organdy.
USES: Good for elegant dresses for French dolls. Drapes well.

NEW   **NAME: Silk organza**
DESCRIPTION: Sheer lightweight fabric with a shiny look. Can be found in rayon also. Comes in many colors.
NOTES: Mousseline de soie was often called French silk muslin. Very expensive.

OLD   **NAME: Taffeta**
DESCRIPTION: Antique taffeta was a crisp fabric with irregular slubs. It was often iridescent.
USES: Dresses, pleated skirts, linings, trim and bonnets.

NEW   **NAME: New fabric substitute is Doupioni silk**
DESCRIPTION: Has irregular threads which cause raised slubs. It has a shiny look and is crisp in texture. It can be pleated, but will not drape well.
NOTES: Silk taffetas were heavily weighted and disintegrated with age. Rayon taffeta has a bright sheen.

OLD   **NAME: Cashmere**
DESCRIPTION: Fine soft fabric made from the downy wool undercoat of cashmere goats.
USES: Coats, cold weather dresses, babies' coats and sacques.

NEW   **NAME: Cashmere**
DESCRIPTION: Soft fabric in various weights, usually in plain colors.
NOTES: Sometimes cashmere is combined with sheep's wool for greater strength.

OLD   **NAME: Challis (shall-ee)**
DESCRIPTION: A flat lightweight worsted wool in plain weave, often printed, sometimes in colors with floral designs.
USES: Dresses for women or girls.

NEW   **NAME: Challis**
DESCRIPTION: Modern wool challis is similar to the old. Also made of cotton, rayon or polyester.
NOTES: Pleats, gathers and drapes well. Can be substituted for grenadine — a silk and wool semi-transparent loose weave fabrics.

OLD   **NAME: Wool crepe**
DESCRIPTION: Soft fabric made with twisted crepe yarn, giving it a pebbly texture.
USES: Cool weather dresses.

NEW   **NAME: Wool crepe**
DESCRIPTION: A textured lightweight wool fabric that is suitable for doll dresses and coats.
NOTES: Cotton, rayon and other synthetics can have a creped finish. Do not use synthetics for dressing antique dolls.

Frilly Bonnet for a 19in Doll with a 10in Head Circumference

by **Hazel Ulseth & Helen Shannon**

Photographs by **Marty Ulseth**

LEFT: Illustration 1. 19in (48cm) doll modeling the frilly bonnet.

RIGHT: Illustration 2. Side view of the 19in (48cm) doll modeling the frilly bonnet.

Who can resist a doll capped in a frilly bonnet with bits of lace framing that lovely face? Who can resist this pattern which makes it possible to create such a frilly bonnet for a 19in (48cm) doll with a head circumference of 10in (25cm)?

Characteristic of little girls' and babies' headgear of the late 1890s, this pattern has been adapted from an illustration of a child of the era mentioned wearing a bonnet just like this.

If a complete costume is being planned for a doll, it would be appropriate to have matching bonnet and frock. Otherwise, any fabric to complement the doll's dress is fine. Sheer silk, cotton batiste, piqué or fine wool challis also make lovely bonnets. Here we have shown wide lace trim with ruching of narrow lace, but other suggestions for trim are shirred or knotted ribbon and tiny flowers.

FABRIC REQUIREMENTS:

9in (23cm) by 20in (51cm) of chosen fabric.
6in (15cm) by 12in (30cm) of unbleached muslin for lining.

1 3/4in (4cm) by 18in (46cm) wide edged lace.
5/8in (1.6cm) by 8in (23cm) narrow edged lace or trim.
5/8in (1.6cm) by 36in (91cm) ruching (may be insertion).
1/2in (1.3cm) by 20in (51cm) ribbon for ties.
Four pieces of lace about 4½in (11cm) by 1/4in (1.3cm) for rosettes.

CUTTING INSTRUCTIONS:

Out of chosen fabric, cut one bonnet body on fold and two bonnet backs.

Out of lining fabric, cut one bonnet lining on fold and two bonnet back linings.

BONNET BODY: Hand- or machine-stitch a tiny hem on each short end. Mark fold line with large basting stitches.

Using bonnet body, mark center front and center back. Hand-stitch two rows of gathering stitches on curved front edge as shown on pattern from * to edge. Fold on fold line, matching stars, and pull stitches to fit; press lightly. Pin and baste edge in place all the way across.

Carefully machine-stitch two rows of gathering stitches 1/8in (.31cm) from edge, then 1/4in (.65cm) from cut edge of brim (which you have just basted in place).

Machine-stitch two more rows as shown on pattern, using previous stitching as guide line.

Machine-stitch two rows of gathering stitches on cut edge (back) of bonnet body as shown on pattern.

BONNET LINING: Using Bonnet lining, fold on fold line and machine-stitch all around except between stars. Clip corners, turn right side out, and press. Mark center front and center back. Mark 3/4in (2cm) on each side of center back (short side), fold on solid lines and pleat to broken center line. Secure by tacking along edge.

COMBINING BONNET BODY and LINING: Match center front of bonnet body to center front of bonnet lining at first row of gathering stitches on brim. Pull first set of gathering stitches to fit lining and distribute the gathers so that more are concentrated at center. Secure gathering threads, and tack lining to bonnet body all across (gathering stitches will be covered).

Pull next two rows of gathering stitches to fit lining, and secure. As

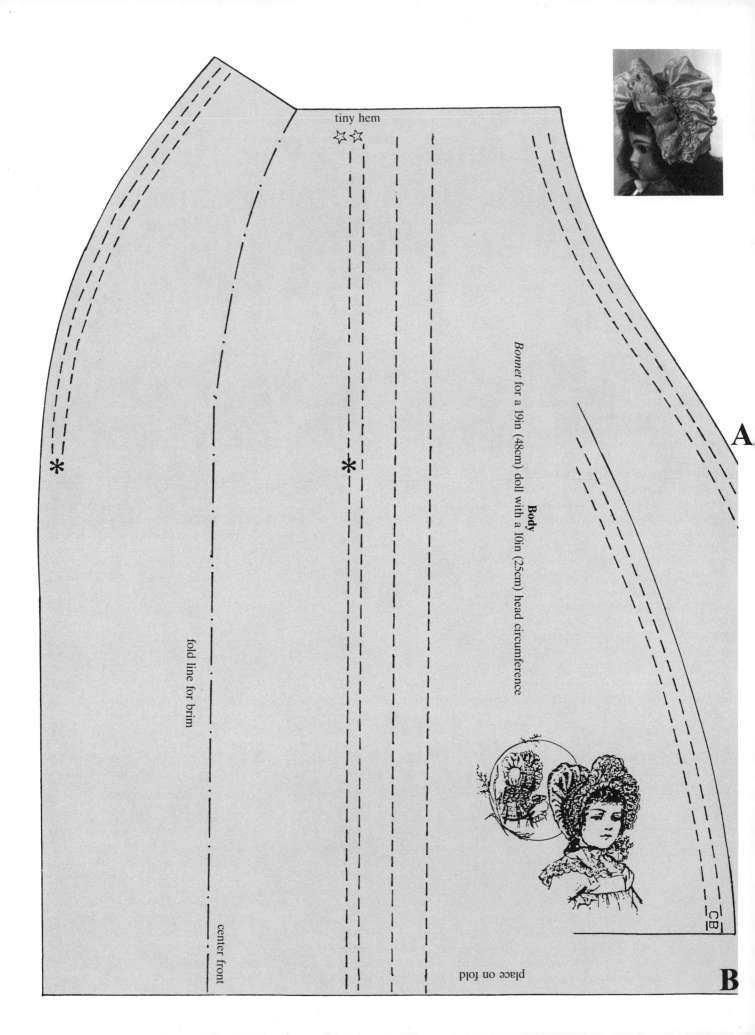

tiny hem

☆ ☆

*

*

fold line for brim

center front

Bonnet for a 19in (48cm) doll with a 10in (25cm) head circumference

Body

place on fold

CB

A

B

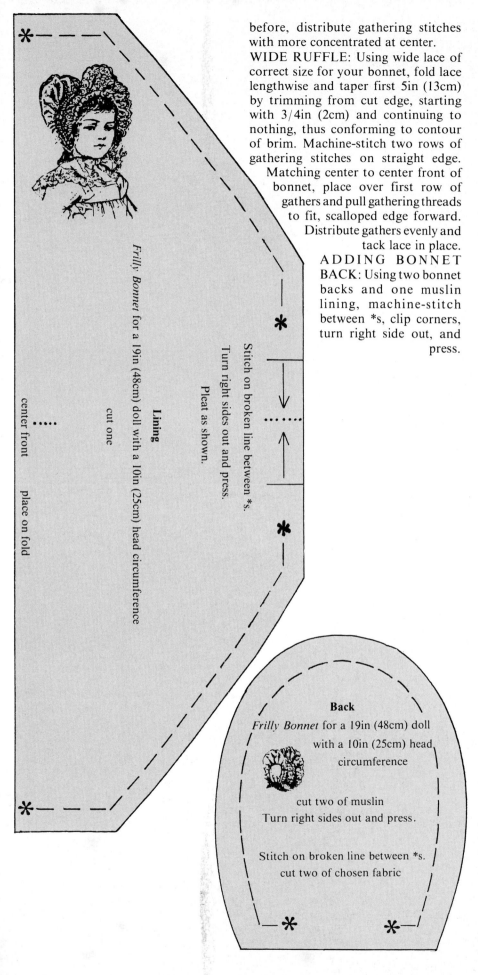

Frilly Bonnet for a 19in (48cm) doll with a 10in (25cm) head circumference

Lining
cut one

center front

place on fold

Stitch on broken line between *s.
Turn right sides out and press.
Pleat as shown.

Back
Frilly Bonnet for a 19in (48cm) doll
with a 10in (25cm) head
circumference

cut two of muslin
Turn right sides out and press.

Stitch on broken line between *s.
cut two of chosen fabric

before, distribute gathering stitches with more concentrated at center.

WIDE RUFFLE: Using wide lace of correct size for your bonnet, fold lace lengthwise and taper first 5in (13cm) by trimming from cut edge, starting with 3/4in (2cm) and continuing to nothing, thus conforming to contour of brim. Machine-stitch two rows of gathering stitches on straight edge.

Matching center to center front of bonnet, place over first row of gathers and pull gathering threads to fit, scalloped edge forward. Distribute gathers evenly and tack lace in place.

ADDING BONNET BACK: Using two bonnet backs and one muslin lining, machine-stitch between *s, clip corners, turn right side out, and press.

Mark center of top.

Pull last set of gathering stitches (on cut edge of bonnet body), match center back with center of bonnet back, and pull gathering threads to fit bonnet back. Again, distribute gathers in such a way as to concentrate more gathers at center back. Place bonnet back over the gathers, and pin in place. Blindstitch securely.

LINING BONNET BACK: Using back lining, machine-stitch all around on seam line. Fold on seam line and baste, then set lining on side of bonnet over the back, thus hiding all the gathering stitches.

On inside of bonnet, match center of bonnet lining to center of bonnet back (where pleat is) and stitch together about 1in (2cm) on each side of the center mark. This leaves part of the bonnet lining detached from remainder of back, but provides support for the "pouf" or stand-up fullness.

ADDING NARROW LACE OR OTHER TRIM: Lightly tack the lace or trim on bonnet top, scalloped edge forward, over gathered edge of lace ruffle. Trim may be fancy braid, lace, shirred (zigzag) ribbon or knotted ribbon.

RUCHING: Using lace for ruching, pleat in 1/4in (.65cm) pleats, tack along one edge, and apply to underside of bonnet brim at edge of lining, loose pleated edge toward front.

RIBBON TIES: Fold ribbon for ties under about 1/4in (.65cm), sew a few stitches. Pull tightly to form a little loop, and sew to bonnet at **s on each side.

ROSETTES: Using two short pieces of lace for each rosette, machine-stitch two straight edges together. Place ends together and hand-stitch to form a loop. Run a gathering stitch around the loop 1/8in (.31cm) from center line, pull as tight as possible and secure thread. Turn both edges upward from stitching, with the shorter edge inside, making a fluffy little rosette. Tack one rosette over each ribbon tie where it is sewn to bonnet.

We are sure you will be pleased with this lovely bonnet and will want to use it for more than one doll. If so, for a slightly different, more piquant look, press center of brim upward to form a point. Do this by placing thumbs under center of brim and pushing upward while your fingers shape the remaining brim. At the point place a tiny flower, a nice finishing touch to your frilly bonnet. □

Illustration 1. *An 8ft (2.4m) green tree highlights small porcelain dolls costumed in passionate tones of red, gold and green.*

Doll Tree Splendor

Nostalgic charm of handmade Christmas ornaments — that will not break!

by **Beverly Bihn**

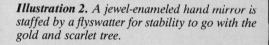
Illustration 2. *A jewel-enameled hand mirror is staffed by a flyswatter for stability to go with the gold and scarlet tree.*

Do I make the dolls to go with the trees or the trees to go with the dolls? Both. I will utilize doll items on my trees and holiday embellishments on my dolls. Since I have been making all of my holiday ornaments for 25 years and the dolls for seven years, they complement each other. The dolls have become a natural outflow of my love to create beautiful objects of art.

As a little girl, I could hardly wait for Christmas time to help my mother decorate the tree. More than once, as the last glass ornament was carefully positioned in its proper place, we would step back to admire our hours of efforts. To our disbelief, horror struck our hearts at the sight of the tree crashing to the floor...smashing years of treasured heirlooms that had been passed from loving hands to loving hearts. I declared I would not endure that heartache again and would begin to make the ornaments myself that would not break.

Twenty five years ago, I could only buy styrofoam balls and colored Easter eggs, so I used both, covering them with ribbons, jewels and flowers. As years progressed, I cascaded

jewels and added laces. I never dreamed of selling the decorations in our furniture business...I just wanted our store to look festive for the holidays. We specialize in romantic elegance, so my decorations are lavishly jeweled and richly enveloped with silk flowers and laces. Clients began to plead with me to sell the ornaments, then the wreaths, garlands, sleighs, gift boxes and trees. Now they want me to decorate their homes for the holidays because they know it will be completely individual and toned to their colors. A doll becomes the icing on the cake...the focal point of all attention...the ultimate of individuality.

The dolls are always on display among the furnishings in the store. Our display rooms are coordinated by color; the dolls and decorations are scattered throughout to blend into the hues of the furnishings. Without the dolls, there would be a tremendous void...they put the finishing "patina" to the romantic atmosphere of their surroundings.

In my article entitled "Doll Wreaths," which appears on page 52, I detailed the wreaths that can be made for dolls (on

Illustration 3. *The opulance of Fabergé has inspired the heavily jeweled tree of rainbow colors.*

Illustration 4. A white bear plays the violin for his "friend" while he nestles among the elegant ornaments.

which I used unbreakable ornaments). An additional delight in making the unbreakable ornaments for the wreaths and trees, is that the wreaths and small trees can be covered to be stored during the year without worry of an heirloom getting crushed or broken. It saves days and weeks of work to have decorations ready to display immediately without having to always put them together. As years progress, other items may be added to these "masterpieces" so that they become an endless collection of "favorite things."

In making unbreakable decorations for the trees and wreaths, I have also used them as "extras" for the dolls. Laces for doll costumes may be gathered into bows or nosegays for the decorations. Pearls draped on trees may also be draped on the dolls. Jewels work for both.

Decorative doll fans may be created for everything. Small fans may be purchased at craft stores for individual embellishments of jewels and flowers. They may also be made from "scratch" from ribbons and laces. Using a 5in (13cm) or 6in (15cm) wide by 24in (61cm) strip of ribbon, fold it like an accordian and secure at one end with a wire or narrow ribbon; this can be encrusted with one's imagination.

Nosegays may be small clusters of flowers with baby's breath interwoven among the stems. Laces may surround the flowers for that nostalgic feeling.

Colored balls, bells, birds, doll hatboxes, straw hats and baskets may have flowers, ribbons and jewels glued for permanent stability. Tassels may dangle from the bottom of ornaments or be individually "flowered."

To create a loose flowing nostalgia, attach individual silk flowers all over the decorations among the ornaments. Decorative fruits may be clustered with ribbons and baby's breath for color. If anything stands still long enough, hang it on the tree. Toys and small musical instruments can be placed on top of limbs or hung with ribbons. Small styrofoam cubes may be covered with foils for "presents" on the trees. Angels and small dolls may nestle in places of honor on my tress, wreaths, sleighs and table arrangements. The trees and decorations may be themed to particular color schemes or jewel-toned to all colors.

Illustration 5. *The Victorian tree is spiced with potpourri embellishments.*

THE TREE OF GOLD AND SCARLET (seen in *Illustration 1*):

For this 8ft (2.4m) tall green tree, I concentrated the colors in passionate tones of red, gold and green, highlighting some small porcelain dolls costumed in red, green and gold. Included on this tree are the following:

10	100 miniature light green cords.
24	large red feathered birds.
12	small red feathered birds.
10	red satin birds beaded with gold jewels.
50	sprays of gold flowers.
30	large gold roses.
15	small gold rose sprays.
6	red-costumed dolls trimmed in gold braid.
6	green-costumed dolls trimmed in gold braid.
12	red velour ribbon fans with gold trim.
24	red satin balls trimmed with gold beads.
24	green satin balls trimmed with gold beads.
24	brass musical instruments.
20	fruit clusters.
100	small red berries attached to the limbs.
24	gold filigree balls.
24	clear plastic balls glued with gold flowers.
20	gold and red 5in (13cm) long tassels.
24	small red foil-wrapped packages for the tree.
24	small green foil-wrapped packages for the tree.
20	gold baskets nestled with red birds.

Illustration 6. *This petite Jumeau doll is fashioned in an enchanting gown made from antique lace lamp shades and collars.*

Illustration 7. A luscious peaches and cream tabletop tree was made to accompany the wreath that was featured in the article on page 52.

Baby's breath.

Packages under the tree wrapped in shades of red, gold and green.

PORCELAIN DOLL GOWNED IN GOLD AND SCARLET (seen in *Illustration 2.*):

This head mold is a Steiner by McNees, robed in royal scarlet and gold interwoven fabric with matching velvet ribbons cascading down the sides. Scarlet, gold and pearl faux jewels cluster over the dress and nestle among the folds of the velvet ribbons. Matching cascades of the jewels have been intertwined into an elaborate hairpiece for the doll's long curled coiffure. A jewel enameled hand mirror has been staffed by a flyswatter for stability, with scarlet sequins sparkling among clustered jewels. Appropriately, the doll has been named "Vanity."

THE FABERGÉ TREE (as seen in *Illustration 3.*):

The opulance of Fabergé has inspired the heavily jeweled tree of rainbow colors. The tree is an 8ft (2.4m) tall white flocked imitation Norwegian pine with wired limbs that fold up for convenient storage and have the strength to hold the weighted ornaments. Scattered among the limbs are the following:

15	100 miniature white cord lights.
24	cranberry satin ribbon and lace trimmed fans.
24	blue satin ribbon and lace trimmed fans.
36	multi-colored flocked fruit clusters.
20	heavily jeweled pink satin egg-shaped balls.
20	heavily jeweled rose satin round balls.
20	heavily jeweled yellow satin egg-shaped balls.
20	heavily jeweled gold satin round balls.
20	heavily jeweled turquoise satin egg-shaped balls.
20	heavily jeweled blue satin egg-shaped balls.
20	heavily jeweled lavender satin egg-shaped balls.
20	heavily jeweled green satin egg-shaped balls.
20	heavily jeweled cranberry satin round balls.
12	round turquoise large balls adorned with embroidered pink flowers.
12	large bone round balls covered in tapestry ribbons, braids and silk flowers.
24	gold filigree balls.
24	jeweled bells in gold and cranberry.
36	cranberry and gold 4in (10cm) tassels.
24	rainbow silk flower clusters with baby's breath.
100	rainbow colored silk butterflies.
12	jeweled green birds.
250	5in (13cm) long gold ball icicle chains.

PORCELAIN DOLL SUITED IN CRANBERRY VELVET WITH WHITE MINK TRIM (seen in *Illustration 4.*):

This 9in (23cm) head circumference Jumeau doll is a Seeley mold number S-26. Her cranberry velvet suit is trimmed with white mink and has a matching hat and muff. The fur was originally collared on one of my sister's sweaters which she bravely relinquished to posterity. The shape made it easier to cut into strips to be curved as the border of the full-shaped jacket on the doll. Old lace has been gathered into ruching to create a long-sleeved heirloom blouse for the suit.

The white bear with the cranberry violin has been placed on a low limb of the tree close to the doll because they are "friends." Packages wrapped in rainbow colors under the tree complete the elegance of this Fabergé detailing. By wrapping the top and bottom separately, the decor is secured to the top only, permitting the gift boxes to be used repeatedly.

THE VICTORIAN TREE (seen in *Illustration 5.*):

Always romantic is the charm of a Victorian-styled tree. Soft colors of pink, rose and cranberry dominate the theme of this 7ft (2.1m) green tree spiced with potpourri parasols, hearts, hatboxes, fans, sachets, cornucopia, handbags, boots, hats and tassels. Sprays of silk flowers mass branches, highlighting the vintage-style ornaments. Most of the balls and potpourri amenities are embossed by flowers, braids, ribbons and laces with baby's breath nestled among silk petals. Garlands of pearls dance in tiers among the mantle of silk flowers. Amply included on this Victorian tree the following:

8	100 miniature light green cords.
20	5in (13cm) bone tassels with various colored ribbons.
12	large lace nosegays of pastel silk flowers.
12	small lace nosegays of pastel silk flowers.
20	lace-covered cornucopia with silk flowers.
10	closed lace parasols filled with potpourri.
10	open lace parasols charmed with silk flowers.
10	potpourri-filled lace handbags fringed with tassels and silk flowers.
10	potpourri-filled lace hearts with silk flowers.
12	potpourri-filled lace bells with flowers.
10	rose satin boots covered in lace and flowers.
10	Victorian straw hats with lace and flowers.
10	Victorian hatboxes covered in ribbons and flowers.
20	pastel lace fans covered in flowers and pearls.
8	jeweled green birds.
20	pink satin balls trimmed in laces and flowers.
20	rose satin balls adorned with braids and flowers.
20	green satin balls covered with ribbons and flowers.
150	pastel silk flowers nestling in the branches.
100	stems of small pink flower sprays.
100	yards of pearl trim, dancing in scallops among the branches.

Baby's breath exploding over the entire tree.

"FANTAISIE" PORCELAIN DOLL (seen in *Illustration 6.*):

"Fantaisie," the petite Jumeau porcelain doll, is a Seeley mold number S110, head circumference 5¼in (13cm). Her engaging gown was made from antique lace lamp shades and collars. Handmade pink and green embroidered flowers and ribbon roses swirl along pleats and tiers of ribbons. To capture the Victorian charm of the tree, she is fashioned in a large hat, holding a matching fan that has been pleated with ribbons and lace. This petite Jumeau doll may also be enthroned on a 24in (61cm) or 36in (91cm) hanging wreath surrounded by laces, ribbons and silk flowers, allowing her pleated train to flow over cascades of matching ribbons and bows.

A LUSCIOUS PEACHES AND CREAM TREE AND WREATH (seen in *Illustration 7.*):

For the glamourous charm of "Eláycee," I created a tabletop tree and matching wreath, lavished in delicacies of peach, green and cream tones. Flecks of pearl beads adorn the ornaments; cascades of pearl garlands enhance the branches; angels of whisper lace enchant the imagination. Scattered over the 4ft (1.2m) tall green tree are the following:

2	green cord 100 miniature lights.
8	peach fans covered in laces and pearls.
6	bone fans covered in laces and pearls.
12	green feathered birds jeweled in peach flowers and pearl beads.
12	pearl covered pears.
12	lace-covered peach balls.
20	laced miniature nosegays filled with peach, green and bone silk flowers.
6	peach ribbon bows adorned with laces and flowers.
12	green satin balls covered in gold beads.
12	clusters of pearl grapes fancied with peach flowers.
26	yards of pearl garlands.
36	small gold balls.
2	lace-gowned angels to recline under the tree.
36	loose stems of peach and bone silk flowers.

Baby's breath to mantle the branches.

For the 36in (91cm) wreath I used:

2	lace-covered angels, feathered and flowered.
2	50 miniature light green cords.
2	gold harps (for the angels to play).
20	small gold bells.
4	small peach hatboxes.
4	satin bone balls lavished with pearls.
4	peach balls clustered in laces and flowers.
18	small peach rosebud clusters.
12	small bone rosebud clusters.
20	sprays of peach flowers.
4	peach 4in (10cm) long tassels.
12	yards of pearls.
26	yards of peach ribbon edged with lace, tied into large streaming bows.

Baby's breath to mantle the wreath.

PORCELAIN DOLL "ELÁYCEE" (seen in *Illustration 8.*):

"Eláycee" has a 10in (25cm) circumference head by Seeley, number S144, and is gowned in peach lace smothered in green ribbons and peach ribbon roses. Her bouffant train is tiered in peach lace and green tulle ruffles which also envelop the large hat. There is more to this doll's artistry than meets the eye. □

Illustration 8. Angels gather around the doll fashioned in peach lace sprinkled with luscious ribbon roses and embroidered flowers.

Doll Wreaths

by **Beverly Bihn**

Because I make all my holiday decorations by hand, I can make them fit any occasion or season. Some people leave them up all year because they go with the color decor of their home. To make a wreath truly special, I create a doll in the color tones to match the wreath. The size of the doll determines the size of the wreath.

A pink silk flower wreath required a small doll with a head about 5¼in (13cm) high. The doll itself came out 13in (33cm) tall, the total length from the top of her hat to the bottom of the flowing costume measures 20in (51cm), perfect for a 20in (51cm) wreath. I split the back of her dress so that I could sit her on the wreath without losing any of the costume under her. The petticoat has rows of hand-pressed pleats which form a train over the bottom of the wreath. Placing her hat to one side made a background for her head without covering facial features or forming shadows over her face. I placed her loosely on the wreath so that she was secure yet easy to remove when needed. At Christmas, miniature lights may be added around the wreath to be hung inside the house on a door, over a mirror or on a wall.

MATERIALS NEEDED FOR THE PINK SILK FLOWER WREATH:

20in (51cm) white styrofoam ring.
12ft (3.6m) white garland.
12 6in (15cm) nosegay holders in bone.
Five dozen miniature pink silk roses.
Five dozen miniature silk azaleas (half in pink, half bone).
Five dozen forget-me-not pink and bone sprays.
Dried baby's breath.
12yd (10.9m) each 1/4in (.65cm) satin ribbon in green, bone, pink and rose.
Five dozen miniature tiger lilies in rose, bone and pink.
6yd (5.46m) each bone and pink satin ribbon 1/4in (.65cm) wide.
3yd (2.73m) each of 1in (2cm) wide lace and 1/2in (1.3cm) wide lace.
White wrapping tape.
S type greening pins to secure decorations to the styrofoam.
Wire for hanging the wreath.
35-light miniature white cord (optional).

OPPOSITE PAGE: Illustration 1. A 13in (33cm) doll adorns a pink silk flower wreath of nosegays.

Illustration 2. A beige and bone lace wreath adorned with a lace fan was created for a portrait doll.

DIRECTIONS:

1. Wrap wire around the top of the wreath to hang on a nail or hook.
2. Wrap the styrofoam ring with the white garland — I completely wrapped it all the way around the styrofoam, not on just one side.
3. To make the nosegays, I filled each with three roses, three tiger lilies, three azaleas, three forget-me-not sprays and baby's breath; make bows with streamers out of the 1/4in (.65cm) pink, bone, green and rose ribbon — secure them with thin wire into the nosegay. Wrap the nosegays' stems with white wrapping tape.
4. Secure the nosegays onto the wreath at different intervals with the S type greening pins.
5. Scatter the extra silk flowers and baby's breath among the spaces between the nosegays, securing them with the S type greening pins.
6. Make large bows out of the laces and rest of the ribbons to flow from the top of the wreath — attach with wire.
7. Miniature lights go on last so that they may be removed when needed.
8. Doll is placed on the bottom to flow the skirt. A ribbon may be

Illustration 3. A wreath with miniature dolls costumed as angels.

tied around her waist to secure her to the wreath.

A beige and bone lace wreath was adorned with a lace fan to coordinate the colors of a portrait doll's costume.

MATERIALS NEEDED FOR THE BEIGE LACE FAN WREATH:
20in (51cm) wire frame in green.
12ft (3.6m) green garland (if you buy a ready-made green garland, omit this garland).
9in (23cm) lace fan.
12 pearl grape clusters.
12 gold metallic apples, 3in (8cm) in diameter.

12 bone satin Christmas balls, 3in (8cm) in diameter.
Baby's breath.
6yd (5.46m) 2in (5cm) lace/ribbon in bone.
12yd (10.9m) gold metallic trim.
12yd (10.9m) 2½mm pearl trim.
50-light miniature green Christmas cord.
Wire to hang wreath and attach decorations.
12 bone silk miniature roses.

DIRECTIONS:
1. If you buy the metal frame for the wreath, wrap the 12ft (3.6m) garland on the front of the wreath

only (if you buy the ready-made wreath, omit this step).
2. Make a bouquet of three bone roses, two pearl grape clusters and baby's breath for the fan.
3. Sew six yards of metallic gold trim on each edge of the lace/ribbon about 1/4in (.65cm) from the edge.
4. Make a large bow of the ribbon/lace and attach it to the fan; attach the grape cluster bouquet on top of the ribbon.
5. Attach the large fan with bow and grape cluster bouquet to the bottom of the wreath with the wire.

Illustration 4. *Christmas colors come to life in this cranberry bird wreath with a doll dressed in velvet with white mink trim.*

6. Make small bouquets using a bone silk rose, pearl cluster and baby's breath. Make bows of the small 2½mm pearl trim and attach it to each cluster.
7. Wire the pearl cluster bouquets at different spaces on the wreath.
8. Wire the rest of the metallic apples, silk roses, bone satin balls and small pearl bows on the wreath at scattered spaces.
9. Place a wire at the top of the wreath to hang on a door, mirror or wall.
10. Place a green miniature light cord on last so that it can easily be

removed when necessary.
11. The beige lace doll measures 26½ in (67cm) to the top of her hat, so the wreath is hung high enough behind her to flow the ribbon/lace beside her costume.

Some wreaths look beautiful with very miniature dolls costumed as angels to become a permanent part of the wreath. For the angel wreath, I accented the gowns in peach so that the main colors in the wreath would be peach and bone.

MATERIALS NEEDED FOR THE DOUBLE ANGEL PEACH WREATH:
24in (61cm) green wreath.
Two angels measuring 18in (46cm) finished from top of head to bottom edge of gowns.
Two gold harps 9in (23cm) high.
12 small gold bells.
Four small peach hatboxes.
Three peach satin balls.
Four bone satin balls.
12 small silk peach rosebud clusters.
12 small silk bone rosebuds.
12 stems of bone forget-me-not sprays.

Illustration 5. A court jester makes an excellent accent for a musical wreath.

12 stems of peach forget-me-not sprays.
Baby's breath.
Wire to hang wreath and to add decorations to wreath.
2yd (1.82m) 1/2in (1.3cm) bone lace trim.
24yd (21.84m) 1in (2cm) bone lace trim.
12yd (10.9m) 2¹/₂in (6cm) wide peach grosgrain ribbon.
24yd (21.84m) gold metallic trim.
12yd (10.9m) 2¹/₂mm pearl trim.
12yd (10.9m) each 4mm, 6mm and 8mm pearl trim.

12yd (10.9m) gold bead garland.
50-light miniature green Christmas cord.

DIRECTIONS:
1. Tie wire at the top of the wreath to be hung over a nail or hook.
2. Tie ribbon or wire around the waist of each angel and attach to the wreath at the upper left and lower right areas.
3. Wire the gold harps close to each angel as though she were holding it.
4. Trim the satin balls with the 1/2in (1.3cm) wide lace and 2¹/₂mm

pearl trim — some of the balls can be covered with the 4mm pearl trim by gluing it onto the balls.
5. Attach the four peach hatboxes at scattered intervals around the wreath.
6. Attach the peach and bone lace-covered and pearl-covered satin balls (from step 4) at scattered intervals on the wreath with thin wire.
7. Make small bouquets of one gold bell, one bone rosebud, one peach rose cluster, baby's breath and bows of the 2¹/₂mm and 4mm

pearl trim. Wire to the wreath at scattered intervals.

8. Sew the 1in (2cm) lace trim on each edge of the peach grosgrain ribbon.
9. Sew the gold metallic trim over those seams on the peach grosgrain ribbon.
10. Make large bows of the peach ribbon, 2½mm, 4mm, 6mm and 8mm pearl trim and gold beaded garland. Let streamers flow 24in (61cm) down; attach the bow and streamers to the left of the lower angel with wire.
11. Place a wire at the top of the wreath to hang it.
12. Place the light cord on last.
13. This wreath can be hung over a mantle, on a wall, mirror or door.

Christmas colors come to life in this cranberry bird wreath, accompanied by a cranberry velvet doll with white mink trim. Shades of red, pink, green and cranberry adorn the wreath with unusual trims. Plastic fruits can be substituted for the flocked fruit clusters.

MATERIALS NEEDED FOR THE CRANBERRY BIRD WREATH:

20in (51cm) green wreath.
5ft (152cm) of green garland.
Large cranberry or red feathered bird.
Six clusters of green flocked grapes (or plastic).
Six clusters of red flocked grapes (or plastic).
Six red apples.
12 cranberry silk carnations.
12 sprays of cranberry forget-me-not silk flowers.
Baby's breath.
Wire for hanging wreath and attaching decorations.
50-light miniature green Christmas cord.
8yd (7.28m) green 3in (8cm) wide ribbon.
16yd (14.56m) bone ¾in (2cm) wide lace trim.

16yd (14.56m) gold metallic trim.

DIRECTIONS:

1. Put wire on the top of the wreath to hang over a nail or hook.
2. Wire the 5ft (152cm) green garland folded at the bottom of the wreath to cascade at least 30in (76cm) on one side.
3. Sew the bone lace on each edge of the green ribbon.
4. Sew the gold metallic trim over the seams between the green ribbon and lace trim.
5. Make large bows of the green ribbon/lace and let it cascade at least 30in (76cm) beside the flowing green garland — wire it to the left of the garland.
6. Wire the red bird beside the ribbon centered at the bottom of the wreath.
7. Wire the red and green grapes, red apples, cranberry carnations, flower sprays and baby's breath at different intervals on the wreath and cascading garland.
8. Miniature lights go on last so they can be easily removed when necessary.
9. The cranberry velvet doll with the white mink trim stands 26in (66cm) to the top of her fur hat so hang the wreath higher in order to let the garland cascade in front of the doll.

A court jester made an excellent accent for a musical wreath, complete with golden trumpets and horns. Since holidays and the decorations have followed particular themes and color schemes each year, I' created one in the colors of the jester — reds and greens.

MATERIALS NEEDED FOR THE RED AND GREEN COURT JESTER WREATH:

20in (51cm) diameter green wreath.
Court Jester head (on a stick).
Four 6in (15cm) gold trumpets and horns.
24 red holly clusters.

12 red satin balls, 3in (8cm) in diameter.
12 small red apples.
24 red ball berries, 1in (2cm) in diameter.
24 small red berry clusters.
Two yards of 1in (2cm) wide red velour ribbon.
Two yards of 3in (8cm) wide red velour ribbon (for fans).
Three yards of 4in (10cm) wide red and green velour ribbon.
Eight yards of green trim (for fans).
Wire for hanging wreath and attaching decorations.
35-light miniature green cord.

1. Put wire around the top of the wreath to hang over a nail or hook.
2. Make a large bow with several streamers of the 4in (10cm) wide red and green velour ribbon and wire to the bottom right of the wreath.
3. Wire the court jester above the bow onto the wreath.
4. Using the 3in (8cm) wide red velour ribbon, cut it into 8in (20cm) long strips to make fans. Sew the green trim completely around all edges of the 8in (20cm) long strips. Fold the ribbon accordion style to make a fan; put wire around the handle. Wire some holly on the handle of each fan and attach to the wreath at scattered areas.
5. Wire some small berries and holly onto the trumpets and horns and attach to the wreath at different areas.
6. Wire holly and berries on the 12 red satin balls and attach to the wreath in different areas.
7. Make small bows of the 1in (2cm) wide red velour ribbon, attach small berries and wire to the wreath.
8. Wire the small red apples, holly clusters and ball berries to fill in any open areas.
9. Place the light cord on the wreath last so that is can be replaced when necessary. □

NOTE: See the companion article "Doll Tree Splendor" on page 42.

Nineteenth Century Jewelry

by **Albina Bailey**

Finger rings have been in use for thousands of years. They have been connected with poetry and saved or lost a kingdom. A ring can symbolize power and has been a mark of slavery. It is also a link to bind together millions for better, for worse, for richer, for poorer; love has placed it where the vein was supposed to vibrate the heart.

In my 1856 *Godey's Lady's Book* it is said a few years ago a ring was found which had belonged to Shakespeare, and it must have been a gift, for the true lovers' knot is there. Who would not desire to possess, who would not like even to see the relic? There is a reason to suppose that the ring was the gift of Anne Hathaway, and we must be allowed to indulge in the idea that it was pressing Shakespeare's finger when those lines were described: "To the idol of mine eyes, and the delight of my heart, Anne Hathaway:-"

1857 *Peterson Magazine*
General Remarks

In articles of jewelry, floral patterns and fanciful devices are much in favor. Some of the most elegant of the new earrings represent roses, marigolds, daisies, hearts'-ease, beautifully executed in jewels and gems. The hearts'-ease is formed of sapphire, topaz and diamonds; the rose of rubies and diamonds; the daisy of emeralds and diamonds; the marigold of yellow topaz and pearls.

An eminent jeweler has recently completed a circlet for the head consisting of lilies formed of diamonds, pansies composed of sapphire and fuchsias of rubies; the stamens are formed of fine pearls.

A complete parure of pink cameos has been made by a Parisian jeweler. It comprises a number of cameos for fastening up the flounces of the upper skirt of the dress, as well as for ornamenting the corsage. A cordon (an ornamented cord or braid) or series of cameos surrounding the head forms the coiffure. It is fixed at the lower part of the head behind, where it is finished by a tuft of feathers twisted spirally.

Some beautiful specimens have recently been formed of coral; and they are almost all encircled by a row of large pearls. For ball costumes, diadems and necklaces are formed of small coral cameos, and are very effective when worn with a white, sea-green or amber-color dress.

Onyx cameos surrounded by brilliants are perhaps the most costly jewelry now worn.

Among the novelties in jewelry are some imitations of flowers. We have seen a daisy composed of a large sapphire, which forms the disc, set round with rays in diamonds. The hearts'-ease has been made in amethysts and diamonds, and the cactus in rubies and diamonds, the cluster of stamens being formed of small pearls. Necklaces will probably be fashionable in full dress evening costume during the coming season.

Chatelaines are regaining fashionable favor; but those recently introduced are somewhat different in style from the same kind of ornament worn a few years ago. The most elegant consist of two long chains of gold, confined together by a slide with jewels, or beautifully enameled. From one of these chains is suspended a watch in the back of which is frequently set a valuable cameo. To the other chain may be affixed a jeweled medallion, or any other trinket which taste may dictate.

As will be seen, the General Remarks given here serve well in their descriptions for making some lovely authentic miniature pieces of jewelry for your dolls, as well as helping one to recognize an antique piece of jewelry.

The "how-to" jewelry and drawings, with descriptions can all be made without difficulty, following the descriptions and using the smallest of beads, pearls and so on.

Godey Lady's Book
The 1860s
General Remarks

The 1861 articles in wear we note the rich long earrings are now the most fashionable; some consist of a double ball, others of a very long pendant, in pearls and jets.

A new style of watch is the rage in Paris at the present moment. It is large, made of ebony, and ornamented at the back with the initials of the owner in silver, or else with fanciful arabesques. The dial-plate, which is small, is surrounded by a thick circle of ebony, the fingers and hours being in silver. The watch hangs from an ebony chatelaine, the rings of which are ornamented with silver and joined together by bars or balls of silver, according to the

pattern of the chatelaine. There is an attempt to introduce brooches and earrings in the same style. As to the watches, they are to be seen at the waistbands of all the most fashionable ladies, especially when they wear the inevitable fancy black dress.

1867 *Peterson Magazine*
General Remarks

Ribbons tied at the back with long streamers, and a large gold locket in front are still fashionable. Necklets of large beads are also worn. Velvet necklaces continue popular, for they are so generally becoming. The "dog collar" necklace, which is tied close around the throat, and has long hanging ends and bows, is sometimes edged with a straw or jet fringe or, for more "dressy" occasions, with tiny rosebuds.

1871 *Peterson Magazine*
General Remarks

Lockets and crosses tied round the neck with colored ribbon, the ends of which are very long, are the almost indispensable adjuncts of evening toilets, unless a necklace is worn. The richest style of necklace is that formed of various precious stones, chased in gold and united by chains of gold; pendants of precious stones and pearls add much to the beauty of such necklaces. The eardrops are worn to match, and sometimes one bracelet.

Ornaments are chiefly of enamel upon gold, silver or copper, and the cinquecento style still prevails; even the form of this jewelry is exciting. An influence on ordinary gold, as bijouterie, lockets, brooches and rings, are modeled in this style, and the marquise ring, in particular, may be cited as an instance of this.

Bracelets of gold are now worn a good deal with visiting toilettes; they are either plain, flat bands of burnished gold, or else of the serpent shape. They are clasped over the long gloves now so universally worn.

1881 *Peterson Magazine*
General Remarks

From Paris, in the way of jewelry, gold pigs are still very popular and are seen sometimes of portentious size. Crabs of massed diamonds are now very fashionable for brooches, and are worn more than were the diamond spiders which have the misfortune to be costly and frightful at the same time. A comical design for a lace-pin is that of a gold pig leaping over a fence, while in white enamel a handpost at one side announces The Road to Good Luck.

1885 *Peterson Magazine*
General Remarks

Necklets, in black and white lace, satin ribbon, velvet and tulle are worn with low and square cut bodices. They are about 1in (2.5cm) wide and are gathered. Some are worn suspended from black velvet ribbon tied closely round the throat. The later ones are of a long slender oval shape and bear the owner's monogram in small diamonds on a background of dead-gold, within a bordering of small alternate pearls and diamonds.

1886 *Peterson Magazine*
General Remarks

The latest novelty in jewelry is a necklace formed of small diamond roses fitting in the curve of the wearer's throat. With this necklace was worn a brooch in diamonds in the form of a rose with stalk and leaves. The roses could be unscrewed, mounted on a pin and worn in the hair.

1891 *Peterson Magazine*
General Remarks

Small brooches are very fashionable. They are usually round and about the size of a silver quarter dollar. The most popular are in artistic enamel: copies of antique and medieval ornaments, and sometimes with small diamonds introduced into the device. Short oblong pins are shown in artistic combinations of colored gems, such as a square yellow diamond finished at one end with a small ruby and at the other with emerald of the same size, each set between two little white diamonds. Others are seen in fantastic shapes such as keys or branches of fruit or rows of birds, and bow knots of diamonds are used to confine clusters of feathers in the hair for evening toilette.

The rage just now in the line of jewelry is for rings which are worn in profusion and are composed of the finest gems. It is in good taste now to display at least three on the ring finger of each hand and two on each of the little fingers. The middle fingers may also be decorated with a ring or two, so that the forefinger and the thumb are alone left unadorned.

A popular style of finger ring is a thick band of gold set with a single round ruby or sapphire cut "encabochon" (without facets) and surrounded with small brilliants.

The most noticeable item at present is the number of bracelets with which a fashionable lady will adorn her arms. In the slender round bangle shape, each bracelet being set with a single good sized precious stone or with three rubies or sapphires or emeralds or diamonds; as many as ten are often seen worn together. Each bracelet must be set with a different kind of gem.

1855 *Godey's Lady's Book*
Bead Bracelet

This bracelet is formed of jet beads strung on India rubber, which then does not need a clasp, but is passed over the hand on to the arm. As the pattern is given, it needs no description.

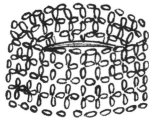

Illustration 1.

NOTE: Any small beads can be used to make this bracelet in the pattern given by Godey. Seed beads, tiny pearls or any small beads of your choice. The bracelet is threaded on elastic; however, very small beads would not pass through elastic. The very fine elastic thread will work nicely for small pearls and other small beads. If the elastic sewing thread is too thick for seed beads, regular polyester sewing thread will be fine. If the sewing thread is used, you would need to allow the ends of the thread to tie round the doll's wrist.

1859 *Peterson Magazine*
Necklace In Imitation Pearl

The materials of this pretty affair are imitation pearl, which not only deserves to be favored for its own sake, but suits every dress, black, white or any color. The beads are large, small and medium size plus a row of those known as the oat bead. A soft cotton is required for stringing them. The mode of threading is so extremely simple, it needs no describing as seen in our engraving.

NOTE: The tiniest of pearls and a package of tiny oat pearls will make this necklace for a large doll. Very tiny pearls can be purchased in many craft shops for this necklace, which will really enhance dolly's dress.

Bracelet

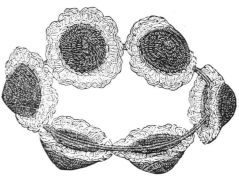

Materials.—Small chenille, without wire: a skein of pure twist, of a color contrasting well with that of the chenille; say gold color silk with chenille, dark green, imperial blue, or claret.

With chenille make 6 ch close in a round work, 3 dc in 1, 2 dc in 1 twice, 3 dc in 1, 2 dc in 1 twice, 1 single stitch.

2d round.—2 dc in 1, 6 dc, 2 dc in 1, 6 dc.

3d.—2 dc in 1, 7 dc, 2 dc in 1, 7 dc.

4th.—With twist, 2 dc in 1, 8 dc, 2 dc in 1, 8 dc.

5th.—With twist, 1 dc 3 tr in the next loop; repeat ten times.

To make up the bracelet, fasten six or seven of these buttons on a piece of elastic braid, the size of the wris

Illustration 3.

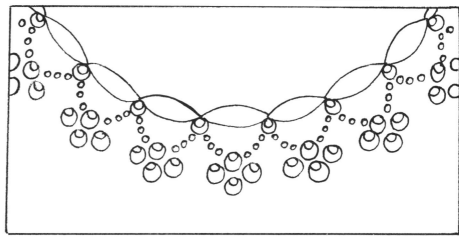

Illustration 2.

Rings Description

The rings shown here in *Illustration 4* are new styles, suited to engagement rings. The first is of gold and dark blue enamel, with a single diamond in the center of the "true love knot."

The second is of richly chased gold, the star having a large brilliant in the

Illustration 4.

center, with five smaller diamonds in the points.

1859 *Godey's Lady's Book*
A Bead Bracelet

Materials: some large-sized chalk beads, three or four sizes larger than seed beads, or shell pearls may be used, or turquoise, and No. 10 steel beads, or uncut jet beads; either will look handsome. No. 20 cotton thread. A fine needle.

1st round. Take ¾yd (.69cm) of cotton; thread thereon 18 beads; tie these up in a circle, not too tight, but sufficiently loose that 20 beads might be tied in, if they were requisite; leave one end of the cotton, about a finger in length; tie the knot of the circle securely.

Illustration 5.

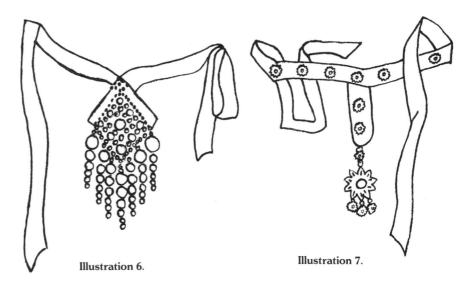

Illustration 6.

Illustration 7.

2nd. Place the circle of beads on the point of forefinger of left hand, with needle and cotton in front, thread a bead*; pass it close up to first circle; make an overcast stitch over the cotton, between first and second bead; with the point of the needle pass up close to this a bead of first circle; hold it tightly; thread another bead. Repeat from * till there are 18 beads in the second row; then pass the needle and thread all through the first circle of beads and tie in a secure knot to the end left on; pass the needle and cotton again through second circle; tie in a knot to the end of cotton and cut the ends off so that the knot is not seen. This running the cotton through the beads makes them firm, strong and even. This forms the first link of bracelet. To make the second after threading the 18 beads, pass them through the first link; then proceed as before. Link as many of these circles together as will enable the bracelet, when joined, to pass tightly over the hand. To join the first and last link together, thread the 18 beads, and, before tying, pass the cotton through first and last link; then tie and proceed as before. When each link is completed, a third row may be added, if desired, worked in the same way; but of course, the preceding row is immovable.

NOTE: This bracelet can be made for dolls by using seed beads, tiny pearls or tiny beads of your choice, threading six to eight beads for each circle, or less, whichever will work nicely for your doll. Work as many links as will slide the bracelet over the doll's hand as described above.

1875 *Peterson Magazine*
The New Fashioned Throatlets
We here give an engraving of a throatlet to be made of blue velvet and pearls. The velvet encircling the throat is lined with white satin and worked in tiny pearls. The ornament depending from the front consists of pearls of various sizes. Roman pearls, of course, are used.

Also shown is a throatlet of black velvet, gilt and enamel. The black velvet encircling the throat is lined with white satin and studded with gold and enamel stars. A single end of velvet falls in front and terminates with a gold and enamel ornament.

NOTE: Illustration 6. Use the very tiniest pearls available and 3mm pearls for the large pearls. *Illustration 7.* The tiny gold sequin stars will work nicely for the center front with the tiny stars attached to its points, as seen in the drawing.

MATERIALS.—Narrow black or colored velvet; some cardboard and beads.
Cut the star or cross out of cardboard; cover with velvet the same color as the neck-piece; then ornament with jet, pearl, steel, or gold beads; or a combination of two, following the designs given.

Illustration 8.

1867 *Peterson Magazine*
Designs For Neck Velvets
1869 *Godey's Lady's Book*
Earrings
Illustration 9. Earring in the Campana style in gold of various tints.
Illustration 10. Earrings, antique cameo, set in gold.

1886 *Peterson Magazine*
Dog Collars
Jet necklace composed of five rows of French jet beads. The clasp in front is also of jet, from which eight rows of beads depend, terminating in large jet pears.
Necklet composed of colored jet beads.

General Remark
Satin dog collars to match the color of the dress and embroidered with beads, also to match, are now often worn round the throat with evening dresses.

Illustration 12.

Illustration 9.   Illustration 10.

Illustration 11.

DRESSING:

DOLL

SOCKS

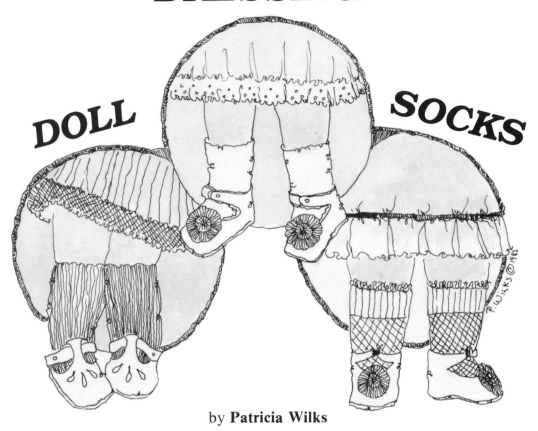

by **Patricia Wilks**

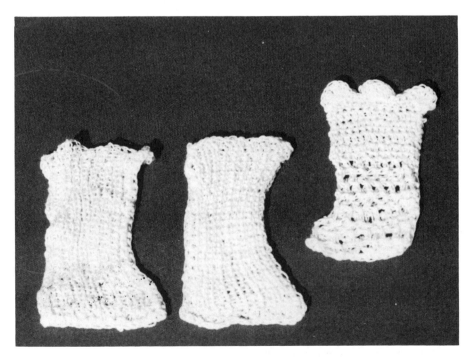

ABOVE: Illustration 1. Knit and crocheted doll socks.

Doll Socks: for a 24in (61cm) German doll

Materials

Size E crochet hook for crocheted socks

Size one knitting needles for 24in (61cm) doll's socks

Size two knitting needles for larger sized doll's socks

Knit-Cro-Sheen in ecru or color of choice

Rib Socks

Cast on 36 sts. Work (in medium tension) in a rib of knit 1, purl 1 for about 5in (12.7cm). Bind off in rib and sew or crochet side seam and bottom seam.

Lacy Socks

Make a chain of 30 sts. Turn, skip 2 sts, single crochet in 28 sts. Chain 1, turn. Work 3 more single crochet rows. Next row: chain 2, skip first st, single crochet in next st, chain 1, skip next st, single crochet in next st, across row (14 spaces made), chain 2, turn. Next row: work as for previous row but work the single crochets in the spaces. Work 6 more rows the same. End off. At top edge of socks attach thread and work one row of shells as follows: In first st work: 2 double, 1 treble, 2 double, 1 single, then 1 single in each of next 3 sts; work a shell, continue across row. End off. Sew seams.

Using smaller sized needles and tighter tension you can make socks for smaller French bébés. □

Dress of the Early 1820s
to fit a 21in doll

by **Barbara Pickering**

Photographs by **Lloyd Pickering**

Fashions around 1820 were noted for simplicity and elegance, based on classical sources. The waistline was immediately under the bust, either belted or girdled. The skirts fell full and long to the ground. The materials used were delicate silks or other lightweight fabrics and colors were subtle. A minimum of underwear was worn. Pantaloons were not in fashion then, although they came in shortly afterwards. A chemise and petticoat was all that was worn. The chemise was knee-length and made of very fine cotton or linen. It was straight, ungathered and often buttoned at the front. It had either a high neckline or an oval or square one. It could be sleeveless or have long or short sleeves. Usually the chemise was trimmed with lace. Silk stockings were worn which reached above the knees and were held up with garters. The stockings often matched the dress in color. The garters could be of silk or fine cloth and were embroidered or adorned with rosettes. From circa 1800 to 1830, slippers of silk, satin or kid were worn, usually decorated with bows and silk ribbons. Pretty bonnets completed the picture. These were extremely feminine, tied under the chin with wide, long ribbons and decorated with artificial flowers or feathers. The crown of the bonnet extended upwards to accommodate the high hair style.

This pattern is based on an old fashion plate of 1820.

Do remember to check the various pattern pieces on your doll, as no two dolls are alike. Some slight adjustments will inevitably be necessary to suit your particular doll.

Materials required:
24in (61cm) by 20in (50.8cm) calico (body)
18in (45.7cm) by 10in (25.4cm) fine white cotton (chemise)
Six small pearl buttons (chemise)
Approx. 37in (93.9cm) by 1/4in (.65cm) white cotton lace (edging of chemise)
17in (43.2cm) by 16½in (41.9cm) white cotton (petticoat)
Approx. 16in (40.6cm) by 1/4in (.65cm) white scalloped lace (edging of petticoat)
Approx. 26in (66cm) by 1/4in (.65cm) white cotton tape (petticoat)
9½in (24.2cm) by 7½in (19.1cm) light blue silk stockings (stockings)
22in (55.9cm) by 1/2in (1.3cm) light pink ribbon (garters)
5in (12.7cm) by 4in (10.2cm) kid (shoes)
3in (7.6cm) by 2½in (6.4cm) leather (shoe soles)
3in (7.6cm) by 2½in (6.4cm) cardboard (inner shoe soles)
Small length of blue embroidery floss (to tie shoes)
Two small fabric flowers (top of shoes)
36in (91.4cm) by 16in (40.6cm) blue silk (dress)
46in (116.8cm) by 16in (40.6cm) cream-colored silk (dress and bonnet lining)
Approx. 23in (58.4cm) by 2¼in (5.8cm) cream-colored lace (bottom edging of dress)
Approx. 62in (157.4cm) by 3/4in (2cm) cream-colored lace (ruching of dress)
48in (121.9cm) by 1in (2.5cm) pink velvet ribbon (sash)
36in (91.4cm) by 1/4in (.65cm) pink velvet ribbon (dress)
Three small old gold tassels (dress, bag)
Three small pearl buttons (dress)
Tiny fabric flowers (to decorate sash)

Illustration 1. 21in (53.3cm) doll shown in her 1820s dress.

Illustration 2. Side view of 21in (53.3cm) doll in her 1820s dress and hat.

15in (38.1cm) by 10in (25.4cm) cream-
colored heavy silk (bonnet)
28in (71.1cm) by 1/4in (.65cm) cream-
colored ribbon (to tie bonnet)
White fabric flowers (to trim bonnet)
3¼in (8.3cm) by 1¾in (4.5cm) sand-colored
silk (bag)
Small length of old gold embroidery floss
(to tie bag)
Matching sewing cotton
Filling
Sobo glue
Wig

Instructions:
Cut out all pattern pieces as indicated.
Sew on wrong side unless otherwise stated.
Seam allowance (1/4in [.65cm]) included.
Press all seams carefully.
BODY: Sew both upper legs to body front,
matching points A and B. Sew seams F to
G. Sew body back from B to H. Sew upper
leg to lower back, matching points B and F.
Then sew together leg seams from D to E.
Now sew in body seat gussets, starting at
C. Sew J to J and G to A.

Next insert the leg into the upper leg
part until the groove of the leg is approximately 1in (2.5cm) from the seam E. Use a
waxed thread and tie the calico fabric
tightly to the leg. Make sure the string does
not slip off the groove. Make the other leg
in the same way. Turn the body right side
out. Stuff the upper leg firmly. Fold the
gussets at the seat inwards and keep them
free from stuffing so that they will open and
close to allow movement. After the rest of
the body is firmly stuffed, turn under raw
edges of neckline and sew up opening.

Proceed with the arms in exactly the
same way as for the legs. Do not put too
much stuffing in them; they should hang
naturally from the body. Then sew both
arms firmly to the top of the body. Finally
place the head onto the body and sew
(again use waxed thread) into position.
CHEMISE: Sew the two fronts and back
together at side and shoulder seams as
indicated by the broken lines on the pattern
(French seams). Fold under front openings and hem neatly. Cut a bias strip of the
same material 1/2in (1.3cm) wide by neckline width. With right sides together sew
the strip to the neckline. Turn the strip to
wrong side of chemise, turn under raw
edges and hem. Do the same with both
armholes. Adjust length of chemise, turn
under raw edges and hem. Mark all buttonholes according to the pattern, make six
small buttonholes and sew on buttons
accordingly. Edge neckline, armholes and
bottom of chemise with very narrow cotton
lace.
PETTICOAT: Fold the material in half and
sew center back seam along broken lines
(French seam). Hem the back opening
with a very narrow hem. Buttonhole stitch
point A and then make a loop across to
prevent the opening from tearing. To

Illustration 3. 21in (53.3cm) doll showing details
of her stockings.

make the loop, pass the cotton thread
from side to side two or three times and
work over them closely in buttonhole
stitch (see diagram). Gather waistband of
petticoat to fit waistband. Place right sides
together and sew. Turn waistband to
wrong side of petticoat, turn under raw
edges, neaten ends, and sew. Adjust hemline, turn under raw edges and sew. Thread
narrow white cotton tape through the
waistband and tie at the back. Stitch white
scalloped cotton lace to the bottom of the
petticoat.
STOCKINGS: If you do not possess a pair
of old silk stockings, use either stockinette
or coarse lace (the latter can be quite
effective). I colored the material to match
the blue silk dress.

Wrap the material around the leg and
tack together, stretching tightly as you go.
Slip the material off the leg and sew along
tacking line. Cut off any surplus material.
Turn under raw edges at the top and hem.
GARTERS: Sew a piece of the pink ribbon
around the leg to hold up the stockings.
Adorn the garter with a small rosette
which is made as follows:

Take a length of your ribbon (approximately 3in [7.6cm]), fold in half lengthwise and pull a gathering thread along one
edge (see diagram), pull tight and secure
firmly with a few stitches. Sew the rosette
to the garter.
SHOES: The pattern given here is only a
guideline. You will have to adjust it according to your doll's feet.

Cut two soles in cardboard and two in
leather. The cardboard ones should be
slightly smaller. Fold the leather top part of
the shoe in half and sew front seam along
broken lines. Turn right side out. Stretch
the leather around over the cardboard sole

matching points A and B and glue. Next
glue the leather sole to the cardboard sole.
Glue a small fabric flower on top of the
shoe and stitch a length of blue embroidery
floss to each side of the shoe and tie into a
bow (see diagram).
DRESS: The dress is made of pale blue silk
and lined throughout with cream-colored
silk. The dress and the lining are cut out
together and sewn as one piece.

Sew the **bodice** front to the back parts
at side and shoulder seams along broken
lines (French seams). Fold the **sleeves** in
half and sew along broken lines (French
seams). Make sure the sleeves are tight
fitting. Gather the top of the sleeves to fit
armholes and sew both sleeves into bodice.
Turn under folding line of back bodice and
hem neatly. Mark and sew three buttonholes and sew on three pearl buttons
accordingly.

Make two front and two back darts in
the **skirt**. I have not marked the darts on
the patterns, as it will be easier for you to
find the correct position when you fit the
skirt to the doll. Fold the material in half
and sew along broken lines (French seam).
Make sure the skirt fits the bodice properly!
Put the dress onto the doll and adjust
sleeve and skirt lengths. Turn under raw
edges and hem.

Sew a lovely piece of lace round the
bottom edge of the dress and sew some
ruched lace round the neckline, and
shoulders and cuffs. I also added pale pink
velvet ribbon to the front bodice and the
bottom of the dress. Place a sash around
the high waistline and finish it off with a tiny
bouquet of fabric flowers. The top of the
shoulders are adorned with two small gold
tassels, so much favored at that time. And,
finally, enhance the elegant dress with a
fine piece of jewelry at the neck.
HAIR: I bought a beautiful auburn wig (real
hair). After several attempts to create the
correct style, I gave up, as it just would not
work out. I asked my very helpful hair-
dresser to have a go. He was most delighted
and created a typical 1820s hair style (see
diagram).
BONNET: Fold the hat part in half and
sew from A to B along broken lines. Insert
the crown, matching points B and C. Sew
the brim to the hat, matching points D and
E. Now topstitch the brim (six rows - see
diagram) which gives it firmness. Make the
same bonnet out of thin silk and insert the
lining into the bonnet (wrong sides together). Turn under all raw edges and
stitch the lining with tiny invisible stitches
to the bonnet. Sew cream-colored ribbons
at points D and stitch artificial flowers to
the hat (see diagram).
BAG: Sew the two pieces together along
broken lines. Turn under raw edges of
opening and hem. Turn right side out and
thread a length of old gold embroidery floss
through the top, gather, make a loop and
secure firmly. Sew a tassel to the bottom of
the bag. □

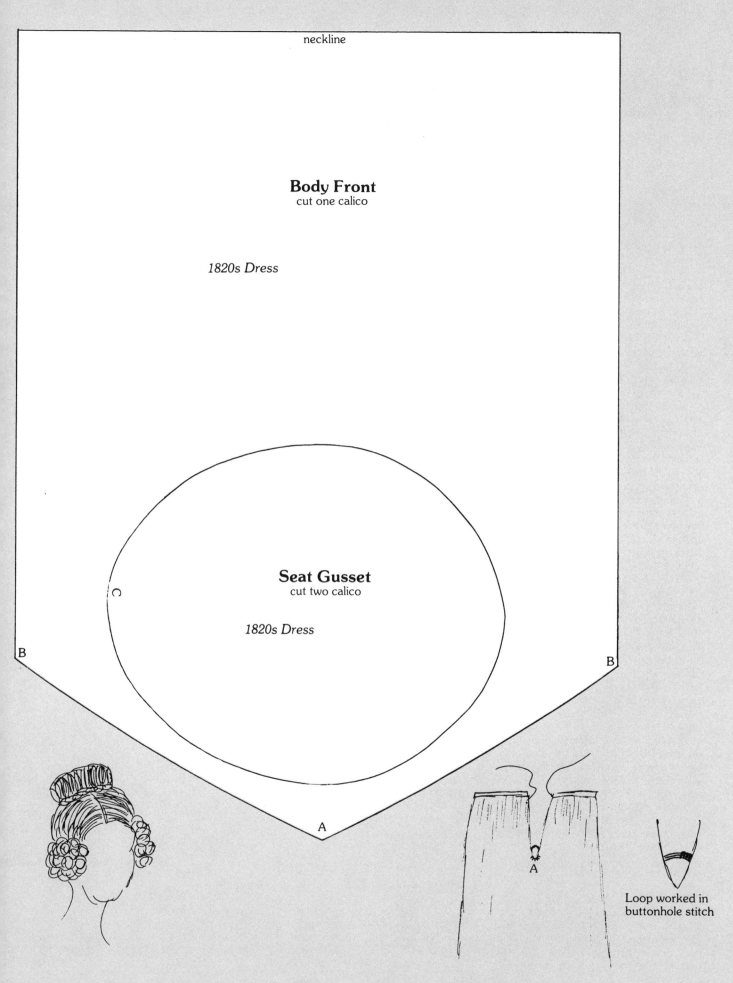

neckline

Body Front
cut one calico

1820s Dress

Seat Gusset
cut two calico

1820s Dress

B

C

B

A

A

Loop worked in
buttonhole stitch

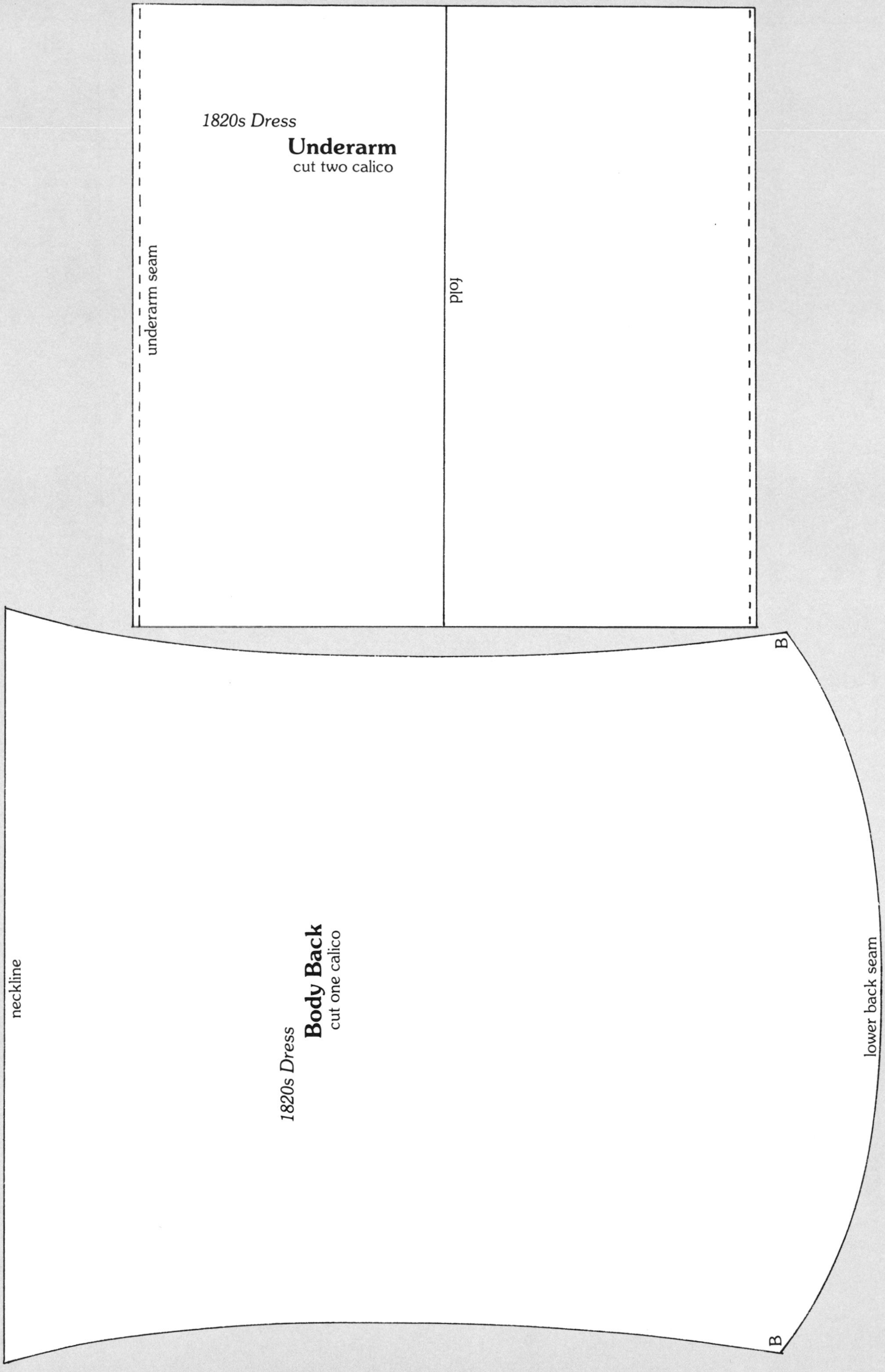

1820s Dress

Underarm
cut two calico

underarm seam

fold

1820s Dress

Body Back
cut one calico

neckline

lower back seam

B

B

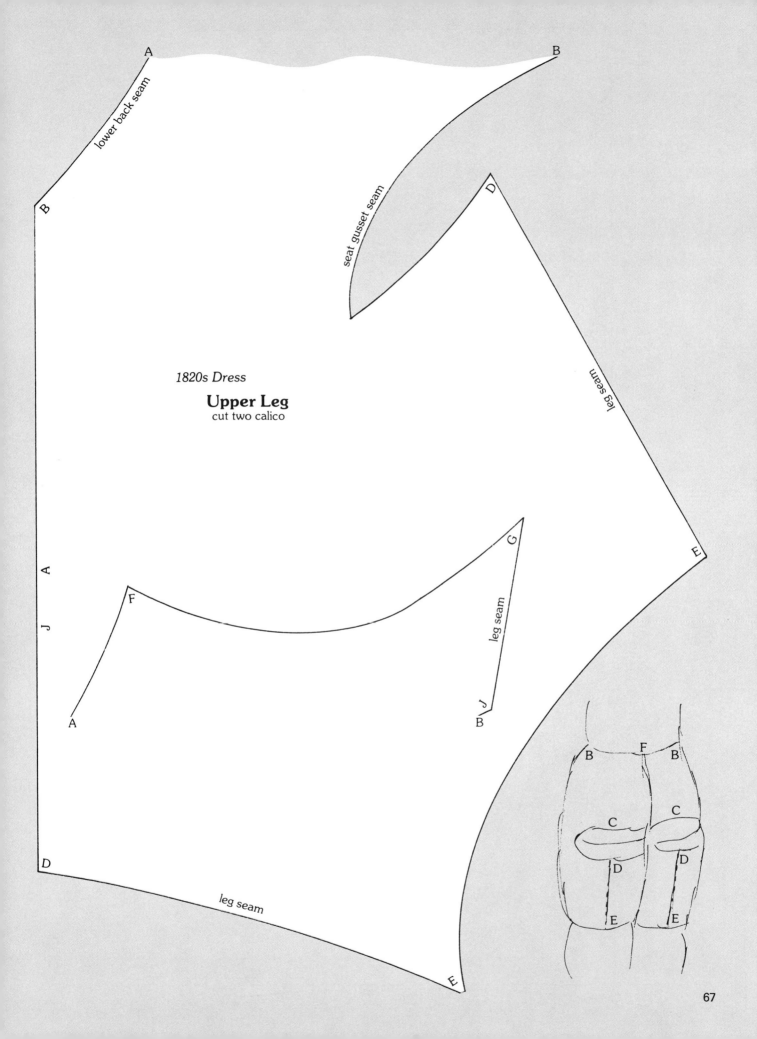

1820s Dress

Upper Leg
cut two calico

lower back seam

seat gusset seam

leg seam

leg seam

leg seam

A · B · D · E · F · G · J

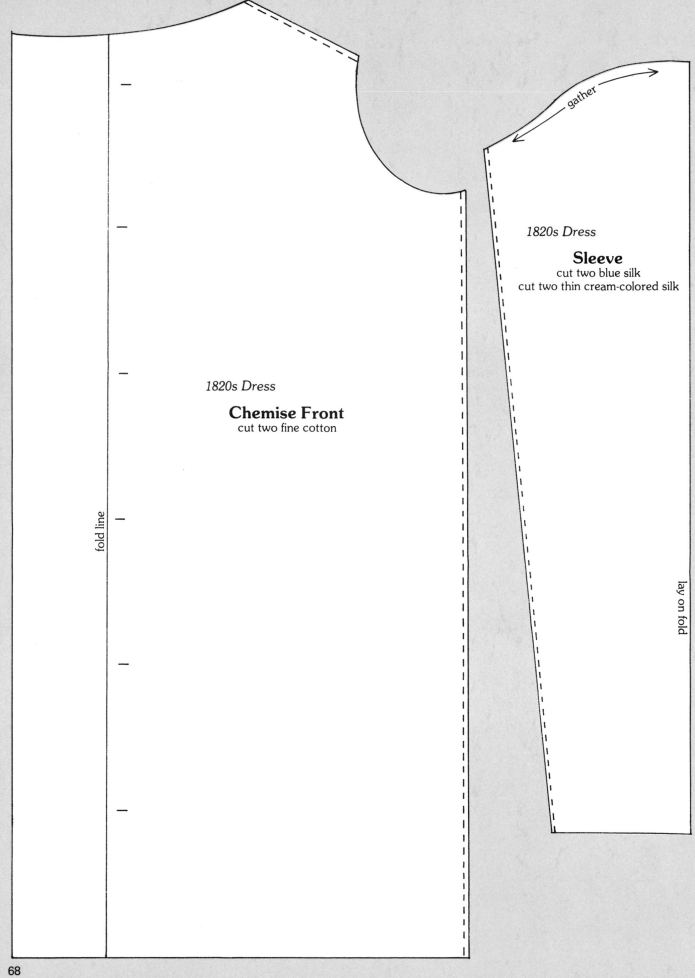

1820s Dress

Chemise Front
cut two fine cotton

fold line

1820s Dress

Sleeve
cut two blue silk
cut two thin cream-colored silk

gather

lay on fold

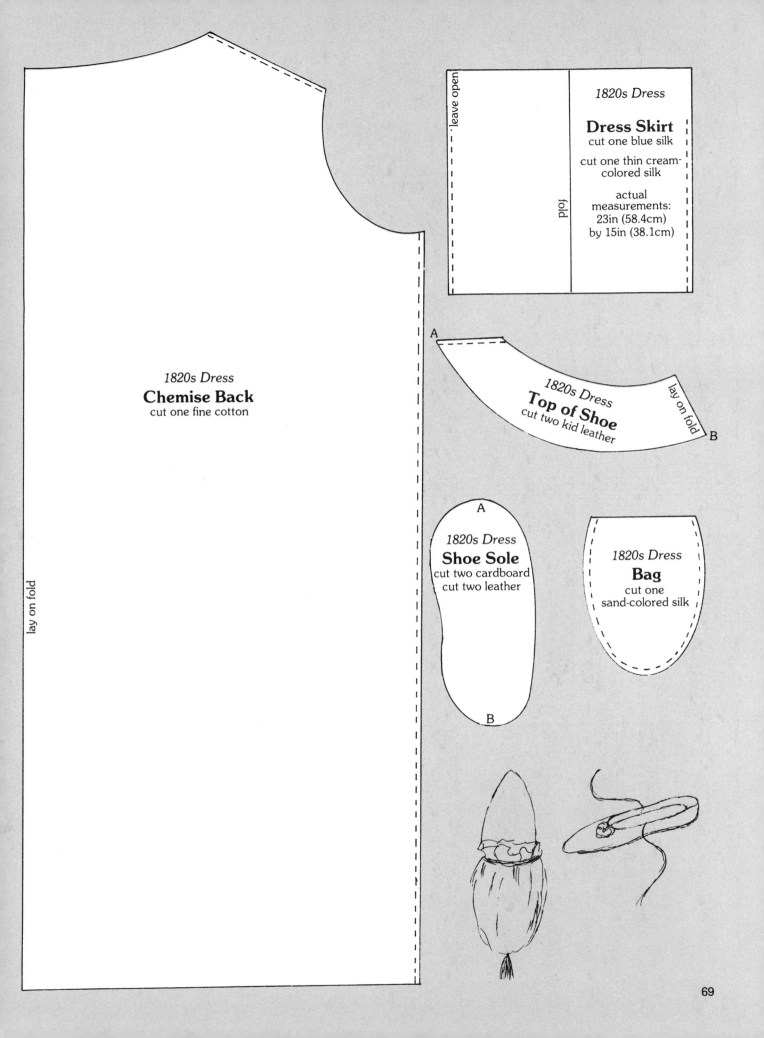

1820s Dress
Chemise Back
cut one fine cotton

lay on fold

leave open

fold

1820s Dress
Dress Skirt
cut one blue silk

cut one thin cream-
colored silk

actual
measurements:
23in (58.4cm)
by 15in (38.1cm)

A

1820s Dress
Top of Shoe
cut two kid leather

lay on fold

B

A

1820s Dress
Shoe Sole
cut two cardboard
cut two leather

B

1820s Dress
Bag
cut one
sand-colored silk

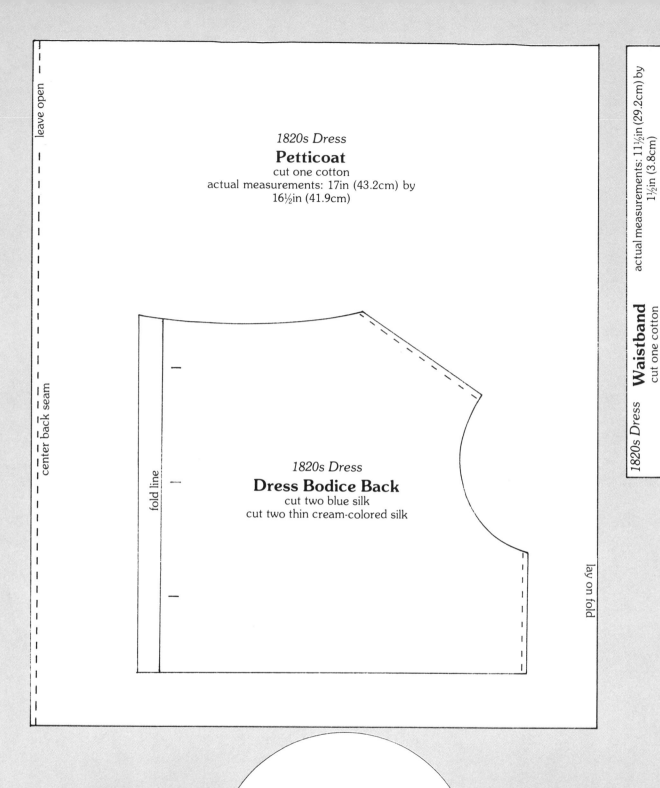

1820s Dress
Petticoat
cut one cotton
actual measurements: 17in (43.2cm) by
16½in (41.9cm)

leave open

center back seam

fold line

1820s Dress
Dress Bodice Back
cut two blue silk
cut two thin cream-colored silk

lay on fold

1820s Dress **Waistband** actual measurements: 11½in (29.2cm) by 1½in (3.8cm)
cut one cotton

1820s Dress
Crown
cut one heavy cream-colored silk
cut one thin cream-colored silk

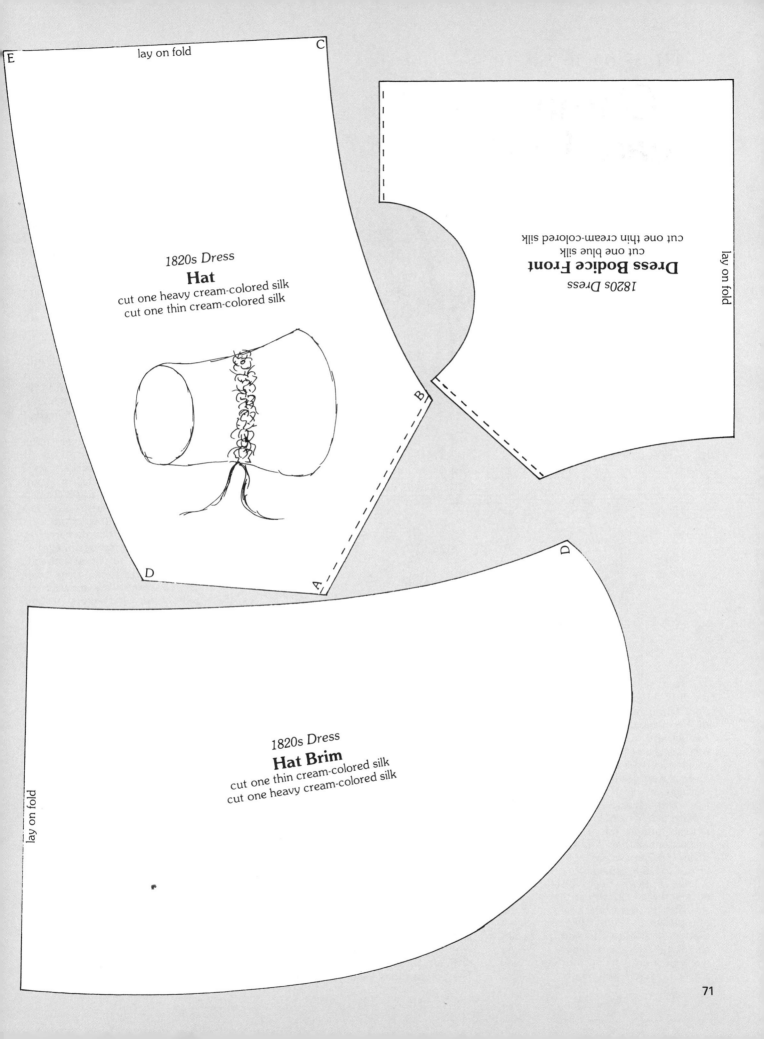

E

lay on fold

1820s *Dress*
Hat
cut one heavy cream-colored silk
cut one thin cream-colored silk

D

B

A

lay on fold

cut one thin cream-colored silk
cut one blue silk
Dress Bodice Front
1820s *Dress*

D

1820s *Dress*
Hat Brim
cut one thin cream-colored silk
cut one heavy cream-colored silk

lay on fold

Dressing a 12½in
China Head Doll

by SANDY WILLIAMS

Pale blue eyes are the focal point on this 12½in (31.8cm) china head doll. She is marked "2½" on the back of her shoulder plate. The markings on her lips, cheeks, nostrils and eyelids are coral tinted. She has black molded curly hair. Her original china limbs were chipped and broken through years of loving play. China legs with black high-heeled boots replace her original broken legs with reddish brown boots. Her undressed measurements are: 7in (17.8cm) chest, 5¾in (14.7cm) waist, 7½in (19.1cm) hips, 2-1/8in (5.4cm) upper arm, 3-1/8in (7.9cm) thigh, 3½in (8.9cm) neck and 5in (12.7cm) crotch.

The patterns are listed in order of placement on the doll: open drawers, chemise, tucked petticoat, chemisette (a short blouse with no sleeves, short, or in this case, long sleeves), skirt and basque bodice.

Since the muslin bodies on china head dolls vary from doll to doll, the patterns should be used as a guide. Finish one garment *before* you measure your doll for the next garment. I like to first try out a pattern in a "pattern tracing cloth" which can be marked on, sewn on and is also semi-transparent - - plus you can take the garment apart and use it as a pattern. Set your sewing machine for 10 to 12 stitches per inch. If sewing by hand, sew with tiny running stitches and occasionally take one backstitch to prevent the stitches from unraveling. The patterns include a 1/4in (0.65cm) seam allowance. Press after each sewing step. I dressed this doll in a medium-blue china silk and trimmed the bodice and skirt with black picot trim. Silk is not difficult to sew with - - just take a few precautions and you will be

rewarded with beautiful results: use a dry iron on a low setting, use fine sharp needles for hand and machine sewing, use silk or extra-fine thread. Carefully lay out all patterns on the straight of grain.

Materials Needed: 1yd (0.91m) of 100 percent white cotton batiste, 1yd (0.91m) of china silk, matching silk or extra-fine thread for lightweight fabrics, seven 3/16in (0.45cm) white two-hole buttons, 1¾yds (1.60m) of 3/8in (0.9cm) fine white lace, 24in (61.0cm) of 1/8in (0.31cm) wide white twill tape, two size oo hooks and eyes, 2yds (1.82m) of 1/8in (0.31cm) wide black picot trim, 20in (50.8cm) of baby yarn for cording, No. 10 sharp hand sewing needles, No. 9 or No. 11 sharp machine needles, No. 22 tapestry (blunt) needle.

Open Drawers: 6¼in (15.9cm) finished length. Cut two drawer patterns from batiste and a waistband 1in (2.5cm) wide by doll's waist measurement plus 1½in (3.8cm) - - I needed 1in (2.5cm) by 7-1/8in (18.1cm). Mark the two tuck fold lines; press on fold lines; stitch 3/16in (0.45cm) in from fold lines to make tucks. Hem drawers 1/2in (1.3cm) and blindstitch lace to this edge. French seam each inner leg seam. Sew the two leg pieces together from CF (center front) waist to dot; narrowly hem each edge of crotch seam. Gather waist of drawers to fit waistband. Attach waistband, tucking in twill tape as you sew. Place drawers on doll; pull tapes; wrap tapes around doll's waist - - waistband will overlap waist about 1/2in (1.3cm). Tie twill tape in a small bow.

Chemise: Mid-calf length, off-the-shoulder. Fold batiste twice so that the shoulders and the CF and CB (center front and center back) edges are on folds. Mark tuck lines. Sew each tuck with tiny backhand stitches; press tucks as illustrated. Gather back chemise between dots to fit doll. Cut a bias strip of batiste 3/4in (2.0cm) wide by the desired neckline width plus 1/2in (1.3cm). With right sides of bias strip and chemise together, sew a 1/4in (0.65cm) seam; trim to 1/8in (0.31cm). Turn bias strip to wrong side of chemise and turn raw edge in; blindstitch closed. Narrowly hem sleeve and sew lace to this edge. French seam each side seam. Turn chemise hem up 1/2in (1.3cm) and blindstitch.

Tucked Petticoat: 6¾in (17.2cm) finished length. Cut a piece of batiste 8in (20.3cm) by 20in (50.8cm) and a waistband 1in (2.5cm) wide by waistline measurement plus

Chemisette Front

Chemisette Back

Basque Front

Basque Back

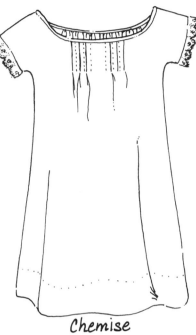

Chemise

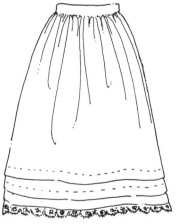

Petticoat

1/2in (1.3cm) plus 1/2in (1.3cm) overlap - - I needed 1in (2.5cm) by 6¾in (17.2cm). Mark hem fold line 1/2in (1.3cm) from bottom edge; mark first tuck fold line 1/2in (1.3cm) above hem fold line; mark second tuck fold line 5/8in (1.6cm) above first tuck fold line (use drawer tuck lines as a guide). Follow drawers' directions for tucks, hem and lace edge. Sew a 1/4in (0.65cm) center back seam to within 2in (5.1cm) of waistline. Press seam open; turn raw edges of center back seam and opening in and blindstitch. Gather waist of petticoat to fit waistband; sew together. Close petticoat with tiny button and thread loop.

Chemisette: Cut chemisette sleeves, bodice front and bodice back from batiste. French seam bodice front to bodice back at shoulders. Stitch five rows of lace across bodice front using the dotted lines as a guide. Gather caps of sleeves between dots; set sleeves into bodice armscyes. Cut two cuffs: wrist measurement plus 1/2in (1.3cm) plus 1/4in (0.65cm) overlap by 3/4in (2.0cm) wide - - I needed 1-7/8in (4.7cm) by 3/4in (2.0cm). Gather sleeve edges to fit cuff. Place right sides of cuffs to right sides of sleeves; sew together; trim seams to 1/8in (0.31cm). Sew undersleeve seam from star to bodice waist in one continuous seam; repeat with other sleeve. Turn raw edge of sleeve opening in and narrowly hem each edge. Turn cuff to wrong side of sleeve; tuck raw edges in and stitch closed. Turn both sides of chemisette back opening in on fold lines, tuck raw edges in and stitch. Cut a waistband: doll's waist measurement plus 1/2in (1.3cm) plus 1/2in (1.3cm) overlap by 3/4in (2.0cm) wide - - I needed 7in (17.8cm) by 3/4in (2.0cm). Gather waist edge of bodice to fit waistband; finish as cuff directions. Cut a piece of self-fabric bias tape approximately 3/4in (2.0cm) by 5in (12.7cm) and with right sides of bias tape and bodice neckline together sew the two together. The neckline of chemisette fits doll snugly so you may need to slightly gather bodice neckline edge before you sew the bias tape on - - this will keep the neckline from gapping

open. Trim seam to 1/8in (0.31cm); turn raw edge of bias tape in and blindstitch closed. Finish bodice back with four buttons and thread loops. Close each cuff with a tiny button and thread loop so that cuffs fit wrists snugly. Place chemisette on doll and push sleeve down over cuff so that it blouses over cuffs.

Skirt: Cut a silk skirt 9¼in (23.6cm) by 31in (78.7cm); cut a batiste skirt lining 8-3/8in (21.2cm) by 31in (78.7cm); cut a silk waistband: doll's waist measurement plus 1/2in (1.3cm) by 1in (2.5cm) wide - - I needed 1in (2.5cm) by 6½in (16.5cm). Sew center back seams: with right sides of silk skirt together, sew a 3/8in (0.9cm) seam 3in (7.6cm) down from center back waist to hem; repeat with skirt lining; press center back seams open. Place wrong side of silk skirt and wrong side of lining together; pin and baste skirts together at their waistlines. Blindstitch silk back opening to lining back opening. Turn up a 3/8in (0.9cm) hem on skirt lining and stitch. Handle the waist of skirt as one piece of fabric from now on. Mark the center front point of skirt

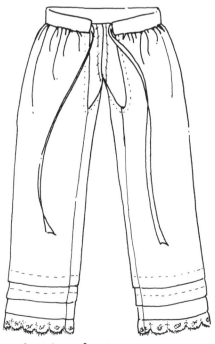

back of drawers

at the waistline. Starting about 3/4in (2.0cm) in from each center back skirt opening (see skirt illustration), evenly space 13 pleats *toward* the center front point; repeat with other skirt side. Place skirt on doll; pin center back opening with about a 1/4in (0.65cm) overlap; gather each skirt between overlap and first pleat to fit doll's waist. Pin up silk skirt hem so it just touches floor. Sew waistband to skirt. Blindstitch silk skirt hem. With tiny stitches sew picot trim around skirt so the trim hides the hem stitches.

Bodice: With pencil, lightly trace bodice patterns on batiste, marking

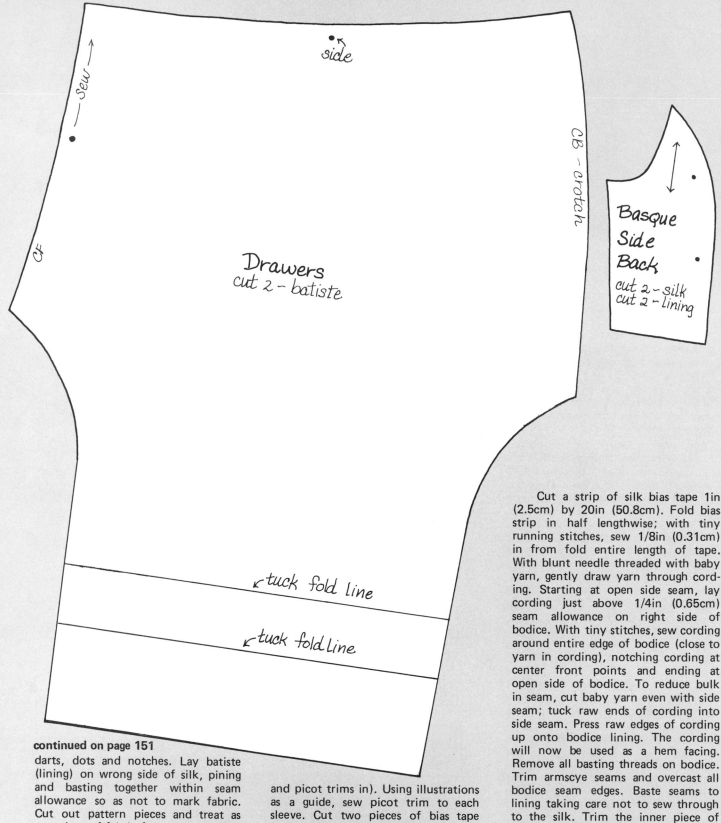

Drawers
cut 2 – batiste

side

sew →

CF

CB – crotch

← tuck fold line

← tuck fold line

Basque Side Back
cut 2 – silk
cut 2 – lining

continued on page 151

darts, dots and notches. Lay batiste (lining) on wrong side of silk, pining and basting together within seam allowance so as not to mark fabric. Cut out pattern pieces and treat as one piece of fabric from now on. Sew darts on front bodices. Match markings on each side back bodice to back bodice; pin at markings. Starting at waist, sew to armscye easing side back where necessary. Sew front and back bodice together at shoulders; press seams toward back bodice. Sew side seams together - - on one side seam leave open 3/8in (0.9cm) above waist (to place raw ends of cording

and picot trims in). Using illustrations as a guide, sew picot trim to each sleeve. Cut two pieces of bias tape from silk fabric 1in (2.5cm) by 5in (12.7cm). With right sides of bias tape and sleeve together, sew bias tape to each sleeve edge. Sew each sleeve underarm seam together; press. Press bias tape up to wrong side of sleeve; tuck raw edge in and blind-stitch bias tape to inside of sleeve lining. Slightly gather cap of each sleeve, set sleeve into bodice armscye matching markings.

Cut a strip of silk bias tape 1in (2.5cm) by 20in (50.8cm). Fold bias strip in half lengthwise; with tiny running stitches, sew 1/8in (0.31cm) in from fold entire length of tape. With blunt needle threaded with baby yarn, gently draw yarn through cording. Starting at open side seam, lay cording just above 1/4in (0.65cm) seam allowance on right side of bodice. With tiny stitches, sew cording around entire edge of bodice (close to yarn in cording), notching cording at center front points and ending at open side of bodice. To reduce bulk in seam, cut baby yarn even with side seam; tuck raw ends of cording into side seam. Press raw edges of cording up onto bodice lining. The cording will now be used as a hem facing. Remove all basting threads on bodice. Trim armscye seams and overcast all bodice seam edges. Baste seams to lining taking care not to sew through to the silk. Trim the inner piece of cording to 1/8in (0.31cm); tuck raw edge of wider piece of cording in and baste to bodice lining - - carefully notching cording fabric at center front points so cording will lay flat against lining. With tiny stitches sew picot trim just inside of cording around entire edge of bodice, using illustrations as a guide. Sew side seam closed. Close bodice center front points with a tiny hook and a thread loop.

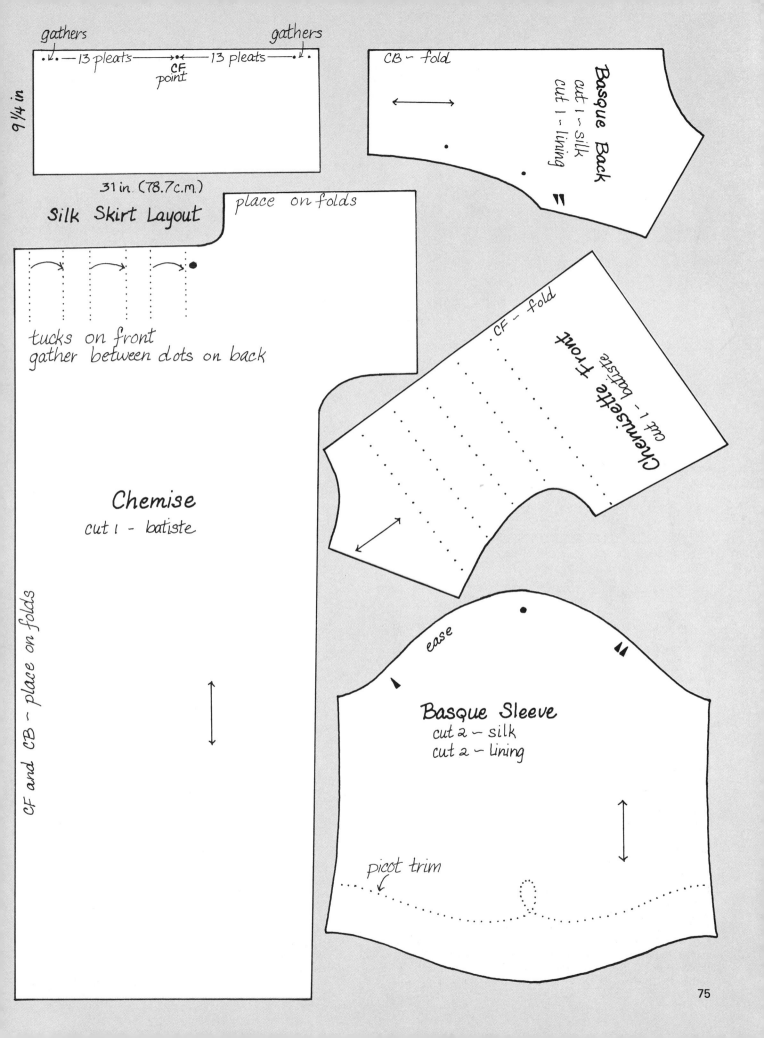

gathers   gathers

|←— 13 pleats —→|←— 13 pleats —→|

CF point

9 1/4 in

31 in. (78.7 c.m.)

Silk Skirt Layout

place on folds

CB — fold

Basque Back
cut 1 ~ silk
cut 1 ~ lining

tucks on front
gather between dots on back

Chemise
cut 1 - batiste

CF — fold

Chemisette Front
cut 1 - batiste

CF and CB ~ place on folds

ease

Basque Sleeve
cut 2 ~ silk
cut 2 ~ lining

picot trim

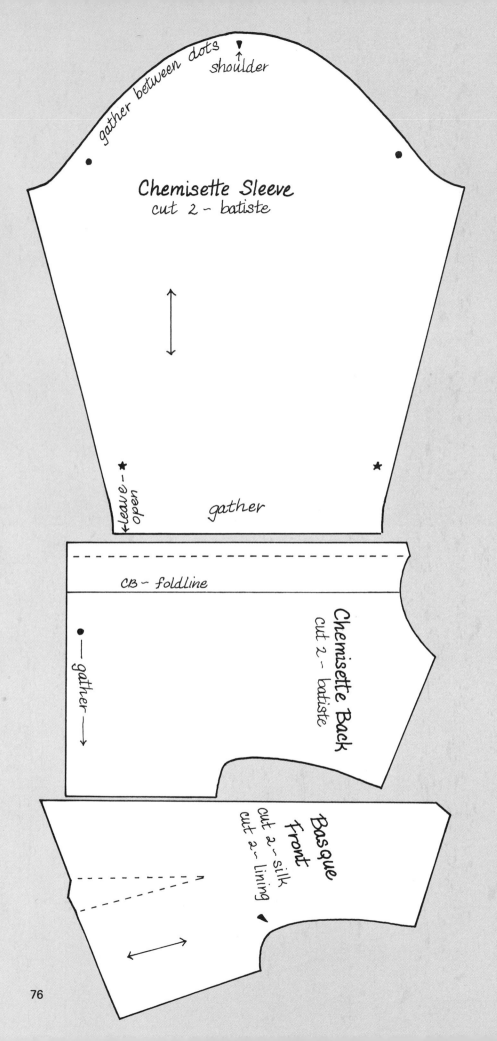

gather between dots

↑ shoulder

Chemisette Sleeve
cut 2 ~ batiste

★ leave ~ open

gather

CB ~ foldline

← gather →

Chemisette Back
cut 2 ~ batiste

Basque Front
cut 2 ~ silk
cut 2 ~ lining

Doll's Coat Pattern from La Poupee Modéle 15 June 1881

An English coat for a Bébé number 1 10in (25.4cm) or 11in (27.9cm)

by **Dorothy S. Coleman**

Patterns redrawn and artwork by **Sandy Williams**

It is very pretty with its two super-imposed square collars; its three large pleats formed at the bottom of each side back; and its belt with a buckle, placed at the height of the pockets through which it passes. The belt will be more original when made of white leather, but if you find it difficult to obtain the white leather, you can make the belt of the same fabric as the coat. The belt should be large enough to go around the coat and should be 3cm (1¼in) high. The bottom fronts of the coat are rounded and four metal buttons form the closure.

1. A front of the coat.
2. A back of the coat.
3. A side of the coat including the three back pleats.
4. A sleeve.
5. A pocket.
6. The smaller collar.
   The larger collar is 1cm (½in) larger all around.
7. Sketch of the front of the coat.
8. Sketch of the back of the coat. □

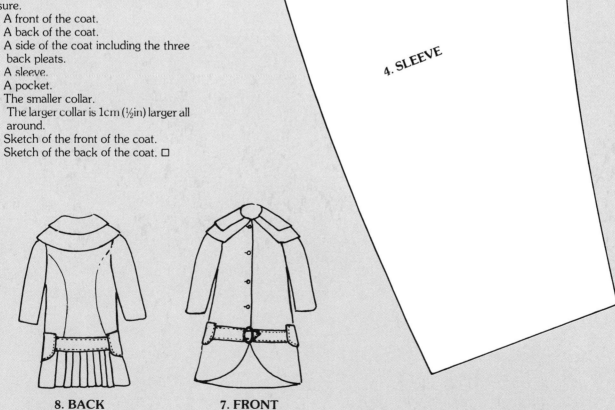

8. BACK   **7. FRONT**

4. SLEEVE

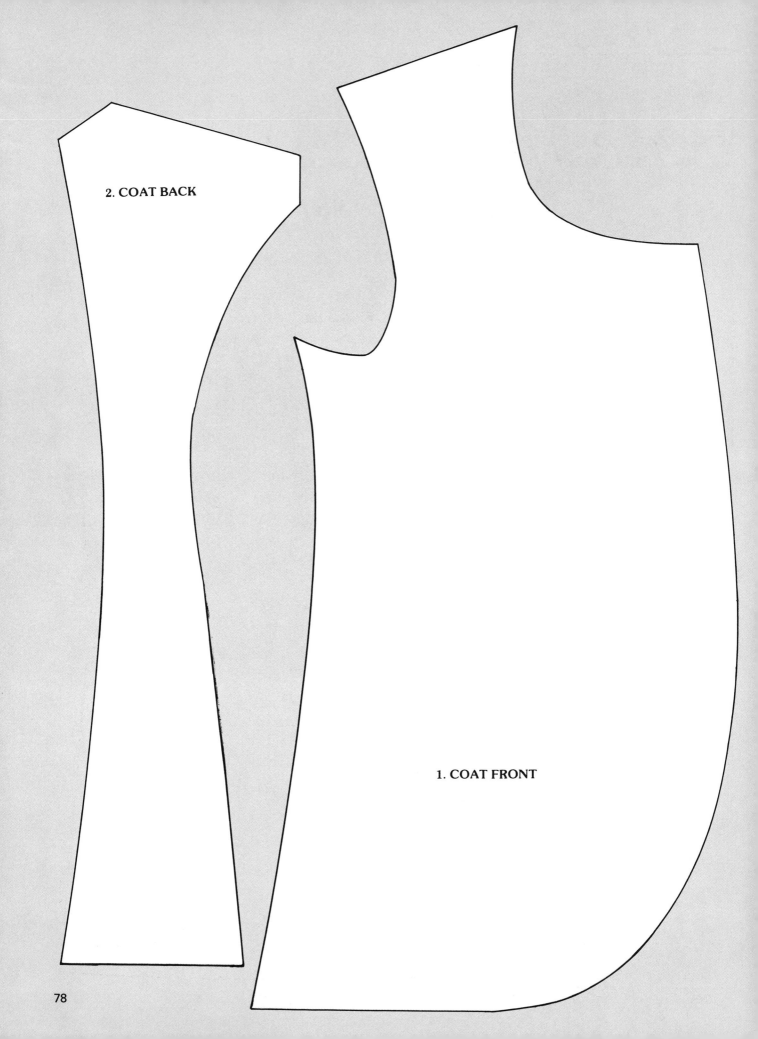

2. COAT BACK

1. COAT FRONT

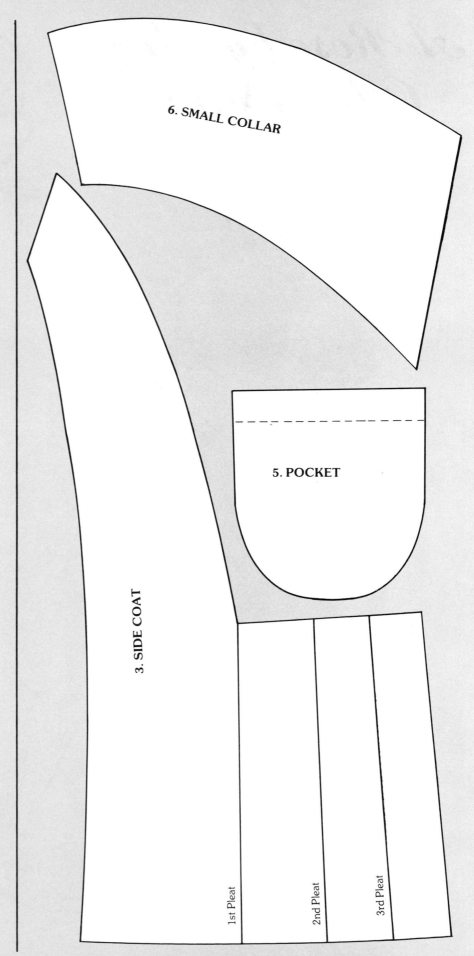

6. SMALL COLLAR

5. POCKET

3. SIDE COAT

1st Pleat

2nd Pleat

3rd Pleat

A Rose by Any Other Name

by Susan B. Sirkis

The souvenir doll of the United Federation of Doll Clubs, Inc., (UFDC) annual convention held in Kansas City, Missouri, in August 1982 was a lovely 16in (40.6cm) doll sculpted by Lita Wilson. The completely dressed, boxed doll was designed to represent Rose O'Neill. Her soft brown wig, flowing caftan and bare feet (not to mention lack of underwear) were characteristic of the *Kewpie* designer's taste in personal appearance. The doll itself, minus her rose petals, is a perfect figure for the doll dressmaker. Neither molded-on shoes nor hair -- no collars, hats or jewelry -- confine the doll to any particular place in time. Hence, visions of many rosebuds bloom in the garden of the mind: Rose Antoinette, in the height of the 18th century French court fashion; Bess, the Virgin rose in 16th century English clothing; Joan of Rose in 15th century armor; Rose Austen, an early 19th century novelist; Madam Rose, an 1870s you-know-what; and, of course, Second Hand Rose, a peddler lady.

This pattern is for the Edwardian Rose, a turn-of-the-century belle. Her lingerie should be made of soft white batiste trimmed extensively with Val lace and insertion. Her dress is of soft rose silk, trimmed with wide lace ruffles and some lace applique. Shoes and stockings should be made to match the dress color. Her original wig is appropriate. A rose may be added to her hair. The doll may also carry a bouquet of roses.

CHEMISE: Use French seams on all lingerie. Sew underarm seams. Gather top of front and back to fit doll. Whip lace beading to top of back and front, extending over shoulders. Whip ¼in (.65cm) lace edging to armholes and around top. Hem bottom. Use narrow silk ribbon to thread through beading and draw up to fit doll's neck.

DRAWERS: Sew leg seams. Trim bottoms with rows of ¼in (.65cm) insertion, beading and edging. Sew crotch seam. Make a narrow casing in top. Run narrow ribbon through casing and draw up to fit doll's waist over chemise.

CORSET: Make the corset of heavy rose-colored cotton. Sew underarm seams. Sew silk ribbon casing to solid lines on corset. Insert pipe cleaners to serve as stays. Bind all edges with ¼in (.65cm) silk ribbon. Work thread loops at Xs on right front edge. Sew corresponding buttons to Xs on left front edge. Work eyelets on dots along each back edge. Metal eyelets may be used instead of hand worked ones if you prefer. Trim top of corset with two rows of lace edging and a row of beading. Thread rose silk ribbon through beading to tie in bow in front. Lace back with rose silk ribbon.

PETTICOAT: Transfer petticoat pattern drawings to a large piece of tracing paper. Place a ruler along each "EXTEND" line. Draw lines long enough so that they extend 1in (2.5cm) below doll's feet. Sew side and center back seams. Leave center back seam open above dot and bind for placket. Make a casing in top and thread with narrow ribbon. Make ½in (1.3cm) hem in petticoat bottom. Trim petticoat with rows of insertion, beading and edging to match drawers and chemise. Place on doll and arrange so most of the fullness is concentrated in back.

STOCKINGS: Make stockings of rose-dyed stockinette. Sew center back seams. Loosely overcast top edge of each stocking. Place on doll and secure with ribbon garter tied under each knee.

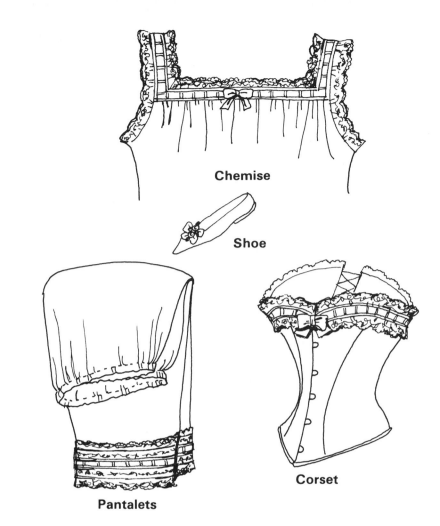

Chemise

Shoe

Pantalets

Corset

SHOES: Make shoes of glove leather or fabric bonded to lightweight STAFLEX. Bind edge of uppers with narrow silk ribbon. Sew center back seam. (Glue may be used if you prefer.) Place uppers on doll. Hold cardboard inner soles in place next to foot. Glue edge of uppers in place around bottom of inner sole. Glue sole and heel to shoe bottoms. Trim toe with cluster of tiny rosebuds (what else?) and a bow.

DRESS: Make the skirt first. Elongate the skirt pattern pieces the same way you did the petticoat except add an extra 2in (5.1cm) in the back for a train. Sew side and center back seams, leaving center back seam open above dot for placket. Face placket with self-material. Gather top of skirt to fit waist, concentrating fullness in back. Mount on narrow, smooth waistband. Close back with hooks and eyes. Make a ½in (1.3cm) hem in bottom, or you may face the bottom if you wish. Trim bias with three ¾in (2cm) ruffles of self-material (or nine ruffles of ¼in (.65cm) silk ribbon dyed to match dress fabric) headed by a narrow band of double-edged lace.

Make pleats in bodice front. Baste in place along top and bottom. Sew bodice underarm seam. Turn under back edges and hem in place. Narrowly bind bottom edge with self-material. Sew sleeve and cuff seams. Gather bottom of sleeves and sew to top of cuffs. Face cuffs with self-material. Gather tops of sleeves. Sew sleeves to sleeve section of bodice top. Narrowly bind all around top of sleeves and bodice with self-material. Gather 1½in (3.8cm) lace to fit around top of sleeves and top of cuffs. Whip in place. Cut lace as shown in sketch and applique to bodice front over pleats at top. Edge top of bodice and sleeves with narrow lace edging.

No doubt it has occurred to you that the Edwardian rose can be changed into a Blushing Rose if her dress is made of cream or white silk and she is given a veil!

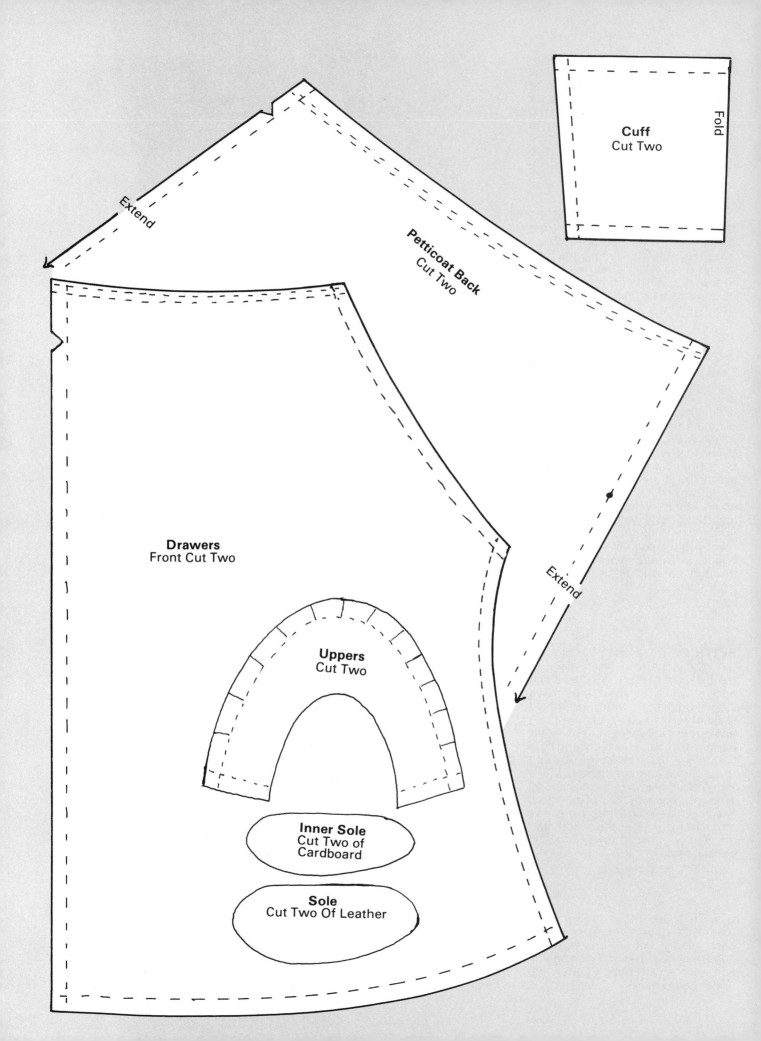

Cuff
Cut Two

Fold

Extend

Petticoat Back
Cut Two

Extend

Drawers
Front Cut Two

Uppers
Cut Two

Inner Sole
Cut Two of
Cardboard

Sole
Cut Two Of Leather

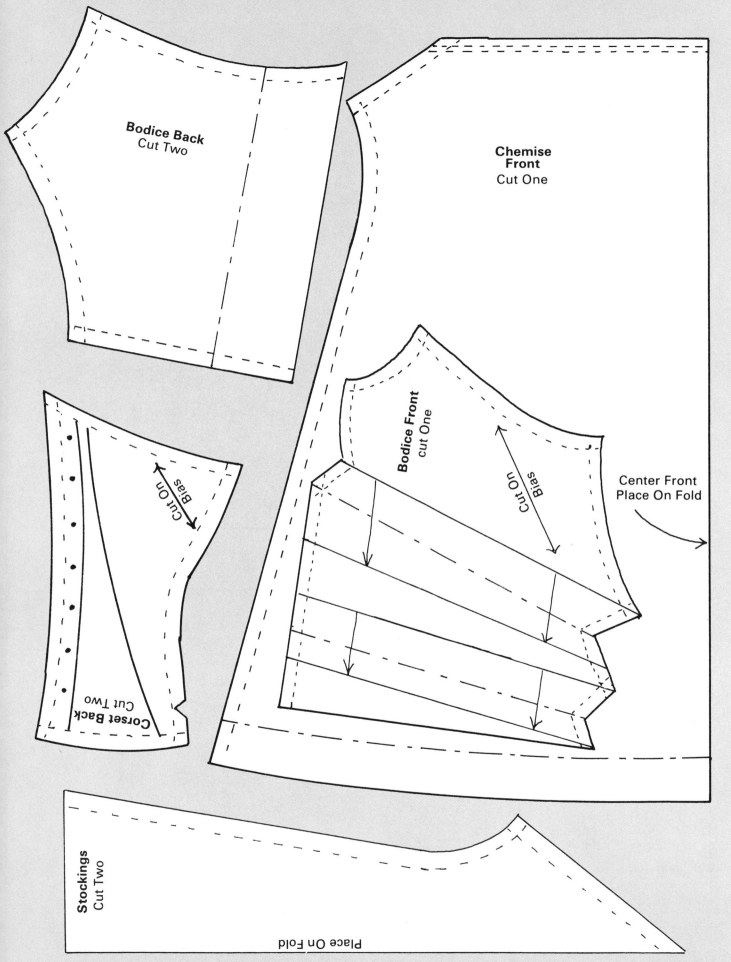

Bodice Back
Cut Two

Chemise Front
Cut One

Bodice Front
cut One

Cut On Bias

Cut On Bias

Center Front
Place On Fold

Corset Back
Cut Two

Stockings
Cut Two

Place On Fold

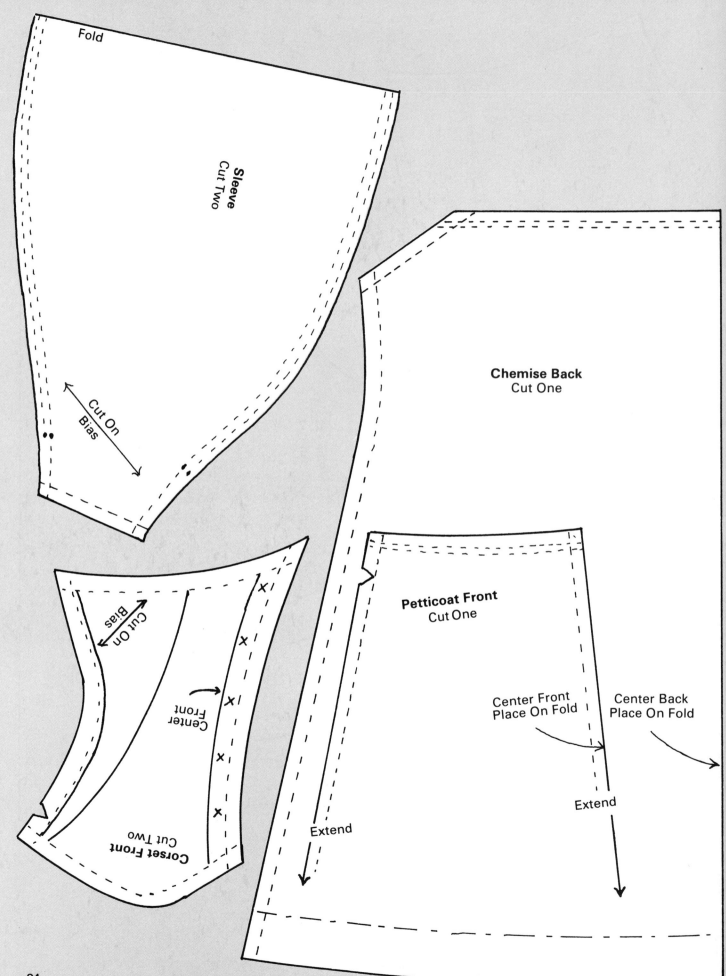

Fold

Sleeve
Cut Two

Cut On
Bias

Chemise Back
Cut One

Cut On
Bias

Center
Front

Corset Front
Cut Two

Petticoat Front
Cut One

Center Front
Place On Fold

Center Back
Place On Fold

Extend

Extend

84

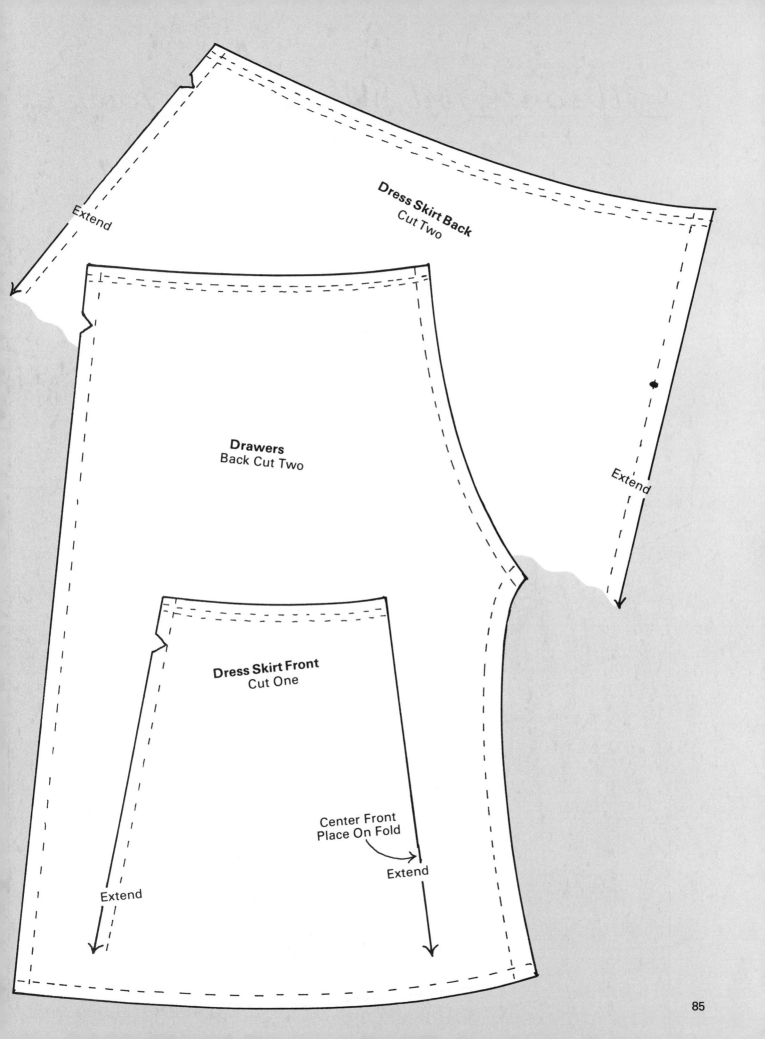

Dress Skirt Back
Cut Two

Extend

Extend

Drawers
Back Cut Two

Dress Skirt Front
Cut One

Center Front
Place On Fold

Extend

Extend

Extend

Gibson Girl Wedding Gown

An Original Pattern © by **Joan Chiara**

Design inspired by *The Delineator* Magazine 1895

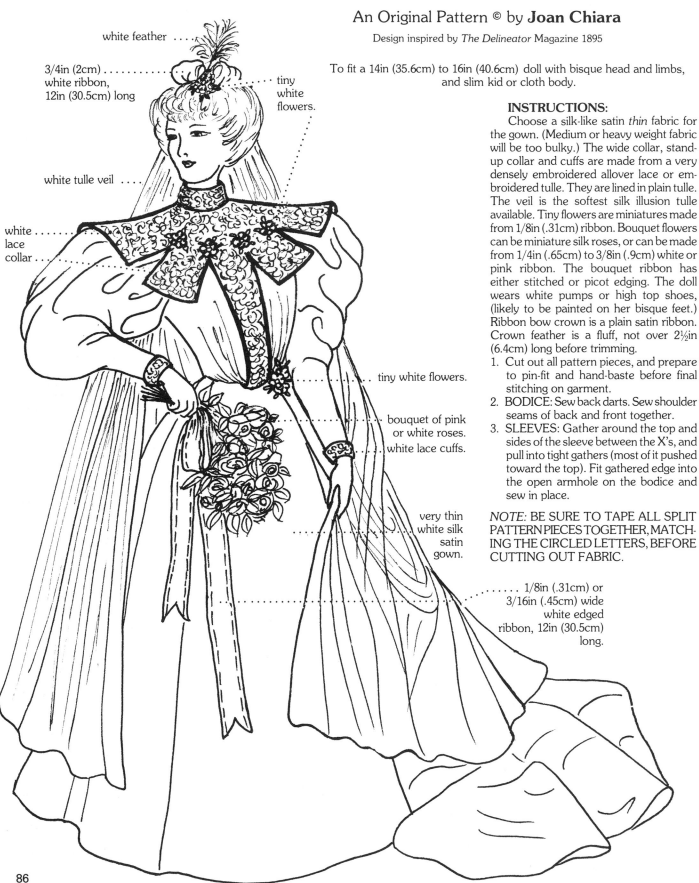

white feather . . . .

3/4in (2cm) . . . .
white ribbon,
12in (30.5cm) long

tiny
white
flowers.

white tulle veil . . . .

white . . . . . .
lace
collar . . .

tiny white flowers.

bouquet of pink
or white roses.

white lace cuffs.

very thin
white silk
satin
gown.

1/8in (.31cm) or
3/16in (.45cm) wide
white edged
ribbon, 12in (30.5cm)
long.

To fit a 14in (35.6cm) to 16in (40.6cm) doll with bisque head and limbs,
and slim kid or cloth body.

INSTRUCTIONS:

Choose a silk-like satin *thin* fabric for the gown. (Medium or heavy weight fabric will be too bulky.) The wide collar, stand-up collar and cuffs are made from a very densely embroidered allover lace or embroidered tulle. They are lined in plain tulle. The veil is the softest silk illusion tulle available. Tiny flowers are miniatures made from 1/8in (.31cm) ribbon. Bouquet flowers can be miniature silk roses, or can be made from 1/4in (.65cm) to 3/8in (.9cm) white or pink ribbon. The bouquet ribbon has either stitched or picot edging. The doll wears white pumps or high top shoes, (likely to be painted on her bisque feet.) Ribbon bow crown is a plain satin ribbon. Crown feather is a fluff, not over 2½in (6.4cm) long before trimming.

1. Cut out all pattern pieces, and prepare to pin-fit and hand-baste before final stitching on garment.
2. BODICE: Sew back darts. Sew shoulder seams of back and front together.
3. SLEEVES: Gather around the top and sides of the sleeve between the X's, and pull into tight gathers (most of it pushed toward the top). Fit gathered edge into the open armhole on the bodice and sew in place.

NOTE: BE SURE TO TAPE ALL SPLIT PATTERN PIECES TOGETHER, MATCHING THE CIRCLED LETTERS, BEFORE CUTTING OUT FABRIC.

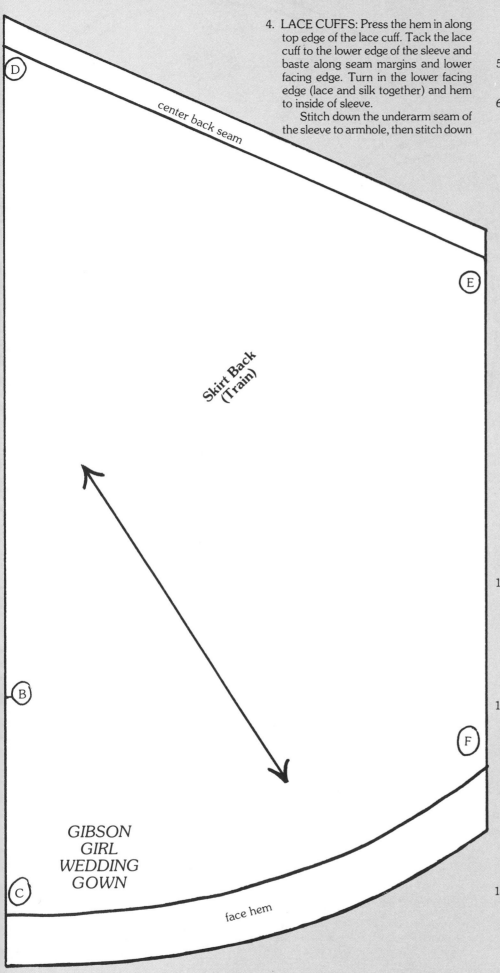

D

center back seam

E

Skirt Back
(Train)

B

F

C

GIBSON
GIRL
WEDDING
GOWN

face hem

4. LACE CUFFS: Press the hem in along top edge of the lace cuff. Tack the lace cuff to the lower edge of the sleeve and baste along seam margins and lower facing edge. Turn in the lower facing edge (lace and silk together) and hem to inside of sleeve.

Stitch down the underarm seam of the sleeve to armhole, then stitch down the bodice side seams to the waist. Repeat steps 3 and 4 for the second sleeve.

5. Gather between the X's on each side of the lower BODICE FRONT, pulling the gathers to fit doll's waist. Staystitch.

6. Sew the tulle lining to the STAND-UP COLLAR along the top edge. Press right side out and set aside.

7. Sew the tulle lining to the large circular LACE COLLAR. Trim the edges close, clip curves, and slit points and center back. Cut out the center for a neck hole. Turn and press the collar right side out. Baste the neck hole around the dress neck edge, with the STAND-UP COLLAR basted into the seam margin. Baste the lower edge of the center front LACE COLLAR, matching the large dot, to the lower edge of the center front BODICE.

8. SKIRT: Matching notches on side seams, sew the SKIRT SIDE FRONTS to each side of the SKIRT FRONT. Now sew the SKIRT SIDE BACKS to the SKIRT SIDE FRONTS. You are working into the train area now. Sew the SKIRT BACK pieces to each side of the SKIRT SIDE BACKS. On the center back seam of the SKIRT BACK, sew from the dot down to the hem edge.

Using bias tape to match fabric or narrow bias strips of the same fabric, face the entire lower edge of the gown and press inward for a faced hem. Hand hem so that stitches do not show on the outside.

9. At the top of the STAND-UP COLLAR back edges, turn each edge in and blindstitch lace to its lining, with collar edges meeting at center back.

10. Sew the BODICE waist edge to the waist edge of the SKIRT. Where the skirt may be larger, just ease or gather it in at the back. Using the same bias tape as on the skirt hem, sew a tape down each edge of the center back BODICE and upper SKIRT. Hem to inside, forming a facing. Close entire back of gown with tiny hooks and eyes.

11. TINY WHITE FLOWERS: Using the narrowest ribbon and a very fine needle and thread, tack five tiny loops of ribbon together for each flower. Bits of light green ribbon can be tacked in the same way, behind the white, to form two or three leaves as background. When attaching each flower (with or without leaves) to the dress waist and lace collar, use a white or pastel embroidery or crochet thread to tack through it and make a French knot for the center of the flower, before finishing the tack inside the dress.

12. The bunch of tiny CROWN FLOWERS are merely strung together on thread or fine florist or jewelry wire, and tied into a tiny bunch. Sew the lower end of the feather into the back of

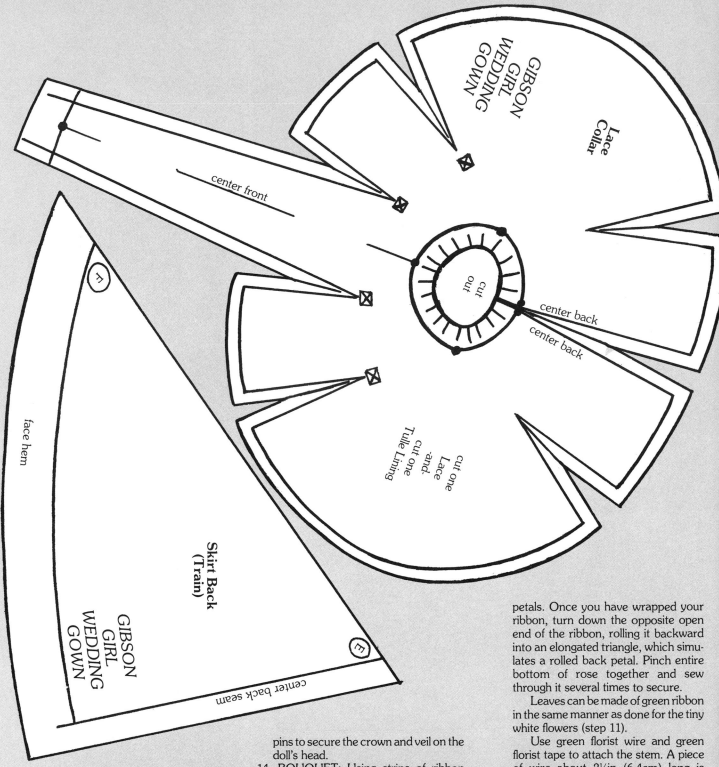

GIBSON GIRL WEDDING GOWN

Lace Collar

cut out

center front

center back

center back

cut one Lace -and- cut one Tulle Lining

face hem

Skirt Back (Train)

GIBSON GIRL WEDDING GOWN

center back seam

the bunch of flowers. Form a wide bow from the plain satin ribbon, that covers only the center top of the head; and finger-press the loops upward. Tack this to the back of the flowers and feather.

13. Cut the tulle VEIL 14½in (36.9cm) by 27in (68.6cm). Gather along one 27in (68.6cm) edge, pulling together as tight as possible; then overcast the gathers together to a semi-circular flat base. On top of this gathered base, tack the crown of flowers, bow and feather. Use pearl-topped straight pins or corsage pins to secure the crown and veil on the doll's head.

14. BOUQUET: Using strips of ribbon from 1½in (3.8cm) to 2in (5.1cm) long, follow the diagram for making RIBBON ROSES, Illustration 1. Fold one end of the ribbon down on the diagonal, forming a point for the center of the rose. Using a fine needle and matching thread, gather through the doubled corner, and along the lower edge, as close to the edge of the ribbon as possible. If you want large buds, do not gather much, and wrap around the bud several times firmly. If you prefer large open roses, gather a more ruffled ribbon, then wrap around. The loose gathers form the appearance of open petals. Once you have wrapped your ribbon, turn down the opposite open end of the ribbon, rolling it backward into an elongated triangle, which simulates a rolled back petal. Pinch entire bottom of rose together and sew through it several times to secure.

Leaves can be made of green ribbon in the same manner as done for the tiny white flowers (step 11).

Use green florist wire and green florist tape to attach the stem. A piece of wire about 2½in (6.4cm) long is pushed through the stitching at the bottom of each rose, and bent to hold at one end. Press one end of the florist tape over the lower portion of the rose, covering the stitching, and wrap around to cover the bottom of the rose and top of the wire stem; pulling to stretch the tape, and pressing the tape to stick to itself, as you wrap. Continue wrapping tightly over the stem. Repeat for each rose.

Gather 9 to 12 roses together and tie with the edged ribbon, forming a drooping bow, as shown in the drawing. □

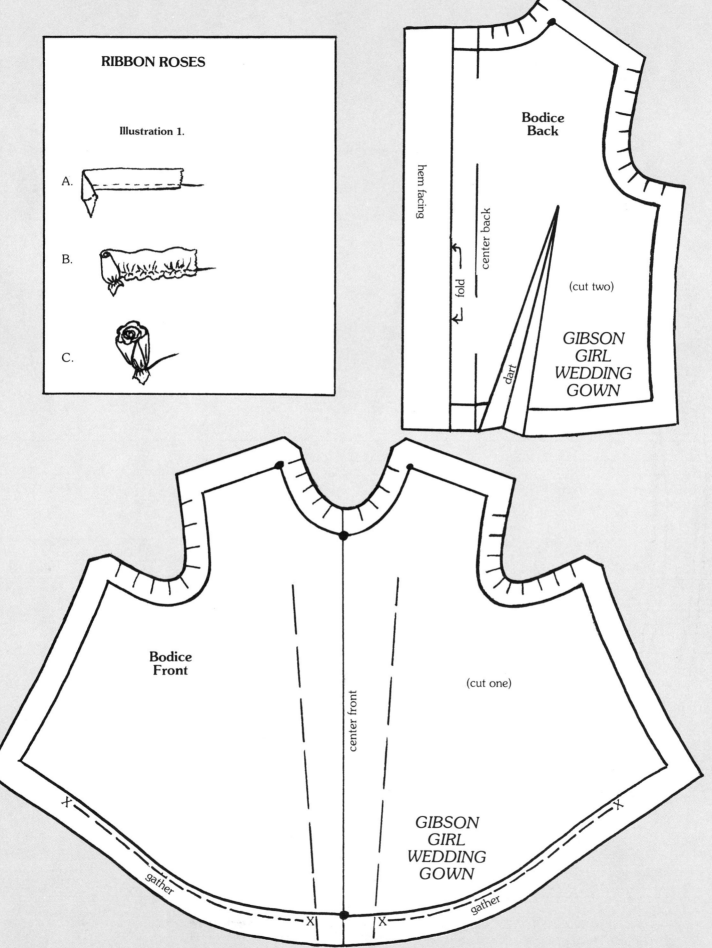

RIBBON ROSES

Illustration 1.

A.

B.

C.

Bodice Back

hem facing

fold

center back

dart

(cut two)

GIBSON GIRL WEDDING GOWN

Bodice Front

center front

(cut one)

GIBSON GIRL WEDDING GOWN

gather

X

X

X

X

gather

89

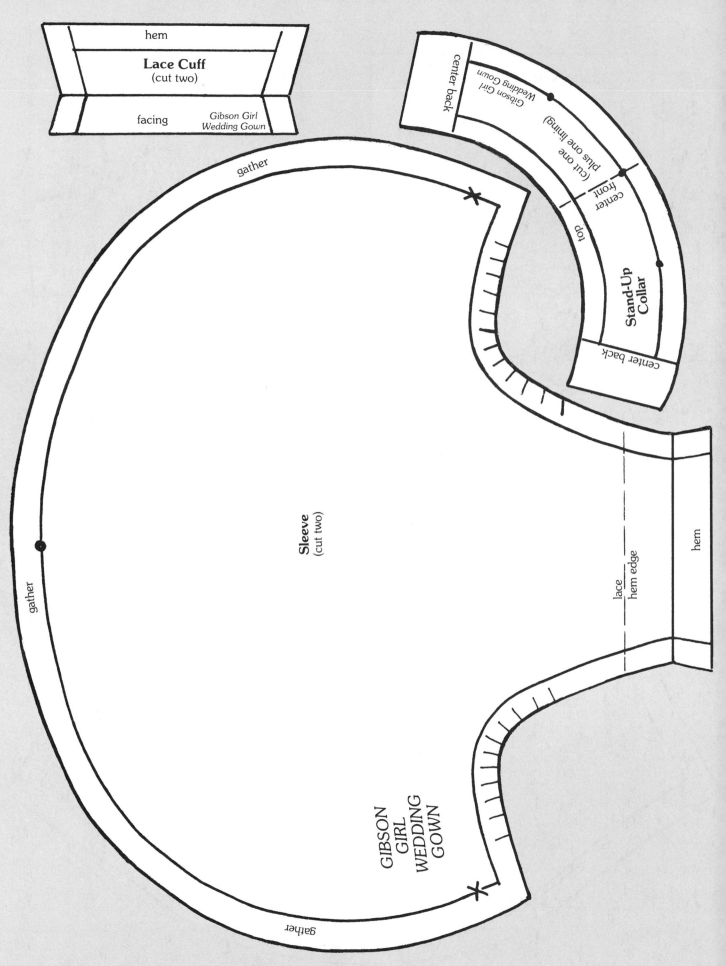

hem

Lace Cuff
(cut two)

facing

*Gibson Girl
Wedding Gown*

gather

center back

*Gibson Girl
Wedding Gown*

center front

(cut one
plus one lining)

top

**Stand-Up
Collar**

center back

gather

Sleeve
(cut two)

lace

hem edge

hem

GIBSON
GIRL
WEDDING
GOWN

gather

gather

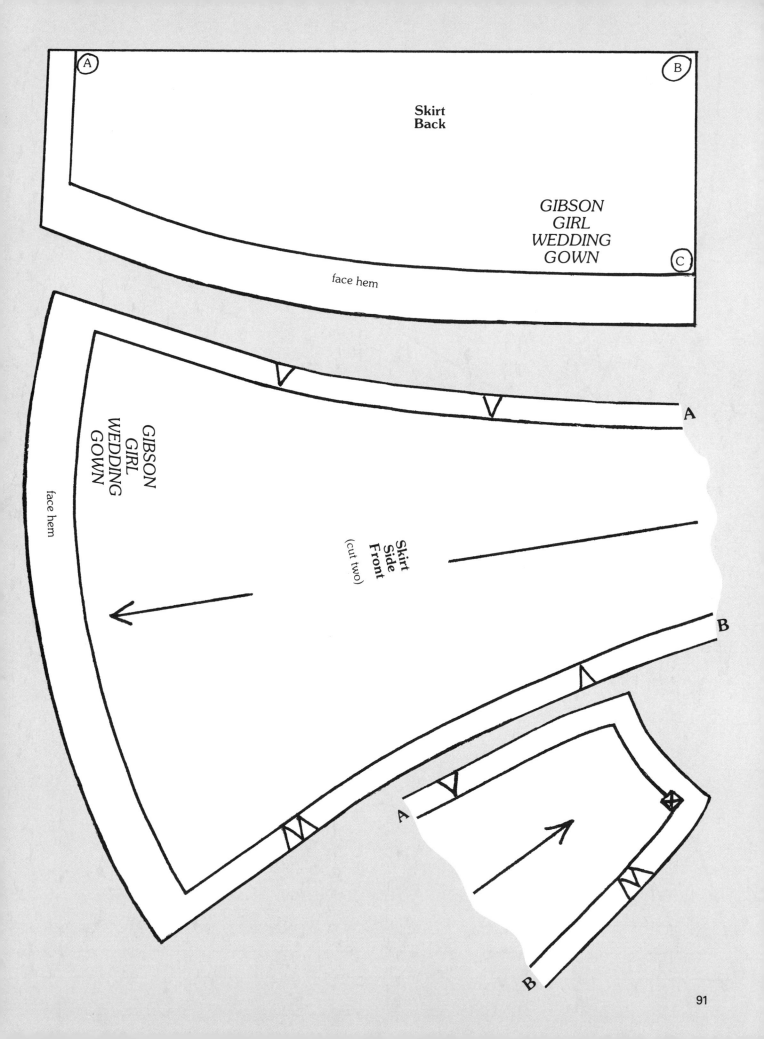

(A) (B)

Skirt Back

GIBSON GIRL WEDDING GOWN

(C)

face hem

GIBSON GIRL WEDDING GOWN

Skirt Side Front
(cut two)

face hem

A

B

A

B

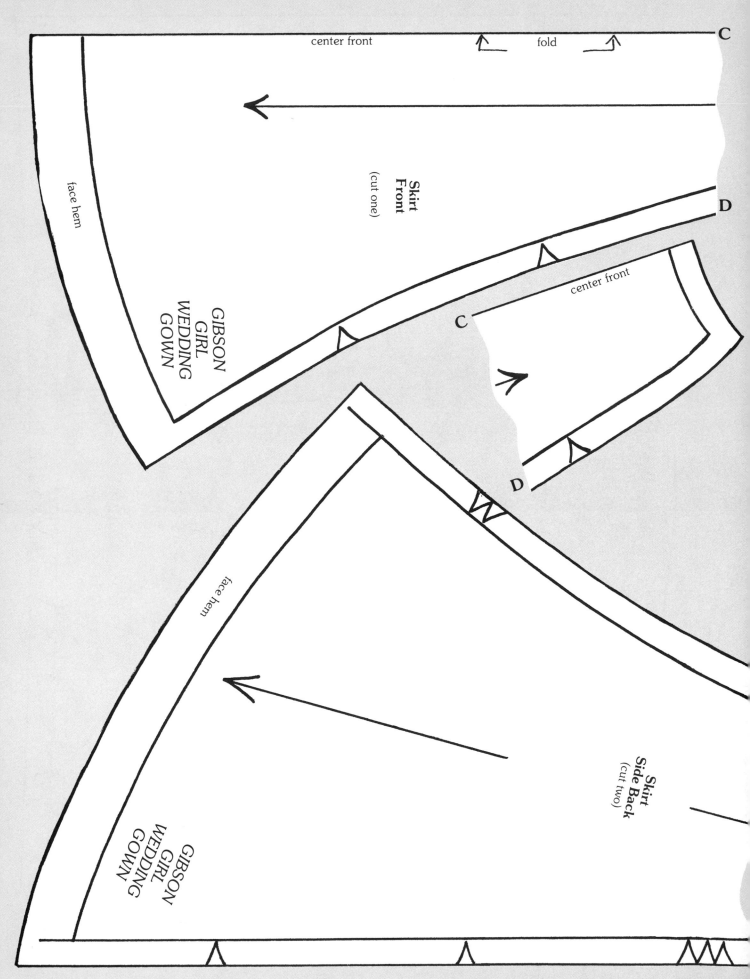

center front · fold · C

Skirt
Front
(cut one)

face hem

GIBSON
GIRL
WEDDING
GOWN

D

center front

C

D

Skirt
Side Back
(cut two)

face hem

GIBSON
GIRL
WEDDING
GOWN

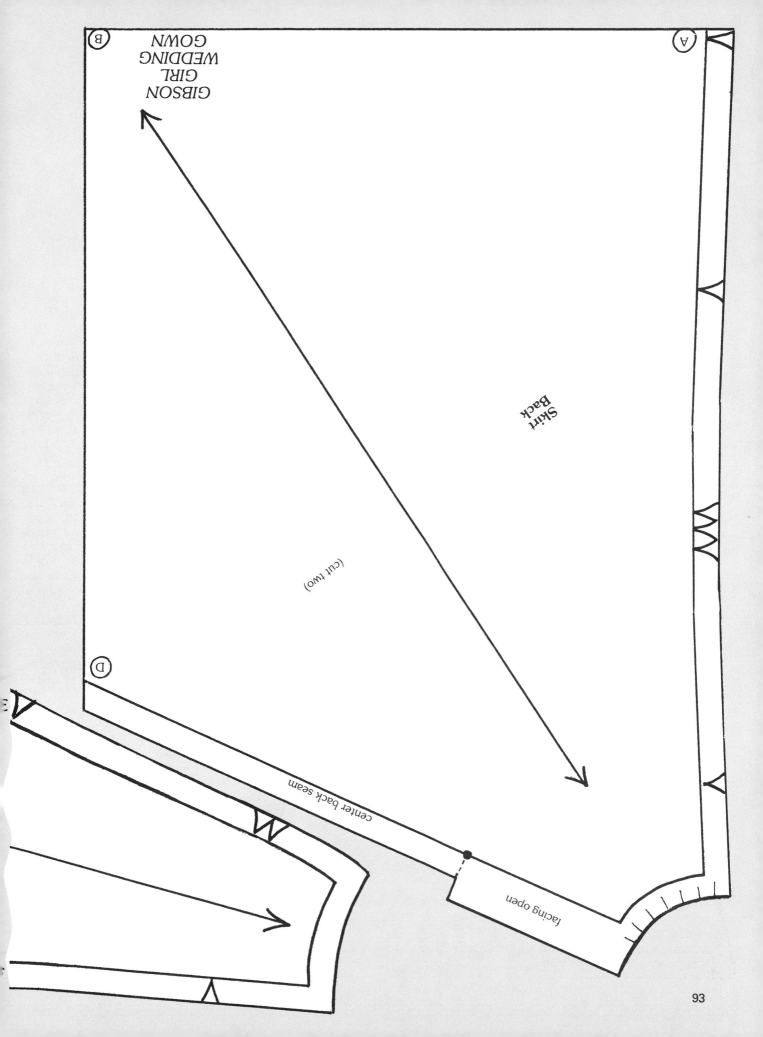

GIBSON
GIRL
WEDDING
GOWN

Skirt
Back

(cut two)

center back seam

facing open

Skirt
Back

GIBSON
GIRL
WEDDING
GOWN

93

A Schoenhut Study
and a Dress to Make

by **Artie Seeley**

Photographs and pattern drafting by **Bill Seeley**

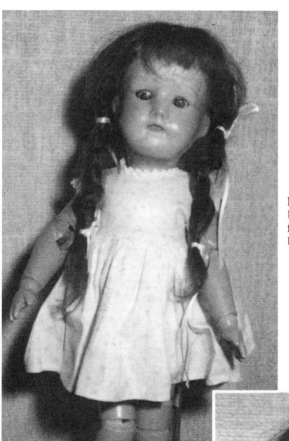

Illustration 1. Schoenhut girl with braids, an open/closed mouth with four teeth and wearing what is believed to be her original dress.

Illustration 2. Close-up of doll shown in *Illustration 1*. Note that the eyes are wooden balls and eyelids are painted.

A Schoenhut doll passed through my hands a few months ago and when the article about "The Mystery Doll" appeared in the June/July 1984 **Doll Reader,**® I thought I knew where to find one. The doll in *Illustration 1* returned for a photograph session; the eyes were open and stuck, but a few gentle slaps to the face and the eyes closed, only to show painted eyelids. There go all thoughts of finding the "mystery" doll. Some paint is off the eyelids and it is easy to see that the eye is a wooden ball. They are brown with a lid painted over the top. She has both upper and lower eyelashes. Her eyebrows are one fine line following another. She has an open/closed mouth with four teeth showing and long hair in braids. Her label is missing. She is wearing what I believe to be the original knit underpants but the undershirt is missing as seen in *Illustration 3* on the right. The dress seen in *Illustration 1* appears to be original. It is creamy white with pale blue polka dots.

I have included a pattern for this 15in (38.1cm) doll if you would like to dress your doll in this simple little house dress or apron; it is sleeveless and open down the back, closed three-quarters of the way down with three old-fashioned white snaps marked "Starlet Dot." The neckline and sleeve openings have cream-colored rickrack for trim.

The doll in *Illustrations 4* and *5* is my own little pride and joy. I received it shortly after reading about the original window display in a New York department store where Schoenhut dolls were all little boys playing football. The unusual spring tension joints allow them to pose in positions typical of little boys at play. The shorts and knit undershirt and the short cropped hair just make me believe this is a boy doll (also seen on the left in *Illustration*

A DRESS ANY LITTLE GIRL
CAN MAKE FOR HER DOLLY

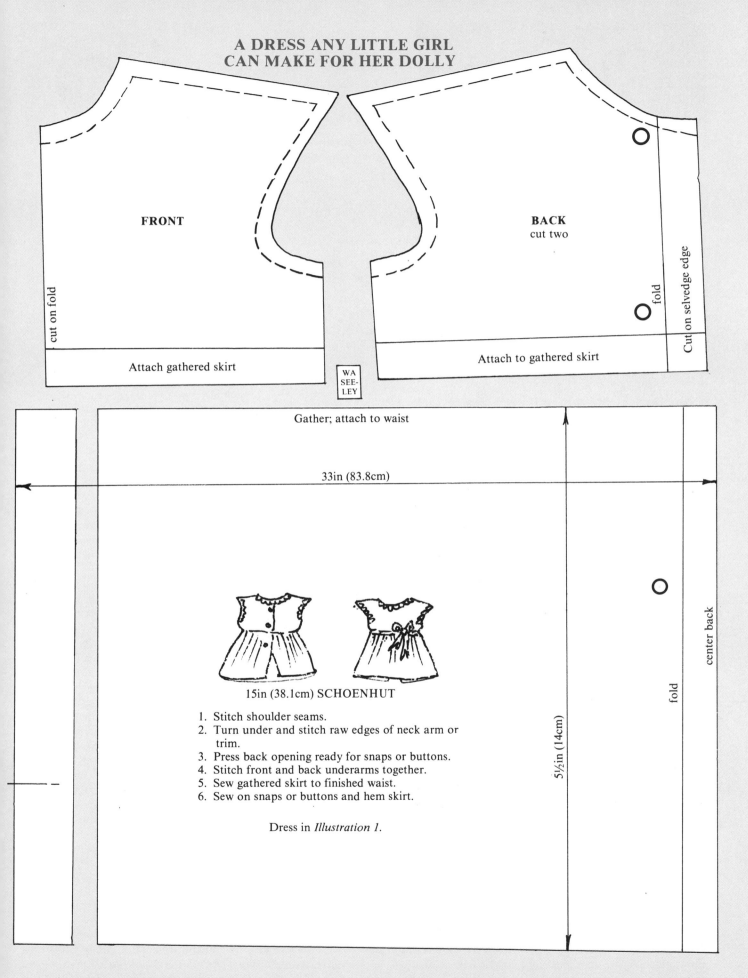

FRONT

cut on fold

Attach gathered skirt

WA SEE-LEY

BACK
cut two

fold

Cut on selvedge edge

Attach to gathered skirt

Gather; attach to waist

33in (83.8cm)

5½in (14cm)

fold

center back

15in (38.1cm) SCHOENHUT

1. Stitch shoulder seams.
2. Turn under and stitch raw edges of neck arm or trim.
3. Press back opening ready for snaps or buttons.
4. Stitch front and back underarms together.
5. Sew gathered skirt to finished waist.
6. Sew on snaps or buttons and hem skirt.

Dress in *Illustration 1*.

LEFT: Illustration 3. Three Schoenhuts shown together.

RIGHT: Illustration 4. Schoenhut boy.

BELOW: Illustration 5. Close-up of the Schoenhut boy seen in *Illustration 4*.

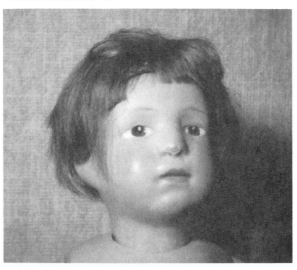

Illustration 7. Schoenhut girl with blonde mohair wig, blue painted eyes and an open/closed mouth with four teeth.

3). The eyebrows are heavier than those on the doll in *Illustrations 1* and *2* and they, too, are a series of fine lines up and down in their strokes which make the eyebrow look thicker. The eyes are intaglio, painted dark brown with a large black iris and a raised white highlight, no eyelashes either upper or lower. The mouth is closed with no teeth showing. The wig is human hair. Except for a chip on the nose, it is in very good condition. *Illustration 6* shows a Schoenhut paper label on the doll in *Illustrations 4* and *5*.

The doll in *Illustrations 7* and *8* is a newcomer to my collection, obviously a girl. She wears a one-piece knit drawers with lace trim, sure to be original, seen in the middle in *Illustration 3*. She also has a red straw sailor type hat with elastic under the chin. Her blonde mohair wig could also be original; it is glued on so firmly that I shall never know. She has shaded blue painted eyes (not intaglio) with both upper and lower eyelashes and an open/closed mouth with four teeth showing and, of course, the usual chipped nose.

The feet of the dolls in *Illustration 9* show the holes that allow the dolls to stand on their own platforms. The strong springs at the joints of wrist, elbow, thigh, knee and ankle allow each doll to assume many positions. The doll in *Illustration 6* does not have the usual paper label. The Schoenhut

Illustration 6. Close-up of the Schoenhut label on the doll seen in *Illustrations 4* and *5*.

Illustration 8. Close-up of the Schoenhut girl seen in *Illustration 7*.

identification appears to be impressed or stamped into the paint between the shoulder blades. It reads: "Schoenhut Doll//Pat. Jan. 17, '11, USA//& Foreign Countries."

Then there is also a Schoenhut baby, shown in *Illustration 10*. Never having seen one, I am most grateful to Marie for letting me share it with you. The baby is so precious, really the prettiest of all. The body looks almost like all baby dolls except that it appears to have been carved from wood and has the same type of wire and spring construction of the other dolls, as seen in *Illustration 11*. See the nails in the back of torso. The feet and hands are not flexible as are the other Schoenhuts. Her eyes are painted with no eyelashes. Dressed, she makes a beautiful sturdy play doll.

I am amazed at the number of nails in the body and can only assume that they are needed for the attachments, whatever they may be, that anchor the head, arms and legs. I have yet to see a Schoenhut that came apart and would certainly be interested in seeing all the parts and the puzzle it must be to put one back together!

Assuming the spring construction dates from 1911 into the 1920s when the dolls were still being made, the springs on these dolls seem as tight as the day they were assembled. Forgetting about being pretty, this must be one of the most practical dolls ever made for a child to play with. □

Illustration 9. Note the holes in the feet of these dolls which allow them to stand on their own platforms. The spring joints allow them to assume many positions.

Illustration 10. Schoenhut baby.

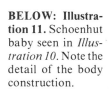

BELOW: Illustration 11. Schoenhut baby seen in *Illustration 10*. Note the detail of the body construction.

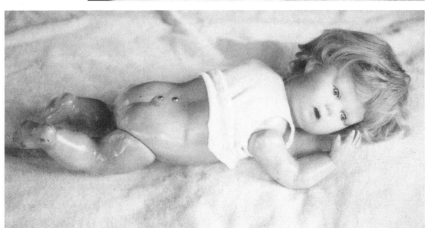

Smoking Flapper's Ethnic Costume

by **Ruth A. Lewicke**

Inspired by **Doll Reader**® article, "Boudoir Dolls," by Margaret Groninger, August/September 1981 issue.

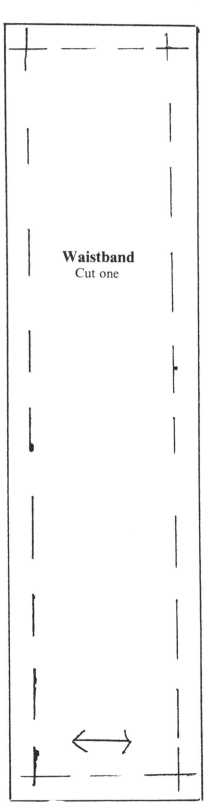

Waistband
Cut one

Toe

Shoe Sole
Cut two

Heel

Doll measurements:
Height: 25in (63.5cm)
Bust: 10½in (26.7cm)
Waist: 6¾in (17.2cm)
Hips: 11½in (29.2cm)
Materials:
1/2 yd (.46m) material with body, but not stiff; suggested color is white.
Two contrasting colors of embroidery trim, 1¼yd (1.14m) each.
1/2 yd (.46m) rickrack, small or medium size.
Pattern instructions: read through first and use illustration as a guide for trim.
1. Sew front shoulders to back.
2. a. Trim on front of blouse may be machine-stitched on as you go; or you may pin it, and hand-stitch it on. If you choose to hand-stitch, use a decorative stitch.
   b. Starting at the middle of blouse, place a strip of trim down blouse center. Leave 1in (2.5cm) at bottom of blouse without trim. Be sure to extend trim over neckline.
   c. Using the other color, put a strip on each side of first trim. Put them next to each other, touching, but not overlapping. Put one more strip of original color trim on each end, just touching.
   d. Take a piece of trim the same color you just used, and place it horizontally on the bottom of

Illustration 1. Blouse for a 25in (63.5cm) smoking flapper.

vertical strips, slightly overlapping; tuck under horizontal trims ends.
3. Turn cuffs under and sew rickrack to sleeves, leaving half of rickrack to show. Rickrack may be sewn to right side of cuffs, if preferred.
4. Sew blouse sides together.
5. Take 13½in (34.3cm) strip of trim, your second color, stitch to bottom of blouse. Make small gathers just past trim decoration.
6. For collar use same trim color as you just used on blouse bottom. Cut two pieces 4½in (11.5cm), turn under each raw edge and sew.
   a. Clip neckline and fold under. Pin.
   b. Now pin collar pieces on. Use edge of center trim to line up collar. Start collar at connecting edges of trim one and two. Place collar piece at neckline back and sew. This will make a stand-up collar that **will** stand up.
7. For blouse back, fold right side of opening under and stitch. Use fasteners you prefer.
8. a. For knickers' leg bottoms, take two pieces of trim color, 5½in (14cm) each, and sew to legs after they have been hemmed. Use small gathers. Sew front seam and lower part of back of knickers together. Now, sew legs together.

b. For waistband, sew right sides of ends together. Place right side of waistband edge to right side of knickers, use small gathers. Sew. Turn waistband over raw edge and sew.

9. Use a piece of trim as a headband.

10. Shoe pattern: use felt or vinyl material. This pattern is shaped for a foot wearing high heels.

a. Sew back of shoe together.

b. Sew right sides of shoe and sole together. Use 1/4in (.65cm) seam allowance, and turn.

c. Use matching material or thin ribbon for tie. Put middle of tie under shoe arch, on the outside. Use opaque sock to make stocking.

The knickers pattern may be used for lingerie and pajamas. Just use a rectangle for a camisole top, and matching trim for straps. Use a kimona style robe, and a string of pearls. □

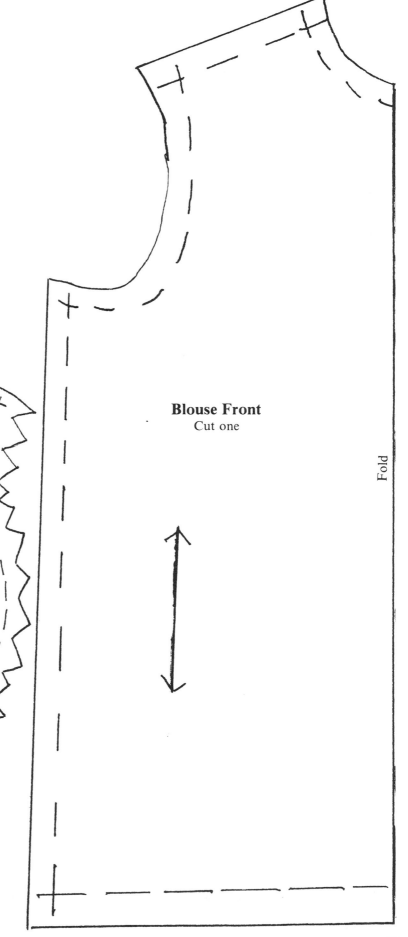

Blouse Front
Cut one

Fold

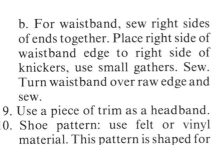

Shoe Upper
Cut two

Toe

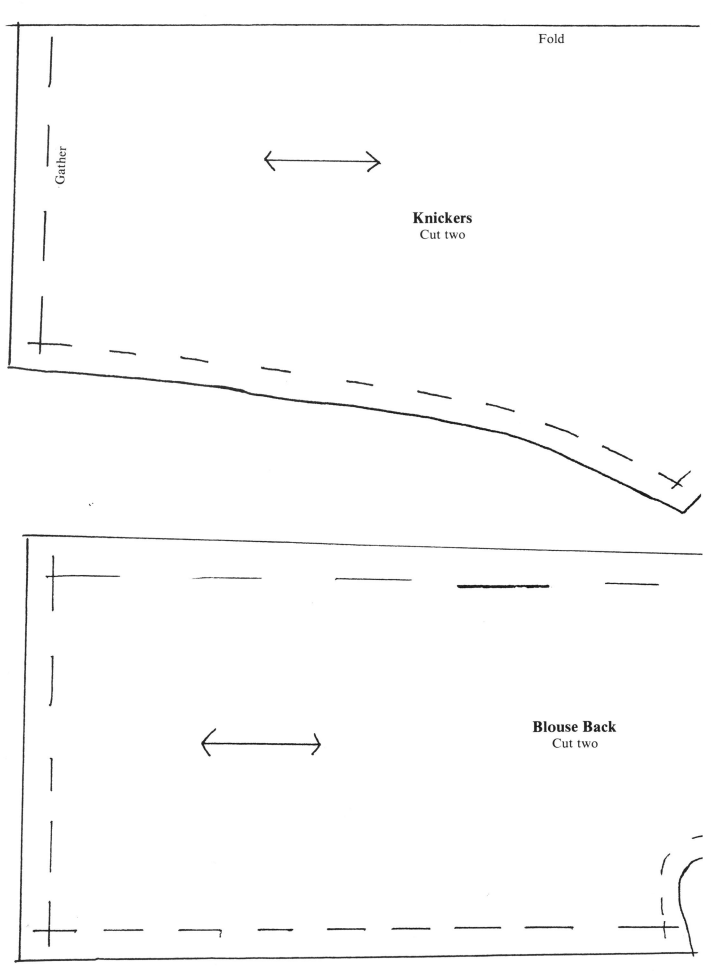

Fold

Gather

Knickers
Cut two

Blouse Back
Cut two

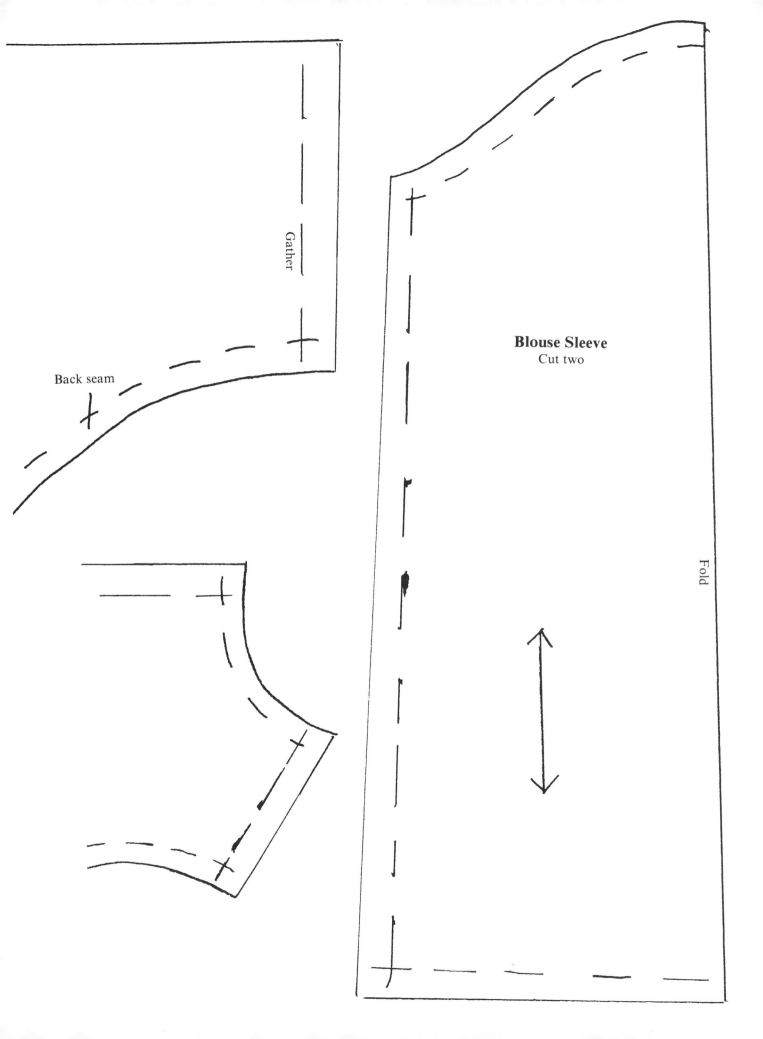

Gather

Back seam

Blouse Sleeve
Cut two

Fold

Scarlett's Golden Anniversary Ball Gown

by **Deanna Sparlin Pinizotto**

Illustration 1. *Scarlett O'Hara* stands a regal 17½in (44.5cm) in her heather blue velvet gown designed by Mrs. LaVerna Jacoby. A blue jewel adorns the neckline. *Scarlett* was sculpted by Lita Wilson. *Muriel Kramer Collection.*

Offered in this issue of **Doll Reader**® is an exclusive ball gown for Scarlett O'Hara to celebrate her 50th anniversary. Scarlett adored a stylish gown for barbecues, weddings and balls to ensnare the hearts of polished gentlemen and stir the envy of rival southern belles. This gown was designed by the late Mrs. LaVerna Jacoby for a *Scarlett O'Hara* doll created by well-known NIADA Artist, Lita Wilson.

Mrs. Jacoby began sewing when quite young. However, her sewing hobby turned profession when her husband died just prior to the Depression and she had five children to raise. In later years, she turned to her sewing to provide a new hobby, dressing dolls. Even though *Scarlett* was very special, *Rhett Butler* was her favorite. His suit is exquisite in each detail, and remains an exclusive pattern with the Jacoby family. However, *Scarlett's* dress pattern is lovingly offered in tribute to the late designer's rich talent and desire for excellence. Now *Scarlett* will have an enthralling new gown to celebrate her anniversary with all who have been captivated by her charm, beauty, stubbornness and courage in the face of disaster and ruin.

MATERIALS NEEDED:

1yd (91.4cm) velvet, at least 45in (114.3cm) wide
1yd (91.4cm) lining material
1yd (91.4cm) white cotton material
Laces, trims and ribbons for slip and pantalets
12in (30.5cm) white seam binding
12in (30.5cm) hem tape to match velvet
Bead or jewel for bodice
Lace for a shawl if desired

Illustration 2. Mrs. Jacoby is seated on the right, next to her long-time friend and NIADA doll artist, Lita Wilson. *Photograph by Walter Kramer.*

Scarlett stands 17½in (44.5cm) tall with her waist measuring 5½in (14cm) and her bust is 9in (22.9cm). Measure your doll to see how closely she equals the above numbers. Adjustments can easily be made in the pattern. The blouse or bodice is very fitted and will need close attention. The skirt is quite full and therefore easily adjusted to suit various doll sizes. The entire dress is lined to give it stability and elegant drape lines. Watch for bulk. Mrs. Jacoby made shortcuts in all her waistbands by using thin hem tape and either stitching the outfit closed or by using fancy bead pins to pin it closed. The pins look like little buttons. Snaps and hooks will not be as satisfactory as they add too much bulk for so dainty a doll.

BLOUSE

1. Sew the darts on velvet pieces 1 and 3. Repeat on lining pieces 2 and 4. On pattern piece 1, slash to dot and pleat the velvet, matching  ○ , □ and △ to its corresponding symbol. This pleated line in velvet will equal the line C in length. (Note lining piece 2.) Pin and stitch along the edge to secure the pleating.

2. Place sleeve lining and velvet, right sides together, and stitch 1/4in (.65cm) along bottom hem. Clip and turn. Repeat on other sleeve. Sew in gathering stitches along top.

3. Sew line A with pleats in velvet, to line A of the sleeve. Stitch opposite edge of sleeve, B - Sleeve to B - Back. Repeat the process for other side of bodice, sleeve and back. The velvet pieces are now all stitched to each other in corresponding manner.

4. Pin front and back lining pieces, right sides together. STITCH SHOULDER SEAMS ONLY (letter D). Finish armhole edge by hand or machine.

5. Place lining and velvet blouse pieces right sides together. Stitch where indicated by dots. (See *Illustration 6.*)

6. To sew the underarm seams with a nice finish, open lining from velvet at side seams. (See *Illustration 7.*) Fold bodice front over bodice back, right sides together, matching X, Y and Z. Sew a continuous seam from base of sleeve, crossing bottom seam and up the back. Turn and the lining is beautifully finished.

7. Evenly gather sleeve top so velvet and lining are equal along the neckline. Double-check the blouse on the

Illustration 3. The celebrated characters from *Gone With The Wind, Scarlett O'Hara* and *Rhett Butler,* sculpted by Lita Wilson. *Rhett* stands 19½in (49.6cm) tall and is dressed in a black suit with a white and silver vest designed by Mrs. Jacoby. *Nelle Sparlin Collection.*

Illustration 4. Close-up of *Scarlett* showing detail of bodice front.

Illustration 5. Mrs. Jacoby finished off *Scarlett's* white cotton pantalets and slip with ruffled eyelet and lavender ribbons. A slip of lace-trimmed netting was also added. *Scarlett* wears stockings and pink leather slippers with gold buckles to complete her ensemble.

doll one last time before the binding is put on the neckline. Seams and darts are still easy to reach if revisions are needed.

8. Baste entire neckline. Cut a bias strip of velvet about 12in (30.5cm) long and 1in (2.5cm) wide. This may vary according to the proportions of the doll. Mrs. Jacoby's finished trim is a narrow 1/4in (.65cm) wide. Sew this piece along the neckline, turn and tack down. This forms a finished edge at the neck.

9. Catch gathered folds at bustline and secure with a jewel, button or ornament.

SKIRT

Place right sides together, velvet and lining, and stitch. Turn to have a finished hem. Place two pleats 3/4in (2cm) deep to fit darts in the blouse. Mark additional pleats at underarm seam and back darts. The skirt is very full, so make adjustments for your specific doll. Experiment before you sew the back seam and trim if needed. The fullness should be drawn to the back with smooth pleats on front and sides. Simply sew skirt to hem tape to eliminate as much bulk as possible. Bodice should fit closely over top of skirt. This will give a pretty silhouette.

SLIP and PANTALETS

Scarlett's undergarments can be sewn and finished as desired. Tucks, eyelet, lace and ribbons may be applied to embellish the simple pattern. Sew gathers or pleats to waistbands as flat as possible and make allowances for doll proportions where fullness may be needed, or minimized. An additional slip can be sewn of netting to enhance the skirt lines. □

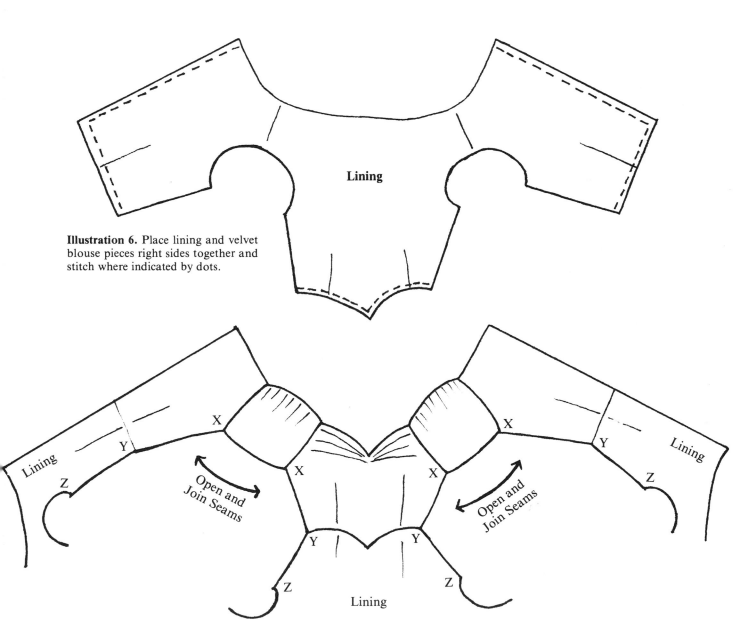

Illustration 6. Place lining and velvet blouse pieces right sides together and stitch where indicated by dots.

Illustration 7. To sew the underarm seams with a nice finish, open lining from velvet at side seams.

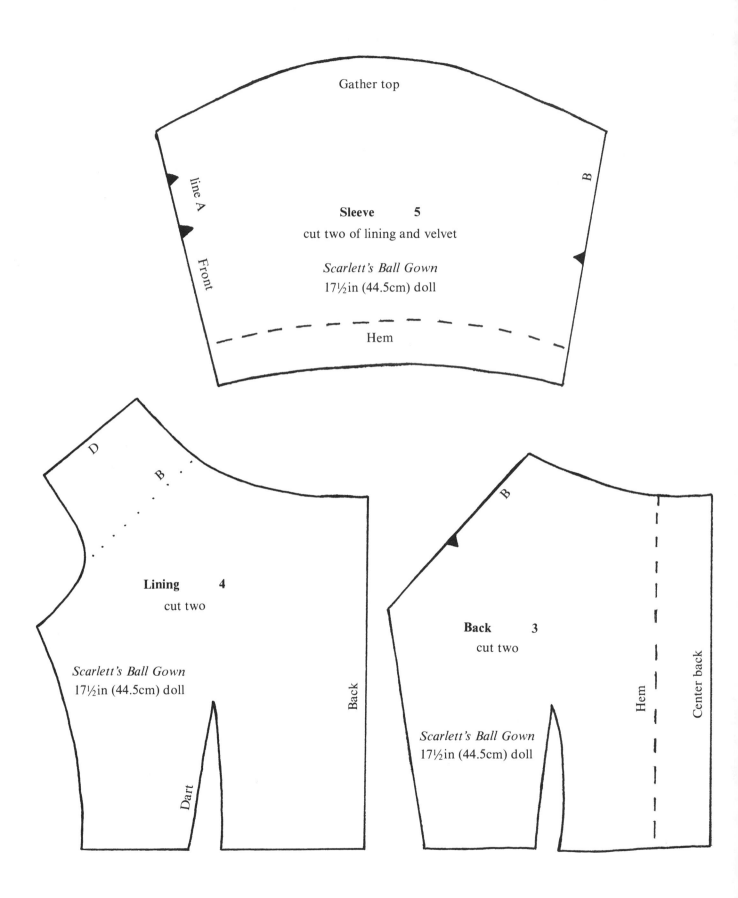

Gather top

line A

Front

B

Sleeve   5
cut two of lining and velvet

Scarlett's Ball Gown
17½in (44.5cm) doll

Hem

D

B

Lining   4
cut two

Scarlett's Ball Gown
17½in (44.5cm) doll

Back

Dart

B

Back   3
cut two

Scarlett's Ball Gown
17½in (44.5cm) doll

Hem

Center back

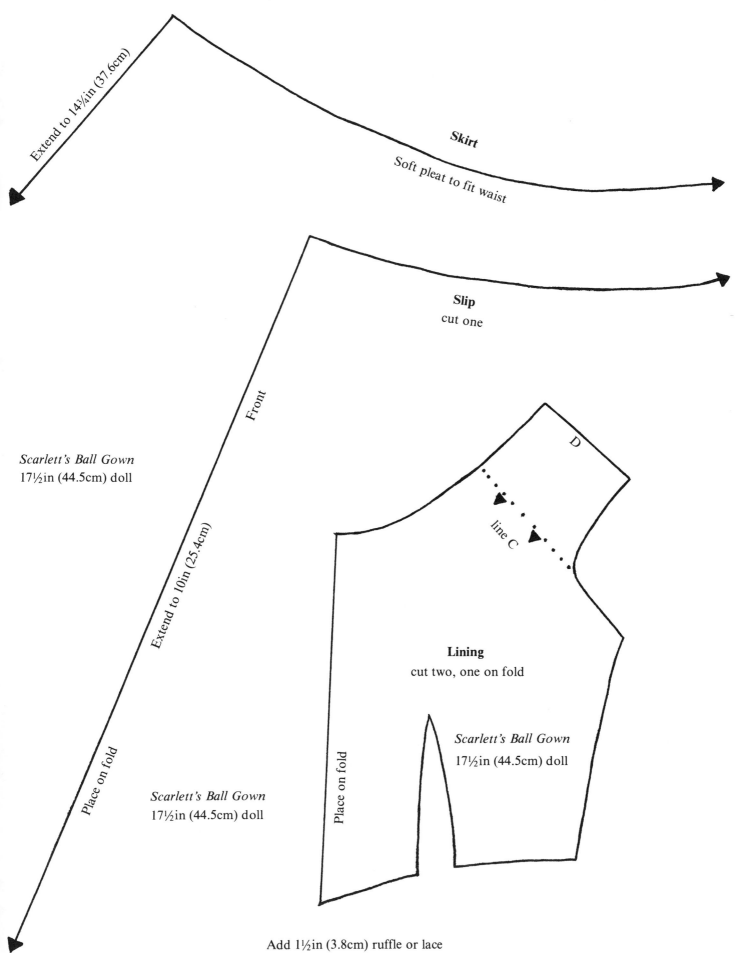

Extend to 14¾in (37.6cm)

Skirt

Soft pleat to fit waist

Slip
cut one

Scarlett's Ball Gown
17½in (44.5cm) doll

Front

Extend to 10in (25.4cm)

D

line C

Lining
cut two, one on fold

Scarlett's Ball Gown
17½in (44.5cm) doll

Place on fold

Place on fold

Scarlett's Ball Gown
17½in (44.5cm) doll

Add 1½in (3.8cm) ruffle or lace

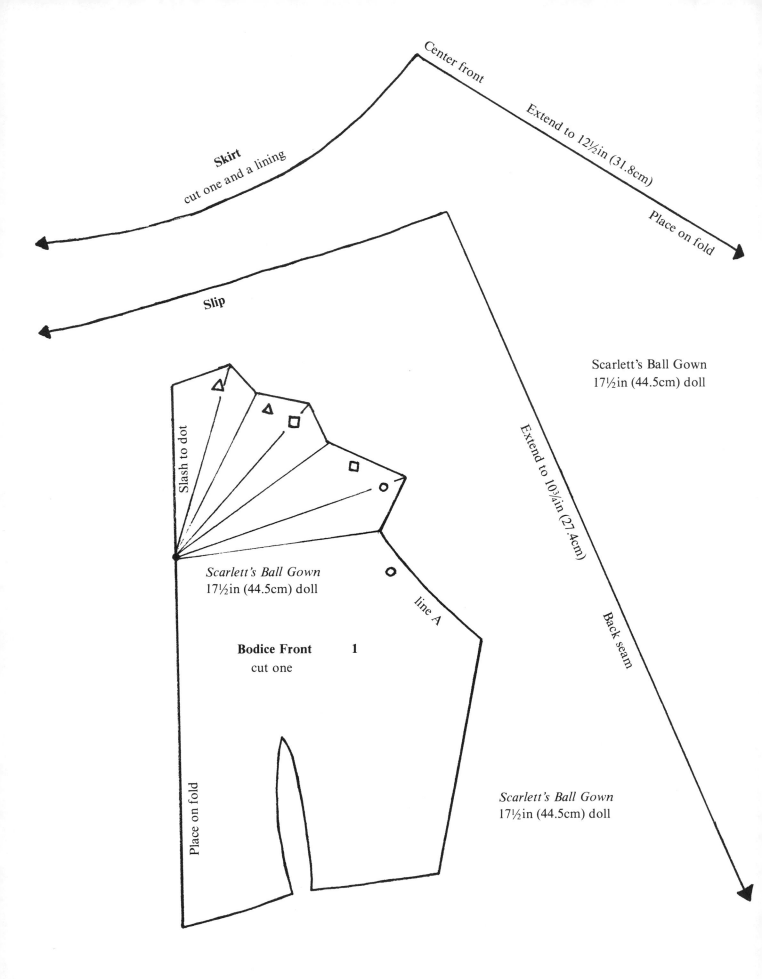

Skirt

cut one and a lining

Center front

Extend to 12½in (31.8cm)

Place on fold

Slip

Scarlett's Ball Gown
17½in (44.5cm) doll

Slash to dot

Extend to 10¾in (27.4cm)

Back seam

Scarlett's Ball Gown
17½in (44.5cm) doll

line A

Bodice Front   1

cut one

Place on fold

Scarlett's Ball Gown
17½in (44.5cm) doll

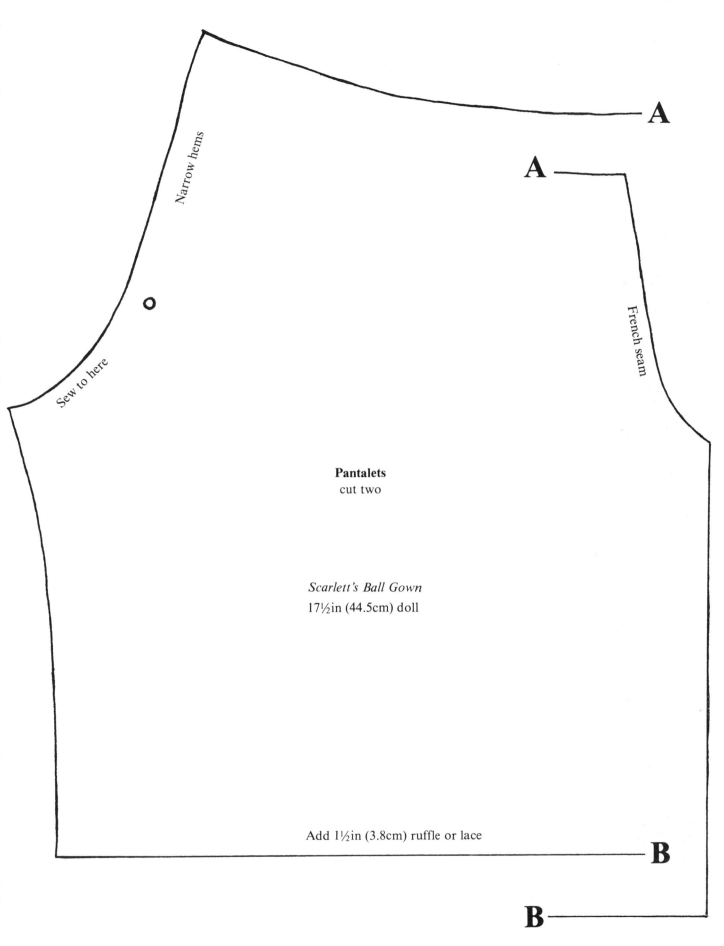

A

Narrow hems

French seam

Sew to here

O

Pantalets
cut two

Scarlett's Ball Gown
17½in (44.5cm) doll

A

Add 1½in (3.8cm) ruffle or lace

B

B

Bleuette's Pattern Wardrobe for 1927: The Fringed Dress

translated by **Lauren Welker**

NOTE: The **Doll Reader**® is pleased to present a series of original patterns for *Bleuette*, a 27cm (10⅝in) S.F.B.J. doll, which appeared on the pages of *La Semaine de Suzette* in 1927. The original articles, by Suzanne Rivière, have been translated by Lauren Welker who has added additional instructions where necessary. These patterns can be reduced or enlarged and, with alterations, can be made to fit other dolls. Other patterns in this series appeared in the June/July 1986 **Doll Reader**, pages 224 to 225, the August/September 1986 **Doll Reader**, pages 238 to 239 and the October 1986 **Doll Reader**, pages 190 to 191.

For further information on *Bleuette* see the May 1984 issue of **Doll Reader**, pages 96 to 101 for the article entitled "Bleuette" by Francois Theimer.

The Fringed Dress

by **Susan Riviere**

Remember as you work on the *Bleuette* patterns that these were intended for use by children. It is not the pattern that makes a quality garment as much as it is the workmanship and the superiority of the materials. In my opinion, this pattern would be improved by a neck facing that would extend low enough in the back to also face the back vent. I would first make the shoulder seams in the garment, then face the neck before continuing on. Have fun making your "shimmy dress."   LW

Fringed dresses are all the rage. You know *Bleuette* is very up-to-date and she looks at the new styles with admiration and a little longing.

"They are so pretty, these fringes," she thinks, "these long strands of silk

Illustration 1. The fringed dress of *Bleuette*.

that dance and flutter with every movement. They are truly charming..."

And *Bleuette* sighs...

If *Bleuette* had been a docile dolly, studious and very wise, she would not have sighed so sadly. Show her this pretty dress, the object of her desires, and get to work.

The pattern consists of the two given pieces which are each cut from fabric folded in half. The dress is made by sewing the shoulder seams and underarm seams along the dotted lines.

A small hem is taken around the neckline. This neckline will be a little décolleté. You make a little slit down the center back from point O to S so the dress will be easy to put on, and you can close the slit with two small snaps.

A little hem is made around the short sleeves. This hem, like the one around the neckline, is trimmed with a row of top stitching. Hem the skirt.

A strip of fabric 20cm (7⅞in) long by 3cm (approx. 1-3/16in) wide folded in half makes the scarf which you wind around the neck of *Bleuette*, letting the ends fall one in front and one in back.

You will now make the fringe trim which gives this charming frock its stamp of originality. It is done using heavy silk thread, threaded through a large needle which you draw through the fabric making a single stitch. Next you reinsert the needle making a simple knot (see diagram on pattern). The thread is cut close to the hem and this makes a strand of the fringe.

You can make each strand with a double thread for a fuller fringe.

In general these fringes are made of silk, but if you do not have any, you can use pearl cotton. One usually chooses the same color fringe as the fabric or, lacking that, one a little darker.

The placement line for the fringe is indicated by a dotted line in the front and back. Follow the curve carefully for a graceful fringe. □

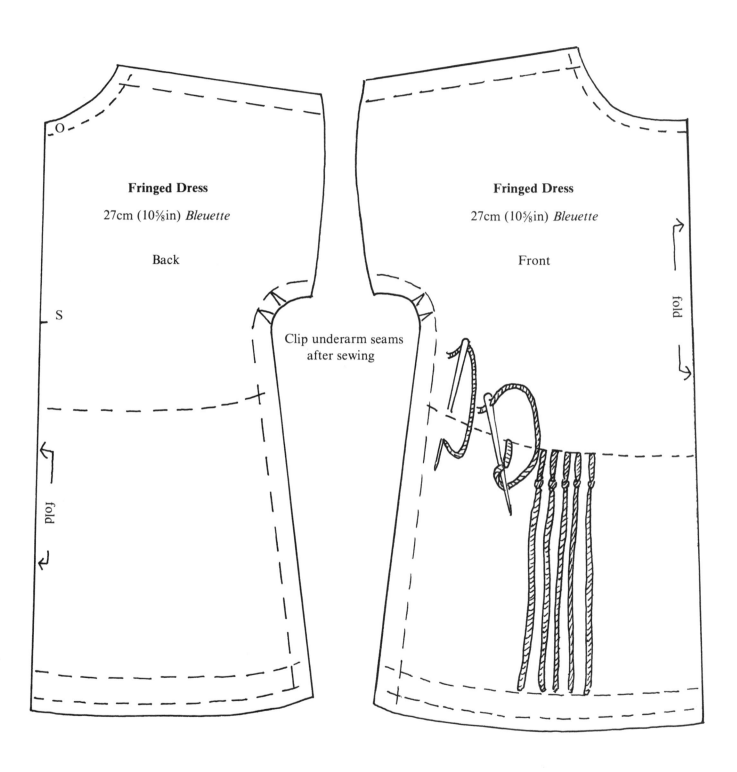

Fringed Dress

27cm (10⅝in) *Bleuette*

Back

O

S

fold

Clip underarm seams
after sewing

Fringed Dress

27cm (10⅝in) *Bleuette*

Front

fold

Illustration 2. The pattern for the fringed dress.

Infant Wrapper from 1895

An Original Pattern by
Joan Chiara

INSTRUCTIONS for the infant wrapper, from 1895, to fit a 13in (33cm) to 15in (38.1cm) baby doll. Specifically designed to fit a 14in (35.6cm) baby doll with composition body, bent limbs.

NOTE: BEFORE YOU PIN THIS PATTERN ON FABRIC, BE SURE TO MATCH THE CIRCLED LETTERS ON SPLIT PATTERN PIECES AND TAPE THE PATTERN PIECES TOGETHER ALONG THOSE LINES.

1. After cutting out all pieces from fine cotton lawn or batiste, tailor tack the black dots that mark top and bottom of four tucks on the wrapper front and four tucks on back. Using these tacks and the lines between them as the center of each tuck fold, baste each slightly over 1/8in (.31cm) in from the fold. Press each tuck. Now stitch each tuck, preferably by hand with very tiny stitches. Pull basting threads out and press tucks toward the sides on each piece. Sew the shoulder seams and side seams.

2. Using white cotton embroidery thread, single strand, embroider the design down the front of the RIGHT side of the wrapper front, around the bottom. (Do NOT embroider design down the left side.) Also embroider the design along bottom of the sleeve. Use a satin stitch or daisy stitch for the leaves and shallow French knots for the buds in the design.

3. Sew a fine cotton lace ruffle of 5/8in (1.6cm) to 3/4in (2cm) wide around the neckline edge. Fold the front facings back and baste the neckline edge over the ruffle seam. Also baste a 3/4in (2cm) wide bias strip of the same fabric along the seam where no facing covers. Stitch both facing and bias strip in place together; turn right side out. Turn under bias strip and stitch down as a facing over the neckline seam, making sure the lace ruffle is pressed to stand straight up. Turn under the notched edge of the facing (the shoulder edge) and blindstitch to the shoulder seam inside. Press the fold edge on each facing from top to bottom.

4. On each sleeve sew a lace ruffle (of the same lace as used on neck edge) along the broken line shown at lower edge of the sleeves. With lace facing upward toward the embroidery, sew the sleeve facing to the sleeve, matching the notches. Sew the underarm seam together on each sleeve,

but do not include the facing. Turn the facing to the inside and turn in the edges and blindstitch carefully along the seam and along the back side of the embroidery.

5. At the top of each sleeve, gather between the X's, pulling to fit into armholes of the wrapper. Match notches, and match the tiny circle to the shoulder seam and sew sleeves in place.

6. Using 1½in (3.8cm) wide bias strips of matching fabric, face the lower edge of the

wrapper all around, sewing it in place. Press this faced hem in; turn in edges and hem with blindstitching to the back of the embroidery. Be sure to catch the bottom of the front edge facing in this hem also.

7. Down the center front of the right side of the wrapper where the buttons are shown you will see a horizontal line. Make your tiny buttonholes across this line, keeping them under 3/8in (.9cm) long. In the same marked spots along the left side

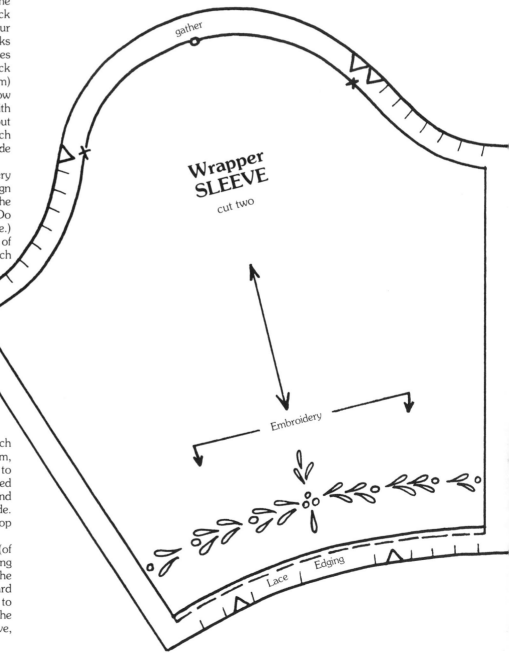

of the wrapper sew the nine buttons, each 1/4in (.65cm) to 3/8in (.9cm) in diameter.

8. Be sure to clip all curves and trim corners and excess seam edges to avoid bulkiness. Press well. This wrapper is very long, much like a traditional christening gown. □

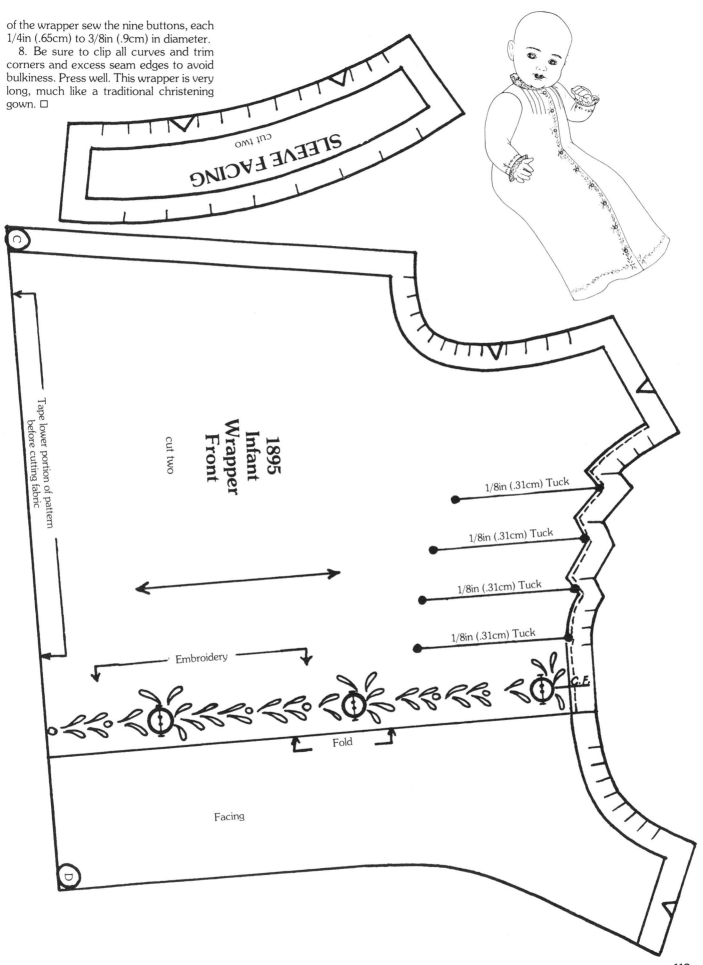

SLEEVE FACING
cut two

1895
Infant
Wrapper
Front

cut two

Tape lower portion of pattern before cutting fabric

1/8in (.31cm) Tuck

1/8in (.31cm) Tuck

1/8in (.31cm) Tuck

1/8in (.31cm) Tuck

Embroidery

C.F.

Fold

Facing

C

D

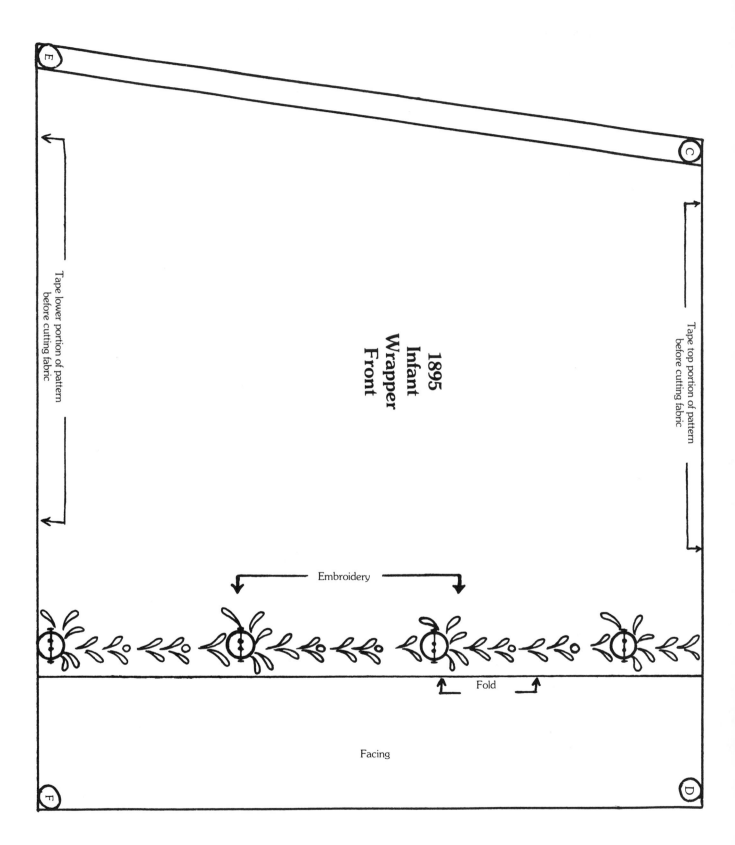

E

C

Tape top portion of pattern
before cutting fabric

Tape lower portion of pattern
before cutting fabric

1895
Infant
Wrapper
Front

Embroidery

Fold

Facing

F

D

114

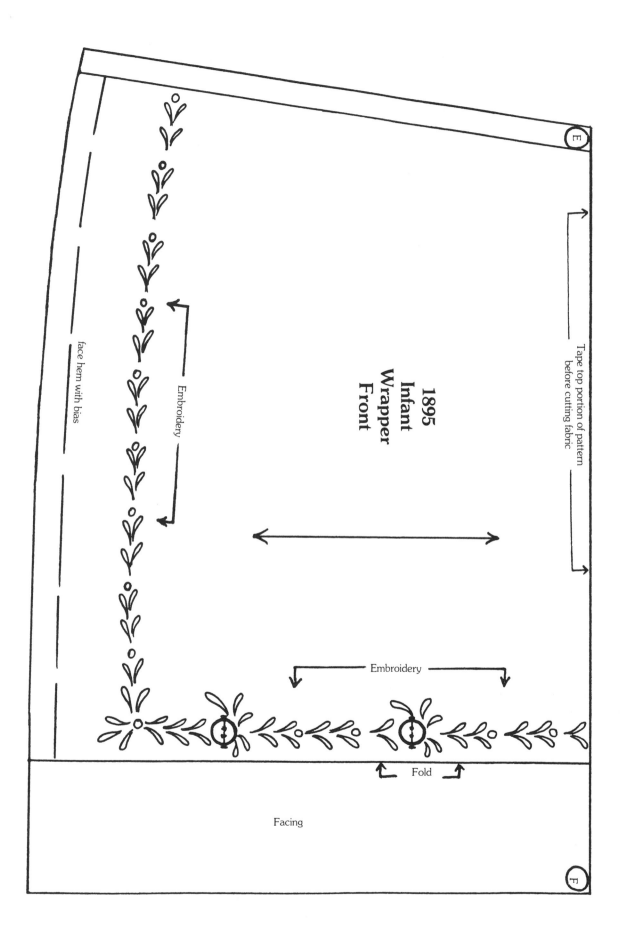

E

Tape top portion of pattern
before cutting fabric

face hem with bias

Embroidery

1895
Infant
Wrapper
Front

Embroidery

Fold

Facing

F

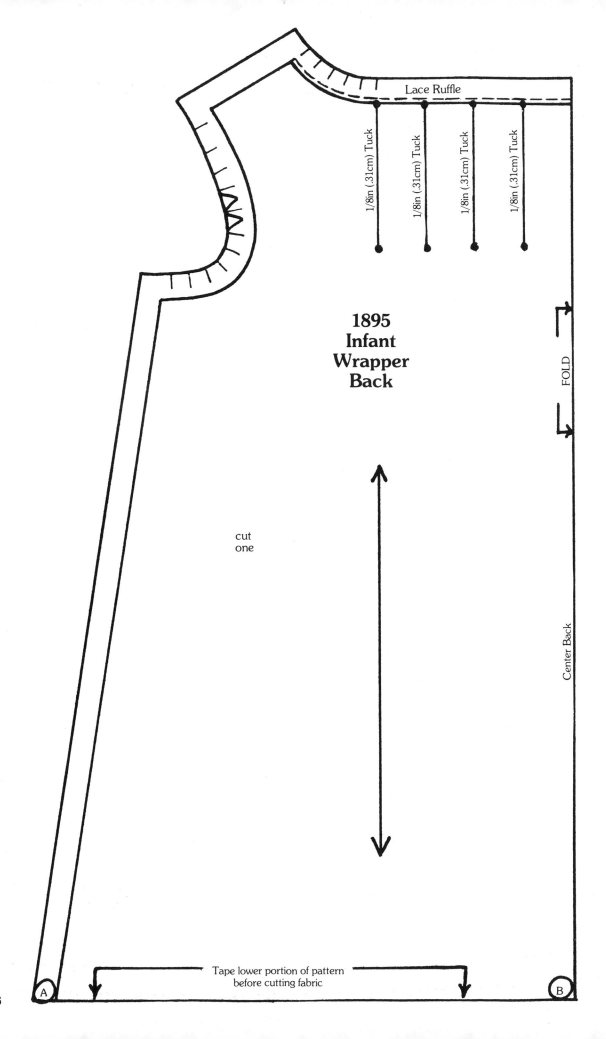

Lace Ruffle

1/8in (.31cm) Tuck

1/8in (.31cm) Tuck

1/8in (.31cm) Tuck

1/8in (.31cm) Tuck

**1895
Infant
Wrapper
Back**

FOLD

Center Back

cut
one

Tape lower portion of pattern
before cutting fabric

A

B

116

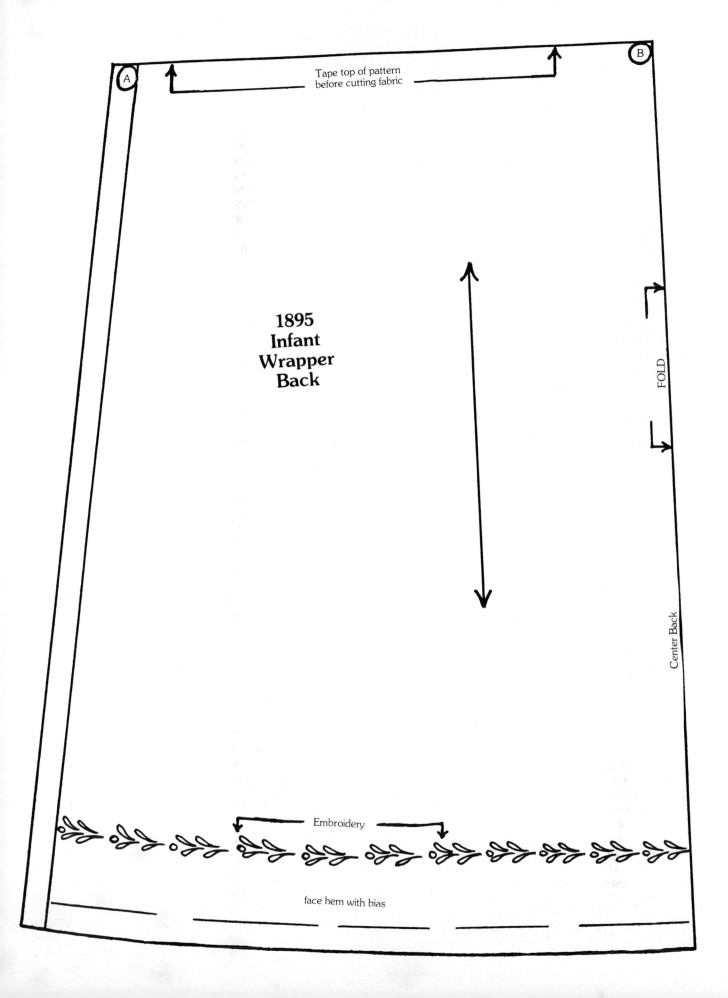

A

B

Tape top of pattern
before cutting fabric

1895
Infant
Wrapper
Back

FOLD

Center Back

Embroidery

face hem with bias

TABLE OF CONTENTS

DOLL MAKING:

St. Nicholas "Real-Life" Pantin Paper Doll Project

by **Beverly Port**

Have yourself a very "Merry Christmas" and select anything you wish for your 1986 Christmas presents, from the many dolls and bears surrounding the good St. Nicholas. Carefully cut out your selections and insert them into his leather carrying-pouch in front, and in both sides of the large cloth bag he carries at his back. This "Real-Life" pantin paper doll is a fun project for young and old.

St. Nicholas makes a wonderful gift containing toys the receiver specializes in collecting, or a super package decoration for a special person.

He can be used as a Christmas Tree ornament or wall ornament and as a free standing ornament on a table or in the center of a Christmas floral arrangement.

He makes an interesting toy for a doll or bear to hold and is a welcome addition to a Santa Claus collection.

Have fun and use your talent and imagination in his completion. Enjoy!

****

Directions as follows:

To activate St. Nicholas, cut him and both his arms out of the pages. Use a glue stick on the back of the three main pieces and glue to medium cardstock, then cut the pieces out. You may also use shirt cardboard or lightweight giftbox cardboard, if cardstock is not readily available. Using an exacto knife, or sharp thin scissors, cut the slits to insert arms and the slits for "present" insertion in the three sack areas as marked in the diagram. Insert the top of the arms from the front and secure them to the body with paper fasteners. Tie a short piece of string from the top of one arm straight across to the top of the other arm. (Arms in "down" position.) Tie a longer string at the center of the "arm" string, as in the diagram.

You may tie a wooden bead on the free end of that longer string. Pulling on this string should move St. Nicholas' arms up and down.

To keep your "presents" from falling through the back of the figure, cut out the shapes marked "A", "B", and "C" from thin paper. Again using a glue stick, apply a thin line of glue along the *edges only* of the three shaped pieces and glue them in the corresponding areas on the back of the figure.

If you decide to use this project as an ornament to hang on the tree or wall, glue a loop of ribbon or wired tinsel to the back top of the head.

For a standing decoration, cut out and attach the "stand-tab" to the back of the figure *after* "B" section is glued on. A more complex base can be made by cutting out *the figure*, the *holly strip* he stands on and the *two large bears* in the bottom corners; all still attached and then bending back the short side pieces containing the two bears. The "stand-tab" at back may still be needed for strength.

Glue the pieces of the pages containing the toys to *thin* cardstock and cut the toys out. Insert those needed into the three slits in the sack areas on the figure. The rest of the toys can be glued to strips of velvet or satin ribbon and used for ornaments or package decorations. They can be put in a paper basket for paper dolls or held by small three-dimensional dolls or bears.

To add sparkling "glitter," spread glue thinly on areas to be covered with glitter and sprinkle it on. Shake off excess when glue dries. Colored "flocking" can be used in the same way. Add extra holly and berries cut from colored paper or old Christmas cards. Holly and berries may also be modeled from red and green Fimo or other modeling clay, that can be cured in the home oven, then glued to the figure. Cotton from pill bottles may give him "real" fur trim or real fur strips of brown may be glued on and cotton used for his beard and hair. Variations are limited only by your imagination. The toys can be "glittered" or "flocked" and tiny ribbons added to the dolls or Teddy Bears. So have fun for a Merry Christmas and a Happy New Year!

See illustrations and diagrams on following pages. Note that diagrams on 201 and 202 are not to scale but are rather presented to illustrate the method of assembly. Trace the actual pantin figure and scale other pieces from it.

ST. NICHOLAS

"Real-Life" Pantin Paper Doll

LEFT ARM

RIGHT ARM

Directions To Assemble St. Nicholas Pantin — Paper Doll

"Merry Christmas to one and all!" St. Nicholas says. He is a Pantin-Paper Doll for you to enjoy this Christmas. Mount St. Nicholas on posterboard. Make a 2 inch slit along the outside of his gold straps (next to green sack) and insert arms. Assemble with small paper fasteners. Put tiny holes just above paper fasteners. Run string through from arm to arm. Then tie another string in middle of section and let last part dangle as shown in diagram. The dangling string becomes the pull string that will make his arms move like the Pantin of old.

To put St. Nicholas's toys in his bags cut along the top of the holly on his gold knapsack and along the top inner edge of the green sack.

Merry Christmas!

(See also following pages for further instructions.)

MERRY CHRISTMAS

St. Nicholas Pantin — Method of Assembly

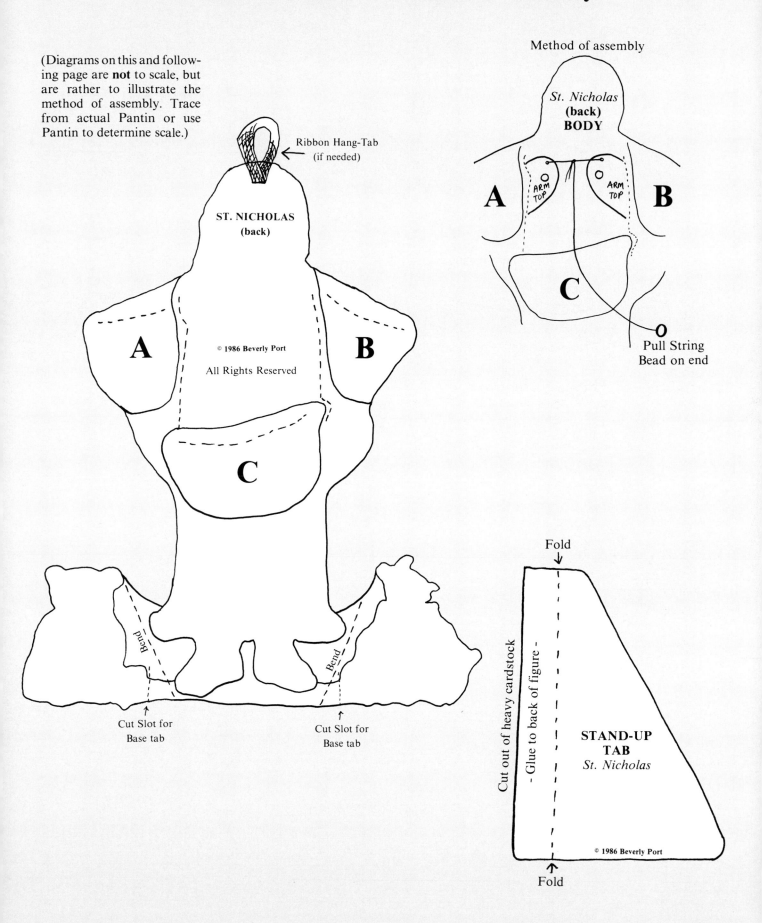

(Diagrams on this and following page are **not** to scale, but are rather to illustrate the method of assembly. Trace from actual Pantin or use Pantin to determine scale.)

Method of assembly

St. Nicholas
(back)
BODY

A

ARM TOP

ARM TOP

B

C

Pull String
Bead on end

Ribbon Hang-Tab
(if needed)

ST. NICHOLAS
(back)

A

B

C

Bend

Bend

Cut Slot for
Base tab

Cut Slot for
Base tab

Fold

Cut out of heavy cardstock

- Glue to back of figure -

STAND-UP TAB
St. Nicholas

Fold

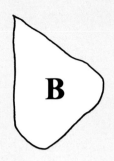

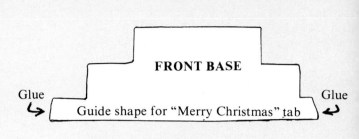

Draw shapes "A-B-C" and cut out. Glue them to corresponding areas on back of the figure of *St. Nicholas*. Put thin line of glue around edges only.

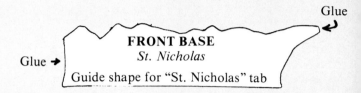

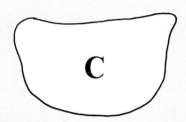

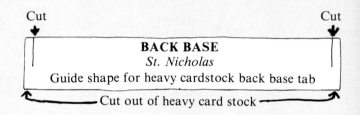

ESTHER,

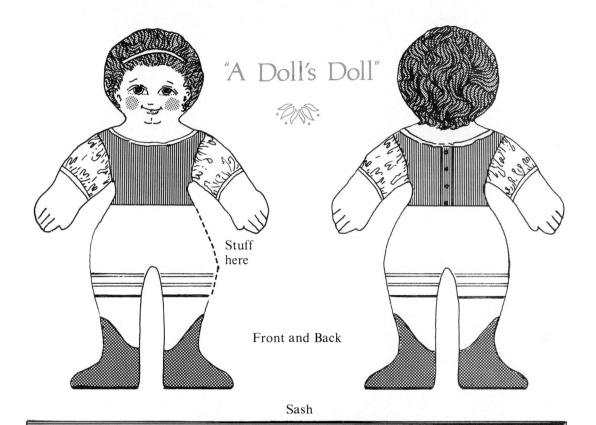

"A Doll's Doll"

Stuff here

Front and Back

Sash

Skirt - Gather waist at dotted line

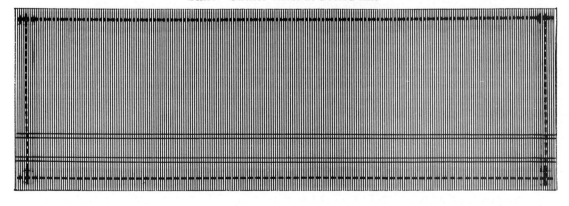

Cut an 8in (20cm) by 10in (25cm) square of beige cotton polyester or muslin. Pin fabric over doll and skirt patterns. Trace patterns with soft lead pencil. Remove fabric from pattern. Do *not* cut out. Carefully fabric paint or embroider details of doll and skirt as desired. Cut around doll body, leaving 1/4in (.65cm) seam allowance. Sew and stuff body. Cut out skirt. Sew back seam and hem. Gather waist and sew to doll body just beneath arms. Cut out sash, leaving 1/8in (.31cm) hem. Turn under and glue or sew. NOTE: If fabric paint is used, hems are not necessary as paint seals edges of fabric. Tie sash around waist, over skirt top. Tack in place.

Rapunzel

by **Katie Richardson**

Now you can bring Rapunzel, the beloved fairy-tale princess we first met as children, to charming "life." Our doll is two-dimentional, 11in (28cm) tall and fashioned essentially of soft cotton, interlining, fabric scraps and a bit of embroidery.

You will need:

1/2yd (.46m) pale pink cotton
1/2yd (.46m) interlining
One small bag polyfill
One skein yellow cotton yarn
Fabric scraps, including 3in (8cm) of 1/2in (1cm) width lace edging
One package assorted color small sequins
Embroidery thread: dark pink, red, medium blue, dark blue, medium green and colors to match fabric scraps
Embroidery hoop
Needle
Pencil
Ruler
Scissors

What To Do:

1. Using outside edge of pattern, cut two pieces of pink cotton fabric. Repeat with interlining material. (NOTE: Inside edge on pattern is for seaming.)

2. Transfer outline of doll's facial features, hands and shoes to one piece of pink cotton using a pencil for the transfer. To simplify this procedure, hold pattern and fabric on window glass and trace *lightly.*

3. Using a backstitch, embroider outline of eyes, nose and cheek with one strand of dark blue thread. Use medium blue thread for crease above eye.

Using a satin stitch, embroider eyebrows with two strands of medium blue thread.

Using one strand of red thread: (a) backstitch center line of lips; (b) satin stitch lips using two strands of pink thread.

Illustration 1. 11in (28cm) *Rapunzel*, a two-dimensional stuffed doll by Katie Richardson.

4. Trace dress bodice onto scrap fabric. (We used white satin.) Cut out fabric and sew into place with a blanket stitch using two strands of embroidery thread in a color to blend with fabric. (NOTE: If you wish, this step can be completed with the zigzag attachment on the sewing machine.)

5. Backstitch hands using two strands dark blue embroidery thread.

6. Repeat Step 4 with two side panels and center panel of skirt, being sure to fit fabric carefully around doll hands.

7. Embroider shoes in a satin stitch using two strands of green thread. Repeat with diamond shape on skirt.

8. Cut and sew lace edging to form collar on bodice.

9. Cut seven 24in (61cm) lengths of yellow cotton yarn. Arrange yarn to form hair by placing yarn strips side-by-side and centering over top of head. Hand-stitch in place to resemble center part.

Bring yarn "hair" down close to each side of face. Sew in place where it meets mid-point of cheek.

10. Trace and cut out crown. Sew sequins onto crown - groups of three at crown point, one long row across bottom. Using two strands of complementary thread color thread and blanket stitch, attach crown to face and hair.

11. Sew each piece of interlining to undersides of pink fabric, approximately 1/4in (.65cm) from outside edge.

12. On 1/2in (1cm) seam line, except for bottom edge, sew right sides of doll together. *Carefully* turn doll right side out. Stuff fully with polyfill. Hand-sew bottom edges together. □

129

Anne of Green Gables — A Sock Doll

by Loraine Wellman

LEFT: Illustration 1. *Anne of Green Gables*, a sock doll, shown in her arrival outfit.

RIGHT: Illustration 2. Close-up of the *Anne of Green Gables* sock doll showing the details of her face painting and her hair.

Anne of Green Gables is a fictional heroine created by Canadian novelist Lucy Maud Montgomery. An orphan sent by mistake instead of a boy to an elderly spinster and her brother, Anne won their hearts and the hearts of millions of readers around the world.

Today, tourists visit "Green Gables" on Prince Edward Island where Montgomery actually lived. Anne continues to be discovered by new generations of readers. Interest in Anne has increased through the made-for-television movies of *Anne of Green Gables* and *Anne of Avonlea* starring Megan Fellows.

This doll is made from a man's tube sock. Needlesculptured with painted features, it combines an element of challenge in doll making with a result that seems charmingly simple.

Clothes are removable for launder-ing. The brown dress represents that worn by Anne on her arrival.

MATERIALS REQUIRED:
Men's white tube sock (size 9 to 15)
*Note: Sock used was 75 percent cotton, 15 percent nylon, 5 percent polyester and 5 percent elastic. Sock **must** be mostly cotton to dye with tea but a slightly different combina-tion or different sock might produce a different sized doll. Check all pattern pieces for size before cutting out clothes.
Tea, alum
Polyester stuffing
Acrylic gesso
Acrylic paints in white, Hooker's green dark, burnt sienna, burnt umber, black, cadmium red medium
Two-ply orange wool
Stick, about 1/4in (.65cm) circum-

ference and 4in (10cm) long
Brown cotton knit (T-shirt or under-shirt type knit)
3/4yd (.69m) fine white cotton or muslin
1/2yd (.46m) brown print fabric
1/4yd (.23m) of 36in (91cm) wide brown plain fabric
1/4in (.65cm) wide elastic
Small amount of black felt
Small size snap fasteners (clear ones are nice)
16 black seed beads
Five 1/4in (.65cm) buttons
1yd (.91m) 1/8in (.31cm) brown ribbon
Small straw doll hat
Threads to match clothing, heavy-duty polyester thread to match body
Needlesculpture needle
1/4in (.65cm) wide flat lace for dress front, 1½yd (1.36m) of 3/8in (.9cm)

wide flat lace
DIRECTIONS:
DYE SOCK:
Dampen tube sock thoroughly and squeeze out excess moisture. Make tea dye by pouring boiling water over two tea bags. Use a bowl large enough to allow the sock to be freely stirred. Add a pinch of alum and enough boiling water to cover the sock. Place the damp sock in the hot tea and stir it until the sock seems one shade too dark — it will lighten when it dries.

MAKING DOLL:
Cut the tube sock according to the diagram.

Stuff head/body firmly. Stuff head area first, rounding with hands. Place a stuffing-wrapped stick of about 1/4in (.65cm) circumference and 4in (10cm) length inside the neck and partly up into the head area (a chopstick works fine). Head will measure 3½ (9cm) straight down the side or 5in (13cm) measured from the center top over the curve of center face. Stuff full enough. Neck circumference should measure about 6½in (16cm). Check appearance with illustrations.

Stuff body firmly. Tie thread at neck, wrapping thread around several times. Add more stuffing if necessary.

Sew the bottom of the body closed, turning in raw edges narrowly.

ARMS:
Right sides together, sew arms, hand and side seams with 1/4in (.65cm) seams. Leave top open. Turn. Stuff lightly in hand area. Divide into fingers with pins (see **Illustration 4**). Using a backstitch and sewing by hand, sew from front to back to form fingers. Finish stuffing arm firmly. Tie thread around to form wrist approximately 1½in (4cm) up arm. At 3½in (9cm), stitch back and forth (see **Illustration 5**) to form elbow. Turn under raw edges and top of arms and pin the arms in place on the body (see illustrations).

LEGS:
Right sides together, sew leg bottoms and side seams. Turn. Stuff legs firmly. Form feet by forcing up the leg bottom at 1¼in (3cm) from bottom. Sew leg tops closed. Pin legs to body and sew. (As they are pinched in at the top, this enables *Anne* to "sit.")

FACE MODELING:
Use heavy-duty polyester thread in a shade to blend in with skin shade and a long thin needlesculpture needle. Following **Illustration 6**, mark dots on face, using pins or fade-out markers. Leave a knot at the back of the head

Illustration 3. *Anne of Green Gables*, a sock doll, shown with her underwear.

and stitch from back to inner eye corner. Take a small stitch but do not pull. Stitch down to opposite mouth corner. Take a small stitch, pulling slightly. Stitch up to same eye corner. Repeat. Stitch to other eye inner corner. Then stitch to opposite mouth corner, pulling slightly as before. Repeat. Stitch to outer eye corner to other outer eye corner and back again. Stitch to inner eye corner. Insert tip of needle where nose will be. With tip into the stuffing, fluff up the stuffing. Stitch from inner eye to nostril and back up, pulling slightly. Stitch to other inner eye and back again. Stitch to 1/4in (.65cm) up from nostril and slightly to center (between 1/8in [.31cm] and 1/16 in [.15cm]). Stitch directly across to opposite side of nose (same positioning from nostril). Take a small stitch and stitch back again. Use the tip of the needle in the stuffing and fluff up the area in between. Bring thread around outside **on top** and hold the thread with your finger to keep the nose in a curve. Insert needle at nostril, pulling thread slightly to secure. Repeat for the other side. Take needle back up to inner eye and, having taken a small stitch, back down to mouth corner. Stitch across to opposite mouth corner, **on top**, pulling only enough to secure thread. Take a small stitch and then sew to back of head. Do not pull. Fasten off thread securely.

FACE PAINTING:
Follow illustrations and check **Illustration 7** for placement of features. It helps to cut out an eye from paper, trace the shape and reverse it for the other eye. Paint gesso where eyes and mouth will be. Always have one coat thoroughly dry before painting over it. A blow dryer can speed drying time. Paint eye white over entire eye. When it is dry, trace the iris shape, looking slightly to one side. Make sure irises are the same size. Mix Hooker's green dark around the outside of the irises and as radiating from the center (spokes effect). Mix cadmium red medium and white to paint the lips. The lower lip is slightly paler but both are pink, rather than red. Add a little more white to make a very pale pink and make one small dot or triangle at inner eye (see **Illustration 8**). Paint the pupil black. When it is dry, add highlights — one dot of white and one small crescent. Use burnt umber and a very fine brush to paint a line around the eyes. Paint the eyelashes, beginning on the line and sweeping gently outwards. Use burnt sienna to paint the eyebrows and to dot lightly to give *Anne* freckles.

HAIR:
To make the curl strip, use hairpin lace loom (or wire bent 1⅛in [3cm] apart) and wrap orange wool solidly on the wire. With the open end to the sewing machine, sew down the center

of the wrapped wool (see **Illustration 9**). Continue to slide the closed end towards you and keep wrapping wool and stitching until a 7in (18cm) strip is completed. Set aside.

The amount of hair needed for the **hair base** may vary according to the sock used and/or the amount of stuffing. Mark lightly with a pencil or chalk, where the hairline will be (check illustrations). Start at the top of the doll and measure from side to side over the top. Cut a piece of cardboard to this length and wrap about 1½in (4cm) width of wool. Slip the wool off the cardboard and pin it on the doll's head, arranging wool evenly to cover the top section. With orange thread, backstitch down the center to form a part and to hold the wool in place. Repeat two to three times until the doll's head is covered. Have all the loop ends curved and pinned at the sides of the head. Sew all loops in place at head sides, using orange thread (see **Illustration 10**).

BRAIDS:

On a piece of cardboard 8in (20cm) long, wrap three loop sections of approximately 12 windings each (amount may vary by wool weight). Slip wool off the cardboard, keeping each section separate. Now tie one end together (using matching wool, tying the three sections together, but keeping the rest of the sections spread out). Braid the three sections together. Tie the end when you finish. Pin the braid to overlap the loops at doll's side head. Sew braid in place. Cut bottom loops open and even.

Take curl strip and pin it, following illustration, across the front of the doll's hairline. If it is a little too long, fold ends under. Pin, then stitch in place, stitching through the machine stitching. Tie 1/8in (.31cm) brown ribbon at ends of braids.

STOCKINGS:

Following pattern, cut two stockings from brown knit material. Have the maximun stretch across the width (old underwear can be utilized for these stockings). Seam very narrow back and bottom seams, leaving top open. Turn right side out and place on doll.

BLACK SHOES:

Following pattern, cut two soles and two shoe tops from felt. Sew, right sides together, in a very narrow seam, seam A-B. Sew sole to shoe bottom. Place on doll, making sure you have a right and a left shoe — overlap goes to outside. Pin. Arrange seed beads evenly spaced (eight per shoe) and take off the shoe and sew beads to top overlap. Sew snaps underneath and on bottom overlap, spacing as needed to hold shoe closed.

CLOTHING:

Note: if the doll is to be a play doll and clothes will have to be washed regularly, **finish** all seams by pinking and zigzagging.

PANTALETTES:

Cut out according to the pattern. Turn up a narrow hem at the bottom. Sew 3/8in (.9cm) wide lace across the bottom. Sew leg seams. Place one leg inside the other, right sides together and sew crotch seam. Turn under 1/8in (.31cm) at waist, turn again to form 3/8in (.9cm) wide casing. Sew at top of waist. Sew bottom of casing, leaving an opening. Measure the doll's waist and cut 1/4in (.65cm) elastic waist measurement plus 1/2in (1.3cm). Insert elastic in casing. Sew elastic ends together. Sew remaining opening closed.

PETTICOAT:

Cut top and lining from pattern pieces. Cut skirt 9½in (24cm) by 34in (86cm). Sew side seams on petticoat top. Repeat for facing. Pin top and facing, right sides together and sew back and top edges and armhole opening. Turn. Press. Sew shoulder seams. Optional finishing: Turn under raw edges and slip stitch shoulder seams to facing.

Sew (ungathered) 3/8in (.9cm) wide lace along the bottom after pressing up a narrow hem.

Gather the skirt evenly along the top (raw) edge. Pin, sew right sides together to petticoat top, keeping facing free. Press under hem on facing and slip stitch facing to petticoat skirt along the seam line. Place petticoat on doll to check fit. Overlap back. Pin. Mark where snaps are needed. Take petticoat off doll and sew on snaps.

APRON:

Cut top, lining for top and armhole facings from pattern pieces. Cut skirt 8in (20cm) by 31in (79cm).

Sew top shoulder seams. Sew lining shoulder seams. Right sides together, sew top and arm opening seams. Trim, clip curves, turn and press.

APRON POCKET:

Cut one pocket. Turn under edge on sides and curved bottom. Press. Turn under top hem. Press. Sew top hem. Set aside while completing apron skirt.

APRON SKIRT:

Turn under hem on apron skirt side and bottom edges. Sew. Turn under hem on curved edge of underarm facing. Sew. Place underarm facings on apron top edges, right sides together, raw edges matching. Facing is 6in (15cm) from back/side of apron. Sew top seam. Trim, clip edges, turn to inside.

Gather top of apron skirt at front and at backs but not where facings are sewn. Right sides together, pin to apron top, adjusting gathers to fit. Leave lining free. Stitch. Press under lining raw edge. Pin in place over gathered seam. Slip stitch in place. Sew two snap fasteners on back opening.

Pin pocket on skirt front. See illustration for placement, but it may vary with individual dolls. Sew pocket in place, sewing side and curved bottom of pocket and leaving top open.

DRESS:

Cut top, front and back facings and collar from pattern pieces. Cut skirt 11in (28cm) by 34in (86cm).

COLLAR:

Right sides together, sew collar pieces to facings on outside curves. Trim seam, clip and turn. Press.

Following pattern guide, sew 1/4in (.65cm) wide flat lace to bodice front. Join bodice front and backs at shoulder seams. Repeat for bodice facing. Baste collar to bodice, matching raw edges and having collar sections meet at center front. Pin bodice to bodice facing, right sides together with collar sandwiched between. Sew back and neck edges. Trim, clip curves, turn. Press.

Gather top of sleeve. Right sides together, pin sleeve to bodice. Sew. Right sides together, sew bodice side seams and sleeve seams. Press under raw edge at sleeve bottom, press up again to form casing 3/8in (.9cm) wide. Sew to form casing, leaving an opening to insert elastic. Measure 1/4in (.65cm) wide elastic the doll's wrist measurement plus 1/2in (1.3cm). Insert elastic in casing, overlap 1/4in (.65cm) and sew elastic ends together. Sew casing closed.

Sew skirt back seam, leaving 1in (2cm) open at the top. Press back raw edges at opening and machine sew. Gather top edge of skirt. Pin, arranging gathers evenly, right sides together to bodice. Sew. Check length on doll. Turn up hem, turning under raw edge and sew. Sew five 1/4in (.65cm) buttons on bodice front between lace. Sew snaps on bodice back opening. □

Illustration 5. Shaping the elbow.

1/4in (.65cm) 1/2in (1.3cm)

2in (5cm) to wrist

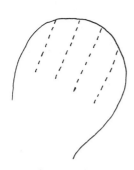

Illustration 4. For stitching the hands, make four rows of stitching to make five fingers.

Illustration 7. Diagram of face positioning.

Illustration 6. Diagram for face modeling.

5/8in   5/8in   5/8in
(1.6cm)   (1.6cm)   (1.6cm)

1in (2cm) between nose end and eyes

1/2in (1.3cm) between nose and mouth

1/2in (1.3cm) apart

Mouth corners 7/8in (2.2cm) apart

1in (2cm) up from neck

Illustration 9. Yarn wrapped on hairpin lace loom showing direction of stitching on machine.

Illustration 10. Loop ends of yarn sewn at the side of the head.

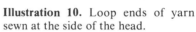

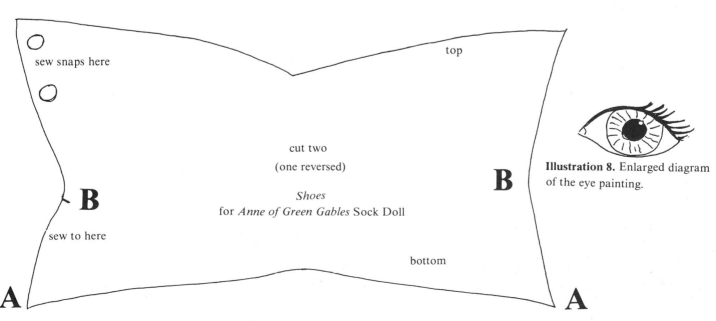

sew snaps here

top

cut two
(one reversed)

Shoes
for *Anne of Green Gables* Sock Doll

B

B

sew to here

bottom

A

A

Illustration 8. Enlarged diagram of the eye painting.

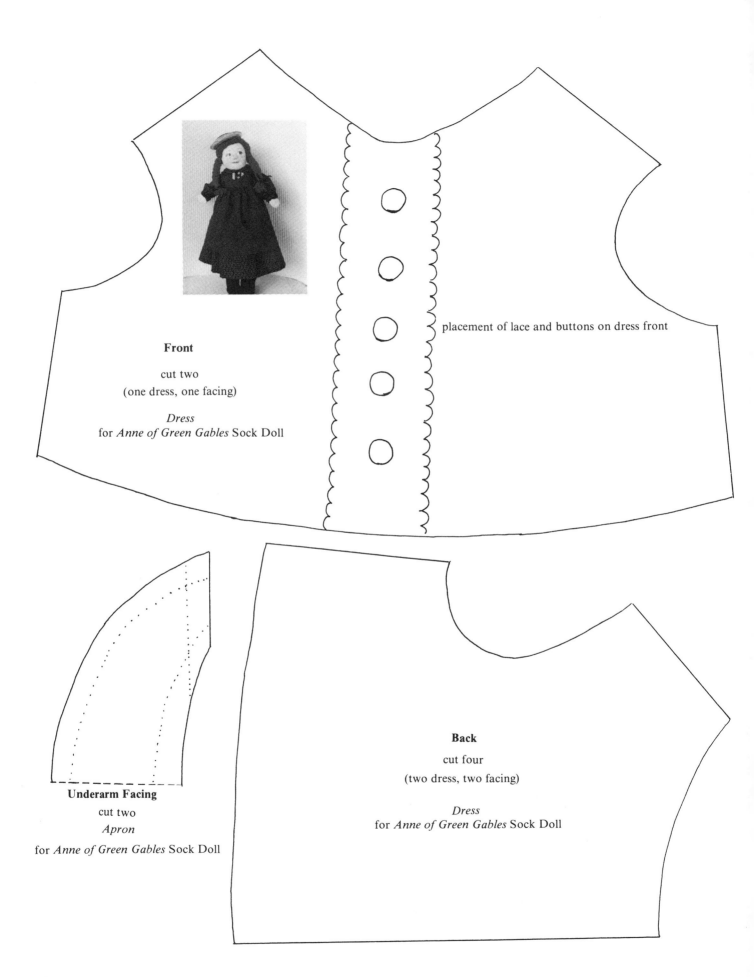

Front

cut two

(one dress, one facing)

Dress
for *Anne of Green Gables* Sock Doll

placement of lace and buttons on dress front

Underarm Facing
cut two
Apron
for *Anne of Green Gables* Sock Doll

Back

cut four

(two dress, two facing)

Dress
for *Anne of Green Gables* Sock Doll

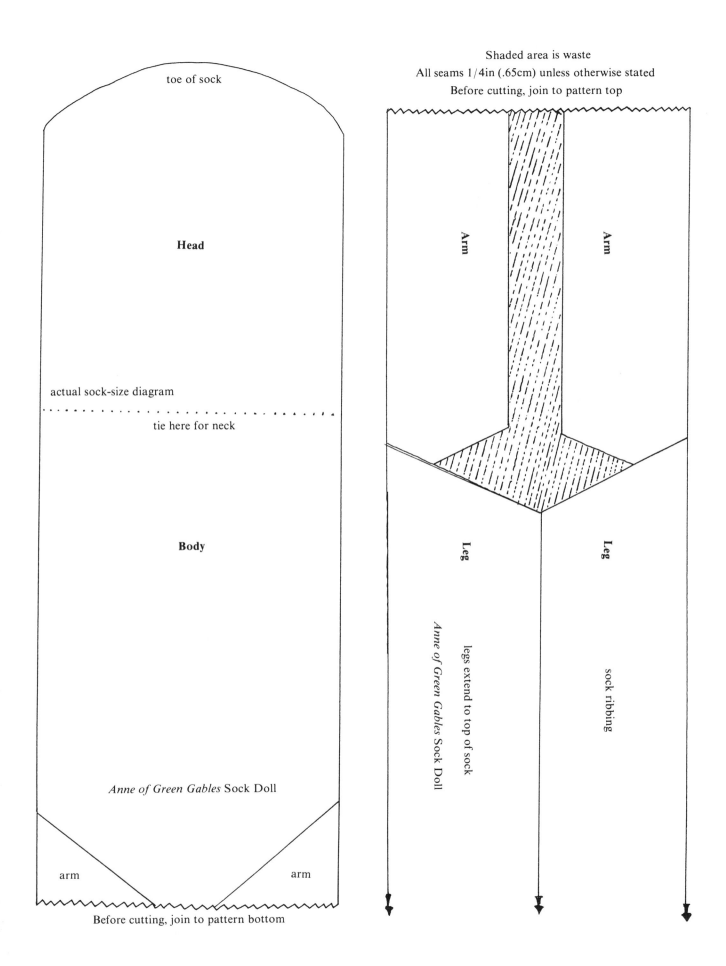

toe of sock

Head

actual sock-size diagram

· ·

tie here for neck

Body

Anne of Green Gables Sock Doll

arm   arm

Before cutting, join to pattern bottom

Shaded area is waste
All seams 1/4in (.65cm) unless otherwise stated
Before cutting, join to pattern top

Arm   Arm

Leg   Leg

Anne of Green Gables Sock Doll

legs extend to top of sock

sock ribbing

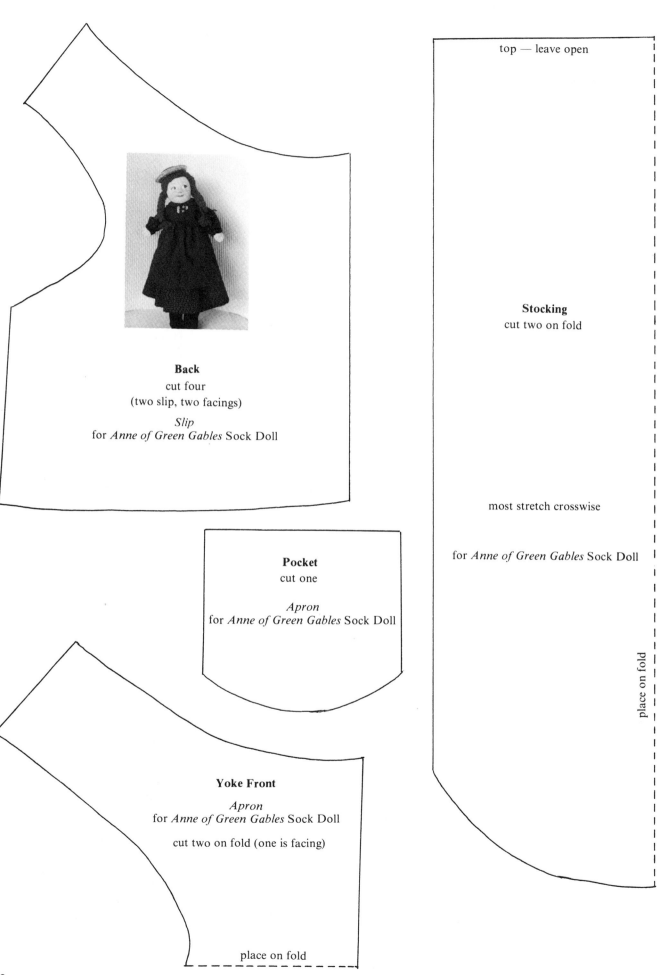

Back
cut four
(two slip, two facings)
Slip
for *Anne of Green Gables* Sock Doll

Pocket
cut one

Apron
for *Anne of Green Gables* Sock Doll

top — leave open

Stocking
cut two on fold

most stretch crosswise

for *Anne of Green Gables* Sock Doll

place on fold

Yoke Front

Apron
for *Anne of Green Gables* Sock Doll

cut two on fold (one is facing)

place on fold

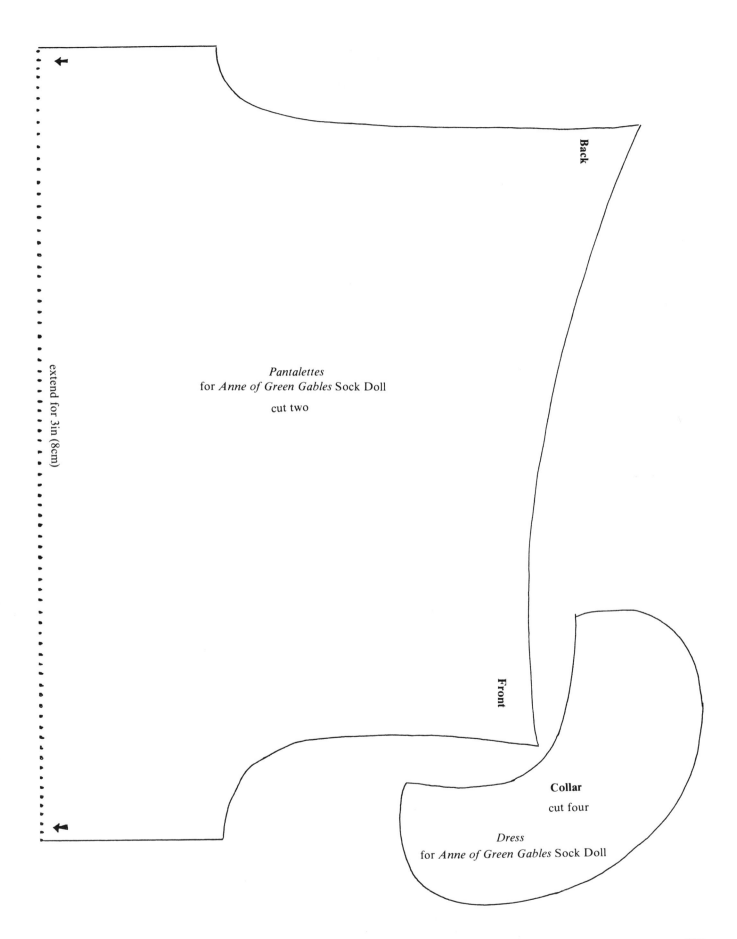

extend for 3in (8cm)

Pantalettes
for *Anne of Green Gables* Sock Doll

cut two

Back

Front

Collar

cut four

Dress
for *Anne of Green Gables* Sock Doll

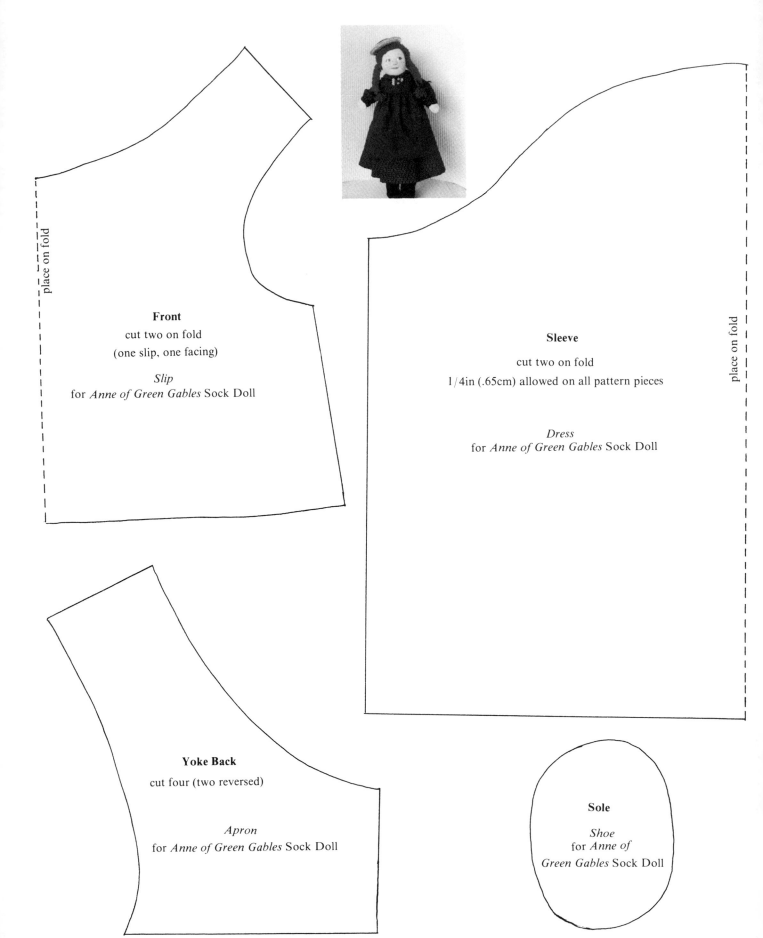

place on fold

Front

cut two on fold

(one slip, one facing)

Slip

for *Anne of Green Gables* Sock Doll

Sleeve

cut two on fold

1/4in (.65cm) allowed on all pattern pieces

Dress

for *Anne of Green Gables* Sock Doll

place on fold

Yoke Back

cut four (two reversed)

Apron

for *Anne of Green Gables* Sock Doll

Sole

Shoe

for *Anne of*

Green Gables Sock Doll

Bettina ... A Peasant Pincushion Doll

by **Patricia L. Wilks**

Illustration 1. *Bettina,* a peasant pincushion doll by Patricia L. Wilks. *Photograph by John Axe.*

Instructions:

1. Pin and cut out pattern pieces in fabric choice. Leave enough fabric around face piece to place in an embroidery hoop. Embroider face. Lay down, side by side, six-strand floss for hair and secure with a couching stitch.
2. Sew and stuff body. Turn under face edge and carefully stitch in place to body.
3. Lightly sew and stuff hands. Sew and stuff arms, gather bottom of sleeve around hand. Sew arm to body with a loop stitch at shoulder.
4. Sew apron and position on body. Sew on beads or small buttons to bodice.
5. Make rosettes with 1/4in (.65cm) grosgrain ribbon and tack to sides of face.
6. Make "babushka" and tie on to finish. Bettina holds a small dried flower/herb bouquet. She makes a handy pincushion.

Helpful Suggestions:

A bit of stuffing inserted between the face and doll head as the face is stitched on will make a more natural rounded face.

Worsted yarn, instead of embroidery yarn, was used on the model shown here. Either can be used.

The "babushka" must be made of a very thin cotton to tie gracefully; or use an old soft handkerchief. Cut it very long and roll the edges under.

The center strip on the "blouse" is a thin white rectangle stitched on and the "buttons" are glass-headed straight pins quite appropriate to a pincushion.

A thin ribbon tied in a small bow is pinned at each side of the hair edges. □

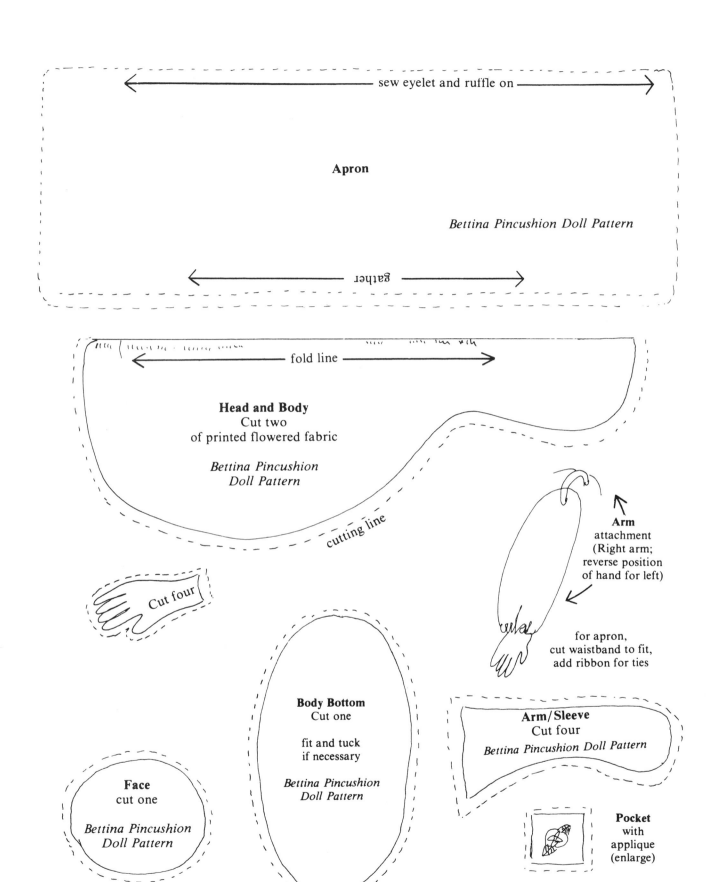

sew eyelet and ruffle on

Apron

Bettina Pincushion Doll Pattern

gather

fold line

Head and Body
Cut two
of printed flowered fabric

*Bettina Pincushion
Doll Pattern*

cutting line

Cut four

Arm
attachment
(Right arm;
reverse position
of hand for left)

for apron,
cut waistband to fit,
add ribbon for ties

Body Bottom
Cut one

fit and tuck
if necessary

*Bettina Pincushion
Doll Pattern*

Arm/Sleeve
Cut four
Bettina Pincushion Doll Pattern

Face
cut one

*Bettina Pincushion
Doll Pattern*

Pocket
with
applique
(enlarge)

Boudoir Doll

by **Doris Rockwell Gottilly**

Long-limbed boudoir or flapper dolls originated in France. Later they were made in other countries and called boudoir dolls. Most of those made represented ladies and were dressed in the latest flapper fashion. They were decorative, elongated and exotic. Many of these figures were thought vulgar mainly because of the elaborate face makeup and gaudy colored outfits. Some held a facsimile cigarette in their mouth. This doll was considered in poor taste in its time.

The boudoir doll was not made for children but was made for young women of the 1920s as a mascot or as a decoration for the bed or dresser. They were made from 1921 to 1929. Some were dressed in Charleston dresses, cloche hats, long beads and high heels. The French Boudoir dolls were usually hand-painted on silk stockinette. The hair styles were thought elaborate for such an inexpensive doll. One of the features that impressed me were the very long legs and arms.

With the above in mind I have designed a long-limbed satin "flapper" for you. It is quite a simple doll to make and can be finished in a few hours. The fun part for me was to apply the makeup to the dolls. I used a simple pattern for the dress with a boat-shaped neck and no waist, the flat "flapper look." The hair is made of small blonde mohair curls styled in a bobbed side part that curls past the ears and onto the side of the face. The complete doll is made from white satin. She is quite a delight to view perched upon a shelf.

Equipment needed:
Sewing machine, scissors, straight pins, needle, tape measure, pencil, 1/4in (.65cm) wood dowel 14in (36cm) long (to use for stuffing arms and legs).

Materials needed:
Tracing paper; 1/2yd (.46m) of white satin; white thread; 1/4yd (.23m) of polyester quilt batting; polyester

Illustration 1. 30in (76cm) boudoir doll completed.

stuffing; acrylic premixed paints in rose, blue and black; small pointed brush to paint features; powdered blush and powdered eye shadow (I used plum for rouge and lavender and purple for eye shadow); curled blonde mohair, 6in (15cm) by 10in (25cm); fabric glue.

There are three main pattern pieces to the flapper doll: the legs, the arms and the body and head.

How to make the doll:
Trace all pattern pieces and transfer to tissue paper, adjusting the pieces so there is no fold and the patterns are one long piece.

Cut out patterns.

Pin pattern pieces to folded satin and cut out two body pieces, four arm pieces and four leg pieces.

Next, place pattern pieces on the batting and cut out appropriate number of pieces as stated on patterns.

Next pin arms together with the satin facing inside and then place the batting on one side and pin at 2in (5cm) intervals. Next pin the leg pieces together in the same manner. Each arm and leg will have two satin pattern pieces. The arms will have one piece of

batting and the legs will have two.

Pin body pieces together with the satin facing inward; pin the two batting interface to one side.

SEAMS: allow about 3/16in (.45cm) for all seams.

Sew all pattern pieces using sewing machine. I used a tight small zigzag stitch to keep the satin from raveling. I set my machine about 18 stitches to 1in (2cm). Be sure to leave the openings for stuffing as shown on the patterns. VERY CAREFULLY, turn each piece right side out and press with a warm (not hot) iron. I had some difficulty turning the hand inside out. What I finally did was to use a rubber eraser to push gently on the hand to turn it right side out and then used the wood dowel to push the rest of the arm right side out. You have to be careful so you do not tear the satin.

Stuff the polyester stuffing (I used about 5oz. of stuffing). For the head and legs, stuff inside the batting as the batting acts as an interface for the satin. The arms have only one batting interface so that will be on the top side of the arm and you will stuff behind it.

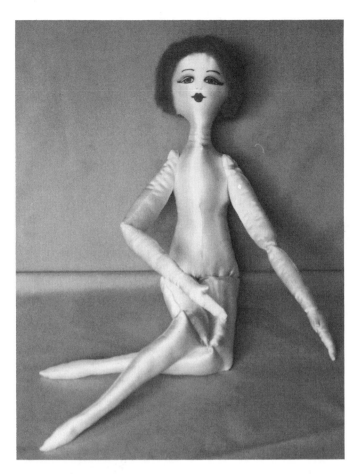

Illustration 5. The completed 30in (76cm) satin boudoir doll. Use button thread to sew arms and legs to doll's body.

Tie thread here after sewing through doll's arms and body twice. Add a drop of fabric glue to knot.

Illustration 2. 30in (76cm) boudoir doll undressed showing body construction.

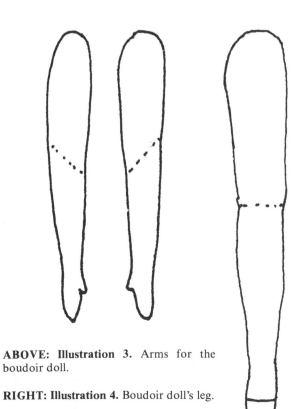

ABOVE: Illustration 3. Arms for the boudoir doll.

RIGHT: Illustration 4. Boudoir doll's leg.

RIGHT: Illustration 6. Doll seated with hands stitched together. Note the stitching on the arms and legs that allow the doll to sit in a seated position with the knees folded and the arms wrapped around them. The hands can be stitched together with one stitch and then tied.

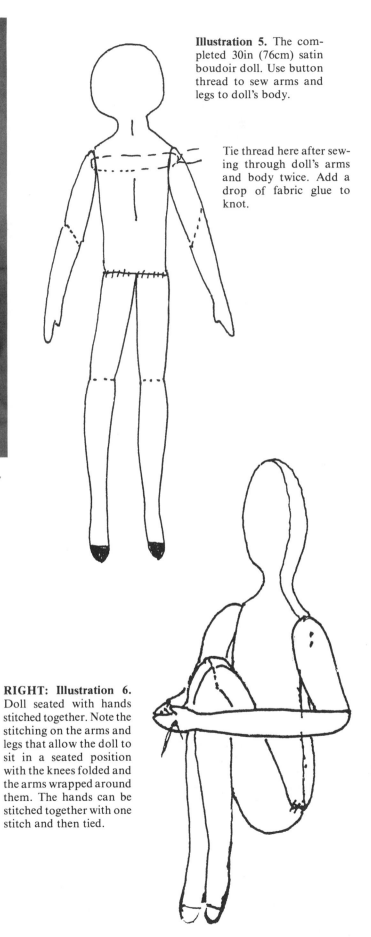

Illustration 7. Outline the eyes with black paint. I gave my doll blue eyes.

black
blue

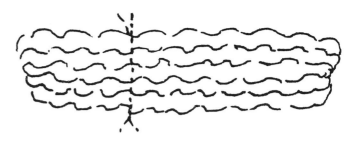

Illustration 10. For the mohair wig, sew the center or side part in the mohair as shown.

Illustration 8. Paint the mouth rose.

Illustration 11. Glue the completed wig to the doll's head with fabric glue. Apply the glue to the head and carefully press the wig to the doll's head. Rubber bands can be used to hold the wig in place until the glue is dry. Then remove the bands.

Illustration 12. Back view of doll's head showing wig.

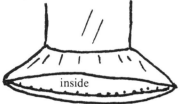

inside

Illustration 9. Press and pin the lining and dress fabric together at hemline, allowing 1/4in (.65cm) fold of the dress fabric so the lining is not visible. Carefully hand-stitch the hem so stitches are not visible from the front. Use a tiny slip stitch.

ARMS AND LEGS: Stuff halfway up arms and legs and then stitch as shown on the patterns. Stitch and then stuff the rest of the arm or leg. This will allow the arms and legs to fold for the sitting position with the arms wrapped around the doll's knees.

Drawing in the doll's eyes, nose and mouth: Before you stuff the doll's head, first sketch in the features. Study the drawing of the doll's face and make sure you place the eyes, nose and mouth in the exact position as the drawing. If you place the features too far down or too much to the right or left, the doll will have a strange look. Check the drawing of the doll's face on the pattern and note how the features are placed in the center of the circle.

The making up of the face with the eye shadow and blush are the fun part. I used the very small sponge applicator that came with the eye shadow to "paint" the eye shadow on the doll. The colors I used were lavender frost and deep violet. After rubbing the color in with the applicator, blow any excess gently away. I cleaned the sponge applicator and then used it to apply the rouge to the doll's cheeks in two round circles. The makeup of the 1920s gave the boudoir dolls a mask-like appearance.

Making the doll's dress: 1/2yd (.46m) of fabric: silk, voile, shantung or any of the silk-like polyester fabrics that are available today. Trace the dress patterns. Cut out pattern pieces. Place the pieces on the fabric and pin in place. Cut out pieces. Sew together at shoulders, sew lining at shoulders. Sew the lining and the dress together at the neckline. Turn right side out and press. (Dress may be made with or without lining.)

Sew lining and sleeve fabric together and turn right side out and press. Gather sleeve at top and pin in place in armhole and sew in place. Sew up sleeve underarm. First sew underarm so the seam will not show and then sew the lining on the inside so the rough seam is not visible. Press and pin the lining and dress fabric together at hemline, allowing 1/4in (.65cm) fold of the dress fabric so the lining is not visible. CAREFULLY hand-stitch the hem so stitches are not visible from the front. Use a tiny slip stitch.

Add a long string of pearls wrapped around the doll's neck to drape down in front and a large sash around the low waistline (around the hips). Pull the doll's knees up and wrap the arms around the knees. She is now ready to perch on your dresser or bed or bookstand. A perky 30in (76cm) long-limbed beauty of a boudoir doll!

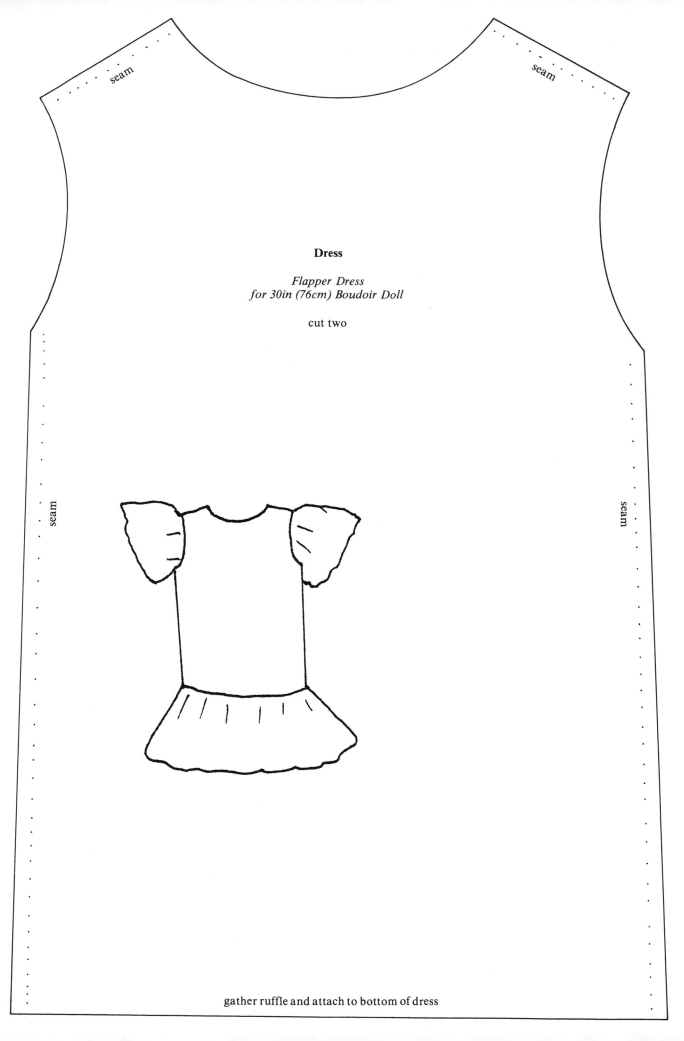

Dress

*Flapper Dress
for 30in (76cm) Boudoir Doll*

cut two

seam

seam

seam

seam

gather ruffle and attach to bottom of dress

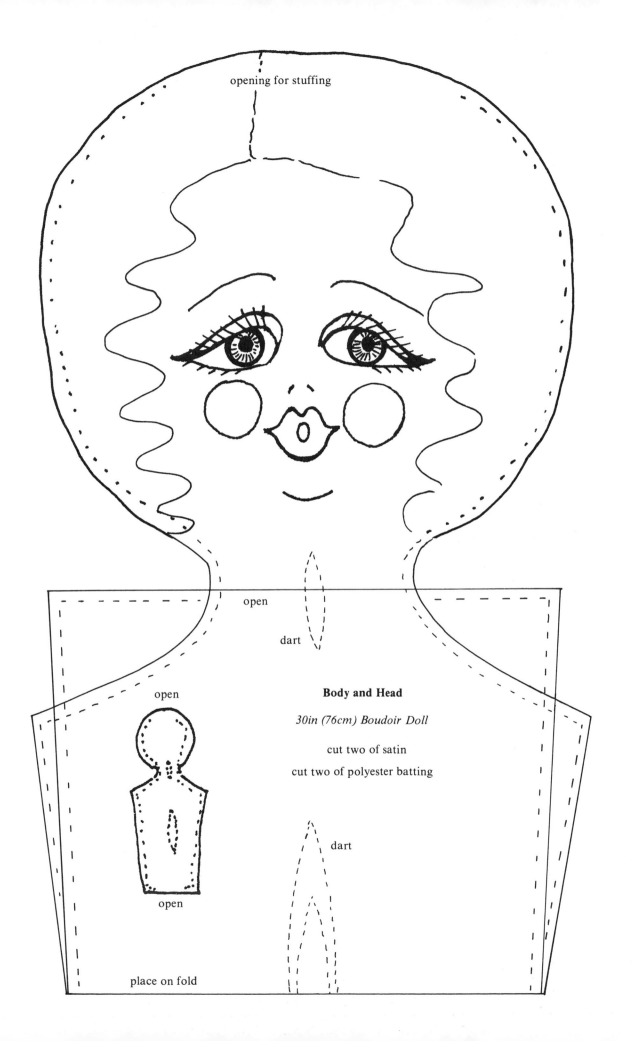

opening for stuffing

open

dart

open

Body and Head

30in (76cm) Boudoir Doll

cut two of satin

cut two of polyester batting

open

dart

open

place on fold

145

Skirt Ruffle

Flapper Dress
for 30in (76cm) Boudoir Doll

cut two on fold

gather fo fit drop waistline of dress

hem by hand

fold of fabric

Arms

30in (76cm) Boudoir Doll

cut four of satin

cut two of polyester batting

Cut on straight of fabric. Place thumbs in toward sides of doll.

open for stuffing

fold

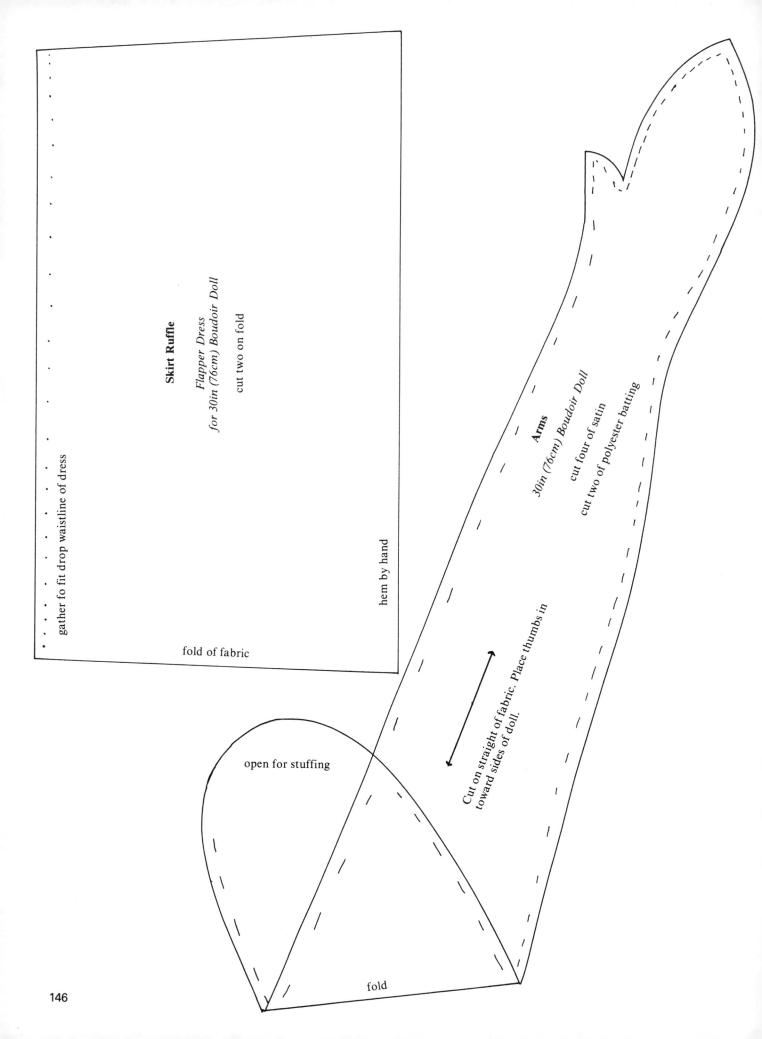

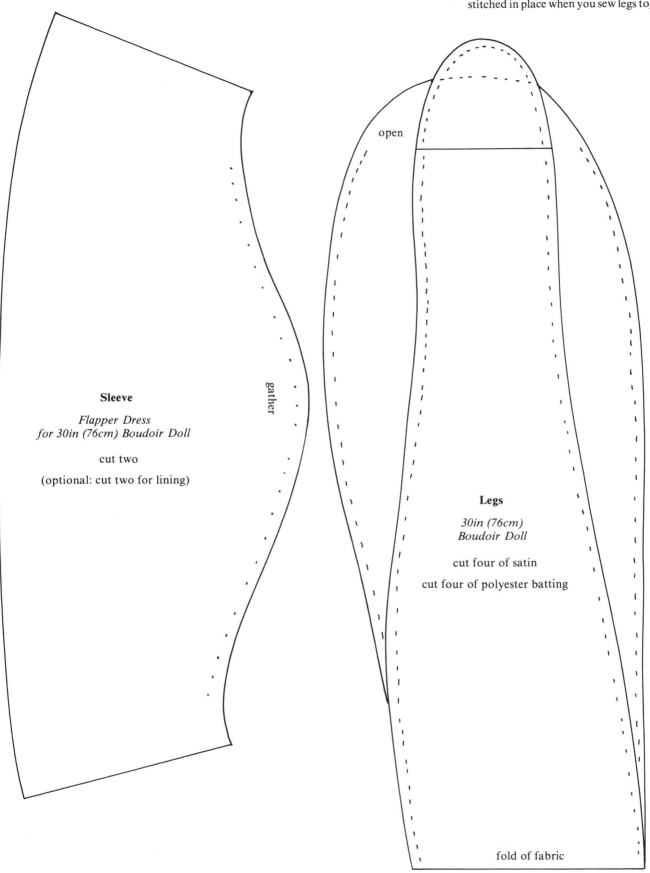

Shoe is 1in (2cm) wide black satin ribbon
stitched in place when you sew legs together.

open

gather

Sleeve

*Flapper Dress
for 30in (76cm) Boudoir Doll*

cut two

(optional: cut two for lining)

Legs

*30in (76cm)
Boudoir Doll*

cut four of satin

cut four of polyester batting

fold of fabric

Baby Doll in Christening Outfit, Part I

by **Mary Huber**

Photographs by **Elspeth**

Illustration 1. 7in (17.8cm) baby doll designed by Mary Huber shown dressed in christening outfit.

Illustration 2. 7in (17.8cm) baby doll designed by Mary Huber.

Doll Reader® is pleased to present a pattern for a 7in (17.8cm) soft-sculpture doll and her christening outfit designed by Mary Huber, just one of the many patterns she designs for her business "Camille's Designs." The pattern and instructions for making the doll itself will be included in this issue and the christening outfit pattern and instructions will follow.

Material List for Doll in Christening Outfit

1/4yd (.46m) body fabric, 100 percent polyester soft-sculpture knit.

3/4yd (.69m) dress, bonnet and petti- coat fabric, soft, lightweight and non- raveling.

Extra-strong button/carpet thread - 1 spool to match body fabric color. 1 spool to match hair fur color.

Polyester sewing thread - match to color of body fabric.

Sewing thread - match dress fabric color.

Fine sewing thread - for doll nose and mouth (medium peach or for black doll, match to DMC floss color 3687).

Elastic thread - small amount for dress sleeves.

1yd (.91m) lingerie-type elastic, 1/4in (.65cm) wide - for panty.

1/2yd (.46m) 1/2in (1.3cm) wide soft lace - for trim on bonnet front edge.

1yd (.91m) 1/2in (1.3cm) woven-edge satin ribbon - for bonnet ties.

Fur fabric - small piece for hair; very soft lightweight, 3/8in (.9cm) short pile. The backing should be a bit stretchy.

Small beads for eyes - actual size ● (round type preferred).

One fine line red ballpoint "Bic" pen -for marking body fabric.

Four 3/8in (.9cm) buttons or doll buttons - for attaching arms and legs.

Dacron or fine quality polyester filling - for stuffing doll.

Lightweight ribbed knit fabric - white, for undershirt, socks and panty

Thin soft felt - small piece for doll footwear.

4 ply strong yarn - match to color of body fabric (for attaching limbs).

One 5in (12.7cm) long thin needle

One 1¾in (4.5cm) long very fine needle - for nose and mouth embroidery.

One 2½in (6.4cm) long thin needle - for adding bead eyes (must fit through bead hole).

One fondue fork - stuffing tool (inex- pensive type obtained in some hard- ware stores, about 10in (25.4cm) long). Also, 4in (10.2cm) long fruit fork, for stuffing hands.

Sequin/styrofoam craft pins, 1/2in (1.3cm) long and very fine. (These are used instead of stickpins for all my small doll making. Note: Some are finer than others so check on this.)

One roll of wide transparent tape - used to reinforce patterns pieces.

1yd (.91m) gathered eyelet, 1in (2.5cm) wide - for petticoat trim.

1/2yd (.46m) 1/4in (.65cm) mesh elastic - for petticoat waist.

Powdered blush and brush - to color doll cheeks.

When sewing this small doll, the choice of fabric and sewing supplies such as thread and machine needles are very important, so make sure you do the following: Select the proper body fabric because the amount of stretch affects the size of the doll and the fit of the clothing. To prevent damage to this knit fabric, a ballpoint sewing machine needle is necessary. Also, you must use a stretchy polyester thread. A straight machine-stitch will be fine if you use the proper thread and if the fabric is stretched slightly as you sew. A notion called "Needle-Lube" is handy when sewing knit fabrics, but use this sparingly.

Whenever you start sewing, always pull back on the two sewing machine threads and turn machine wheel towards you. Use the 1/2in (1.3cm) very fine sequin pins instead of regular stickpins because this will eliminate the need for basting for work on the doll body and clothing. The pins should be on top of the fabric when stitching by machine.

Trace pattern pieces on paper. To make the paper patterns for Skirt, Bonnet and Petticoat, follow the measurements given on the Dress Fabric Layout. Before cutting out any patterns, apply wide transparent tape, to the back side. Large pattern shapes could be taped around edges only. This taping enables one to trace around patterns more easily and accurately. It also strengthens the patterns for reuse. After taping, cut out the patterns.

Sewing The Small Doll Body

Check the Body Fabric Layout and note that parts are traced for two dolls. (Since such a small amount of fabric is needed, trace parts for more than one doll.) Use a fine line red ballpoint pen to trace parts as shown. Always make a few pen marks on paper to get ink flowing so that fabric marking will be as light as possible.

The tiny-dotted line on Body Fabric Layout indicates a machine-stitching line for legs, arms and bodies, so follow this. Do not stitch between large dots (openings for stuffing), foot part of legs or neck and bottom part of bodies. Stitch 1/8in (.31cm) inward from your line to allow for seam except for hand area which is stitched close to red line. Set machine-stitch length for tiny stitching around hand. Now, cut out the fabric pieces.

Transfer the ear mark and face on head side and head front fabric pieces.

Match the edges of the fabric pieces to the patterns and place on a white paper. Use red pen to mark lightly. (Note: Although this doll has no ears, the ear mark is needed for reference when the mouth is stitched.)

Sewing The Doll Head

(Use thread a bit lighter than body fabric color. Remember to pull back on two threads at the start and to gently pull on fabric in back as you continue to sew.)

Follow the illustrated steps from 1 through 7 for sewing the head.

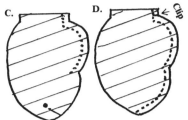

Step 1.

Step 1. Arrange parts as shown, then flip one SIDE over HEAD FRONT.

Step 2.

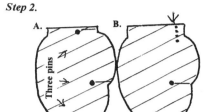

Step 2. A, B, C and D. Pin parts in three places, then sew from neck to head top. Repeat for other side. Note: Use tiny very fine sequin pins.

Step 3.

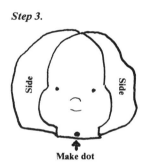

Make dot

Step 3. Trim the seams along head front.

Step 5.

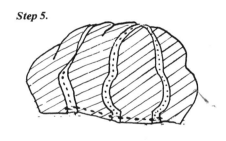

Step 5. Baste neck at seams so they are open and flat. Stretch fabric as you do this.

Step 4.

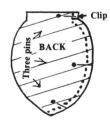

Clip

Step 4. Connect one side to back.

Step 6.

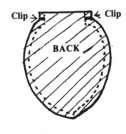

Step 6. Connect other SIDE to BACK.

Step 7.

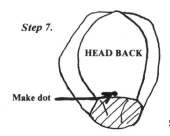

Make dot

Step 7. Turn sewn head right side out.

149

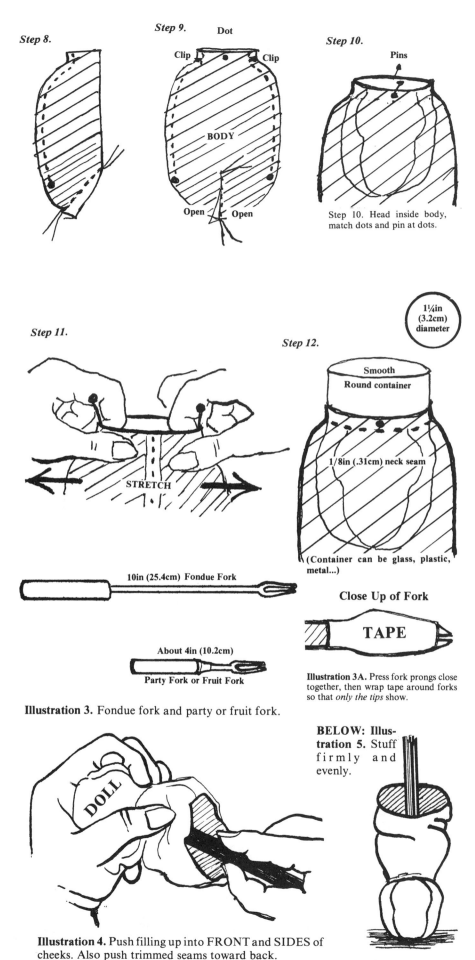

Step 8.

Step 9.

Dot

Clip   Clip

BODY

Open   Open

Step 10.

Pins

Step 10. Head inside body, match dots and pin at dots.

1¼in (3.2cm) diameter

Step 11.

STRETCH

10in (25.4cm) Fondue Fork

About 4in (10.2cm)

Party Fork or Fruit Fork

Illustration 3. Fondue fork and party or fruit fork.

Step 12.

Smooth
Round container

1/8in (.31cm) neck seam

(Container can be glass, plastic, metal...)

Close Up of Fork

TAPE

Illustration 3A. Press fork prongs close together, then wrap tape around forks so that *only the tips* show.

BELOW: Illustration 5. Stuff firmly and evenly.

DOLL

Illustration 4. Push filling up into FRONT and SIDES of cheeks. Also push trimmed seams toward back.

Sewing Doll Body And Attaching Head

Follow the illustrated steps from 8 through 12. After stitching the darts and knotting thread ends, clip at neck and sew seams open and flat. Make a dot at neck of both Body Front and back because this will help when attaching the head. Head is right side out as it is inserted into the body which is wrong side out. Match dots of head and body and pin at dots. Stretch neck opening with pins and even edges of head and body, then pin between dots. Some round container, measuring about 1¼in (3.2cm) in diameter, could be inserted into the neck opening before basting the neck seam. After basting, remove the container and stitch by machine. Make sure that fabric is stretched a bit as you sew, otherwise the neck opening will be too tight for stuffing. Turn work right side out.

Stuffing The Head And Body

When stuffing, always support the opposite end FIRMLY, making use of your hand, body or table. For stuffing tools, use a "fondue fork" which is inexpensive and found in most hardware stores. The fork prongs must be hammered or pressed close together before use. Another tool, good for small areas is a "fruit fork." This works well for the doll hands. Again, the fork prongs must be pressed together. These tools make stuffing faster and easier; however, reasonable care must be taken to avoid snagging the fabric.

Begin stuffing by inserting a large wad of filling into top of head, pack firmly with tool. Continue filling evenly all around until head is about half full, then start filling cheeks. Push a large wad of filling up into the front and side of one cheek starting from center of chin. The trimmed seams are pushed backwards as you stuff. Try to achieve a smoothly rounded cheek. Next, add filling in other cheek, the same way, checking so that both sides are evenly rounded. Press your thumbs across eye area to make sure it is even and smooth across. Now add filling firmly into sides and back of head.

When you are satisfied with the shape of the head, pack filling firmly into neck and body. Fill body only about two-thirds full and pin shut for now. (Note: If a run occurs, usually by the neck seam, it is caused by failure to support opposite end as you stuff. Apply Elmer's glue over run using the tip of a needle to apply. Let glue dry before continuing.)

Pull In Doll Neck

Babies do not have much of a neck showing, so pull neck in at four points; the seams on each side of Head Front, at neck and at sides of head, at neck, below ear mark. Use a long thin needle and strong button/carpet thread which matches the color of the body fabric. Only a single thread is used, so knot one thread end. Start and end at center back of head. From back, bring needle out at one Head Front seam, then turn around with needle and go diagonally ⟍ to back of head. Pull a bit on thread and secure. Repeat steps, but this time go to the other Head Front seam. Turn around with needle, return diagonally ⟋ the other direction to Head Back. Again, pull a bit on thread and secure. Now, pull in the sides by simply going directly across sides. Pull thread a bit as you do this. Secure thread well. (Note: If you wish, center of neck can also be pulled in.)

Adding Bead Eyes

Check placement of your traced eye dots and nose mark. After head is stuffed, you may want to make some changes. If you do, wrap the tiniest bit of filling around the tip of a toothpick, dip this into nail polish remover or rubbing alcohol and press lightly on red marking. Blot with paper toweling at the same time. Let this dry before making new markings.

Use strong thread and a long thin needle which fits through bead hole. Insert needle from back of head and come out at eye dot on head front. Add the bead, then return to start at back of head. Pull a bit on the thread. Repeat steps for adding the other eye bead. (Note: Never pull too hard on thread because this pushes the eye in too much and is unattractive on a finished doll.)

Doll Nose

After bead eyes are added, embroider the doll nose using a simple outline stitch. Only a single strand of thread is used so knot one thread end. Use a very fine needle for this. Insert the needle from side of head to reach the nose. The same medium peach very fine thread used for the nose can be used for the mouth. (For a black doll, use a very dark brown for the nose and a shaded raspberry color for the mouth. Match this to DMC floss color No. 3687.)

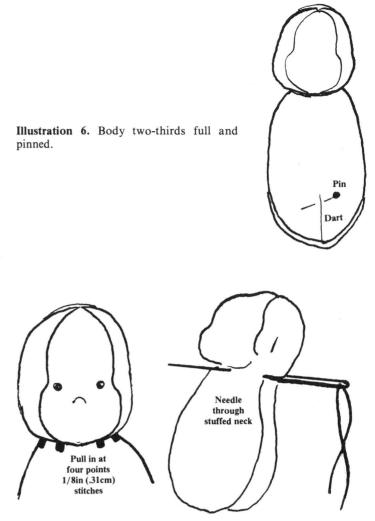

Illustration 6. Body two-thirds full and pinned.

Pin

Dart

Needle through stuffed neck

Pull in at four points 1/8in (.31cm) stitches

Illustration 7. PULL IN NECK: All stitching is done IN and OUT of groove of neck seam. A tiny 1in (2.5cm) by 1in (2.5cm) piece of sandpaper can be used to grasp needle.

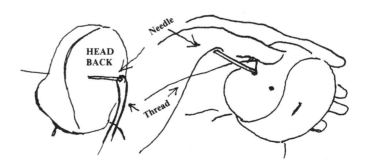

HEAD BACK

Needle

Thread

Illustration 8. Bead size is just a bit larger than seed beads. Size of bead is related to the size of the stuffed head. Bead eyes located across center of head, 1/4in (.65cm) from each side seam.

Illustration 9. Outline stitch.

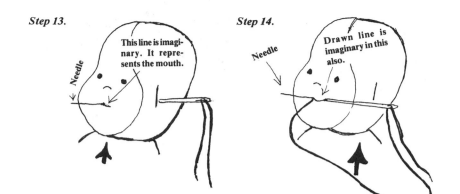

Step 13.

This line is imaginary. It represents the mouth.

Needle

Step 14.

Needle

Drawn line is imaginary in this also.

Step 13. Mouth - Use fine sewing thread and fine needle. Knot single thread, insert from behind ear mark. Pull thread all the way out at mouth corner, but DO NOT PULL ANY MORE! (Mouth location is slightly over 1/4in (.65cm) below center of nose.)

Step 14. Needle inserted from other mouth corner, come out just in front of thread at start. Make about 1/4in (.65cm) stitch. Thread should be all the way through, but DO NOT PULL ON THREAD!

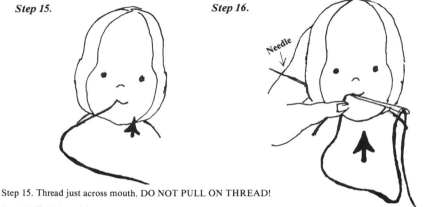

Step 15.

Step 16.

Needle

Step 15. Thread just across mouth. DO NOT PULL ON THREAD!

Step 16. Hold thread, insert needle (above thread) inside at mouth corner and come out in front or behind lower part of ear mark. DO NOT PULL ON THREAD!

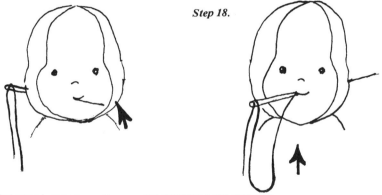

Step 18.

Step 17. Turn around, return to mouth corner. DO NOT PULL ON THREAD.

Step 18. Needle in at mouth corner, out below ear (needle and thread inserted to the other side). DO NOT PULL ON THREAD.

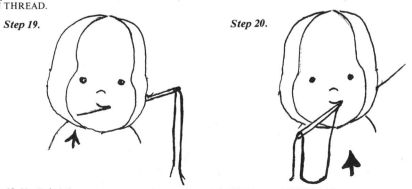

Step 19.

Step 20.

Step 19. Needle in below ear, come out at mouth corner. DO NOT PULL ON THREAD.

Step 20. Needle in at mouth corner, come out below ear. * REPEAT STEPS 16 and 17. PULL ON THREAD NOW. * REPEAT STEPS 19 and 20. PULL ON THREAD NOW. (Note: Insert needle from inside to get to points shown in steps 16 and 19 for this step.)

Mouth Sculpturing Stitches

(Follow steps 13 through 16.)

The ear mark on each head side is important when making the mouth because your needle and thread will be inserted in and out from behind this mark.

Note: It is very important that the needle is above mouth thread in steps 16 through 20. Make sure of this by simply sliding your needle up from under mouth thread as shown in *Illustration 10.*

After the mouth is made, remove red pen markings under nose and mouth thread in same way as mentioned before. Do not do this after blush is applied or face will be discolored. Let remover dry completely, then apply blush to doll cheeks and along neck seam.

Closing The Body Opening

First, check the doll face to see if more filling should be added to cheeks. If more filling is needed, remove pin and filling in body and add some.

Now, turn doll upside down and complete filling neck and body as firmly as you can. Start sewing the bottom opening shut with a "ladder stitch" from one side to the other. It is best to sew part way, then pack more filling inside and continue doing this until the body is firmly filled.

Finish the body by rounding out the bottom with a long thin needle and strong button/carpet thread. Insert needle from center crotch, inside and bring needle out at dot shown in *Illustration 11.* Repeat same step making sure needle and thread are carried over the dart on body. Pull on thread until the bottom is rounded, then secure by going in and out from dot to crotch. Add a touch of glue at crotch.

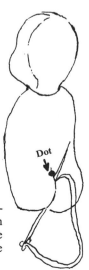

Illustration 10. Mouth thread *over* needle.

Dot

Illustration 11. Insert needle from center crotch, inside and bring needle out at dot.

152

Doll Arms

Turn the already sewn arms right side out and start filling hand part lightly but evenly. Also fill thumb. Check steps 21 through 26. The X's on the hand indicate spaces between thumb and fingers where your needle goes in and out. First, do the thumb space, then do the center finger space. Knot thread end, insert needle from spot directly behind the X for thumb, go in and out twice. Now, bring the needle to the top and return to starting point making sure that needle and thread go over the outside of the hand. Hold thread exactly where you want it, then pull a bit to define the space. Secure the thread by going in and out of X spot. Use this technique to form two fingers and a thumb on one side of the center space and two fingers on the other side of the center space.

Continue stuffing arm firmly, then sew opening shut with a ladder stitch. In step 25, show bend in arm in the same way that the finger spaces were made. Thread goes around the outside of arm. Pull tightly and secure. For the wrist, tack thread at the bottom of wrist, then wind around the wrist. Elbow dimples are made by going in and out of X's as shown.

Doll Legs

Attach soles to the partly sewn legs by first pinning both together at heels and toes. Stretch sole at pins and keep stretched as you baste sole on, by hand, close to the edges. After basting, sew by machine, stretching fabric as you sew. Turn leg right side out and stuff foot part lightly but evenly. Start making the toes. Use the same techniques that formed the fingers, except make sure that you plan for a right and left big toe. A big toe and one small one are made on one side of the center leg seam and three small toes are made on the other side. When toes are completed, fill the rest of the leg, stuffing firmly. Close the opening by hand-stitching, then define the bend in the leg, the ankle and knee dimples.

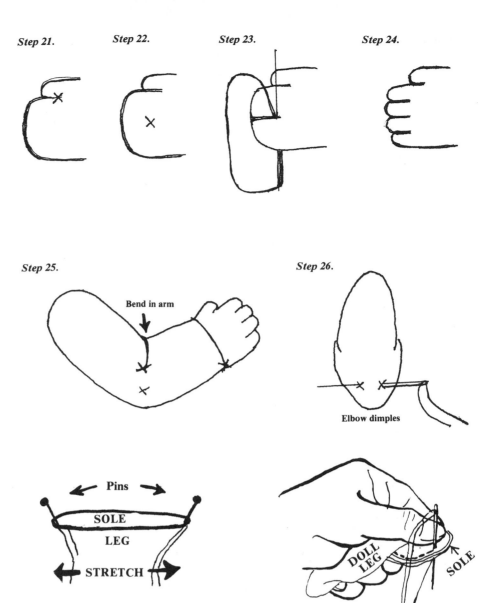

Step 21. *Step 22.* *Step 23.* *Step 24.*

Step 25.
Bend in arm

Step 26.
Elbow dimples

Pins
SOLE
LEG
STRETCH

Illustration 12.

Illustration 13. Baste sole on by hand.

Illustration 14.
Make a RIGHT and LEFT big toe.

Illustration 15. Bend in leg.

Illustration 16. Knee dimples.

Illustration 17. Actual size of fur pile, soft and even.

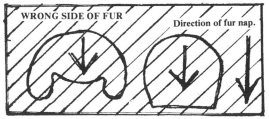

WRONG SIDE OF FUR

Direction of fur nap.

Trace patterns on backing.

Illustration 18.

Illustration 19. Ready for sewing (use 1/2in [1.3cm] sequin pins).

A.

Pin front to back wrong side

B.

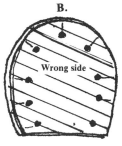

Wrong side

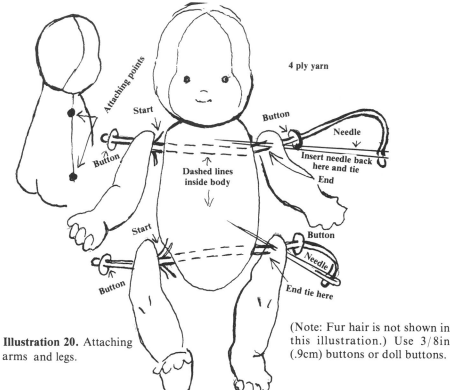

Attaching points

Start

Button

Button

Dashed lines inside body

Button

Needle

Insert needle back here and tie

End

4 ply yarn

Start

Button

Button

Needle

End tie here

Illustration 20. Attaching arms and legs.

(Note: Fur hair is not shown in this illustration.) Use 3/8in (.9cm) buttons or doll buttons.

Doll Hair

Before attaching the arms and legs to the body, make the fur hair and stitch it in place. Choose a very soft lightweight fur that has an even 3/8in (.9cm) pile and a thin slightly stretchy backing. Stretch the backing, by hand, in all directions before tracing the patterns.

Place the two patterns on the backing, checking carefully that fur nap runs in the proper direction. Use a ballpoint pen to trace around the hair patterns, then carefully cut parts out on your traced line through the fur backing only.

With right sides of Hair Front and Hair Back facing, start pinning together. Check *Illustration 20.* As you pin, push the fur inside, stretch the backing so parts fit well and make sure pins will be on top of fabric for machine sewing.

Stitch the pinned hair by machine, stretching the fabric as you sew. Turn sewn hair right side out and again, stretch it out. Try the fur hair on your doll's head and check for loose areas along top and sides. Pin any loose area to mark the place for restitching but do not worry about length of head front at this time. This part can easily be trimmed after the other parts fit.

Restitch any part of head top or sides, then try the hair on doll's head again. Now you can trim the *backing only* along head front areas that need it. After this, use regular stickpins and pin the hair on doll's head, pulling hair for a snug fit before stitching it on. Use a 5in (12.7cm) long very thin needle and extra-strong button/carpet thread which matches the fur hair color. Note: The back part of the hair can be turned to the inside or trimmed for the length you want. Knot one thread end.

Insert needle under hair to hide the knot, then bring needle to the outside. Stitch the hair onto head securely by going in and out through the stuffed head. With the tip of the needle, push fur nap aside as you stitch and also keep pulling down on the fur fabric. Make sure that hair is sewn on through all areas, secure needle by going in and out a few times before cutting thread. The fur hair can be brushed carefully with a wire brush, old toothbrush or hairbrush, but be careful not to snag face fabric.

Now the arms and legs can be attached to the body.

Attaching The Arms And Legs

For attaching the limbs, you need four 3/8in (.9cm) small buttons or doll buttons, a 5in (12.7cm) long thin needle, 4 ply strong yarn which matches the color of the body fabric and a tiny 1in (2.5cm) by 1in (2.5cm) piece of sandpaper for grasping the needle. Tape the yarn end to insert it into the needle, double the yarn and knot the ends. Trim off any yarn beyond the knot.

Check *Illustration 21.* Start by inserting the needle into the inside of one leg, making sure the big toe is on the inside of the foot, pull needle through to the outside. Add button, inserting needle through one buttonhole, then turn around back into other hole and through the same leg. Continue pushing needle through the same leg. Continue pushing needle through the stuffed body, the opposite leg and button. Turn around with needle, going back through the same button and leg ending up on the inside of the leg, next to the body. Pull tightly on yarn, drawing limbs into body a bit, then secure yarn by knotting several times. Reverse direction as you knot.

Repeat these steps when attaching the arms.

The doll itself is now completed. NOTE: The pattern and instructions for the christening outfit appear on page 157.

Note: When cutting out fur fabric pieces, make sure you only cut through backing, not fur.
Use soft, very short pile fur, only 1/4in (.65cm) to 3/8in (.9cm) long.

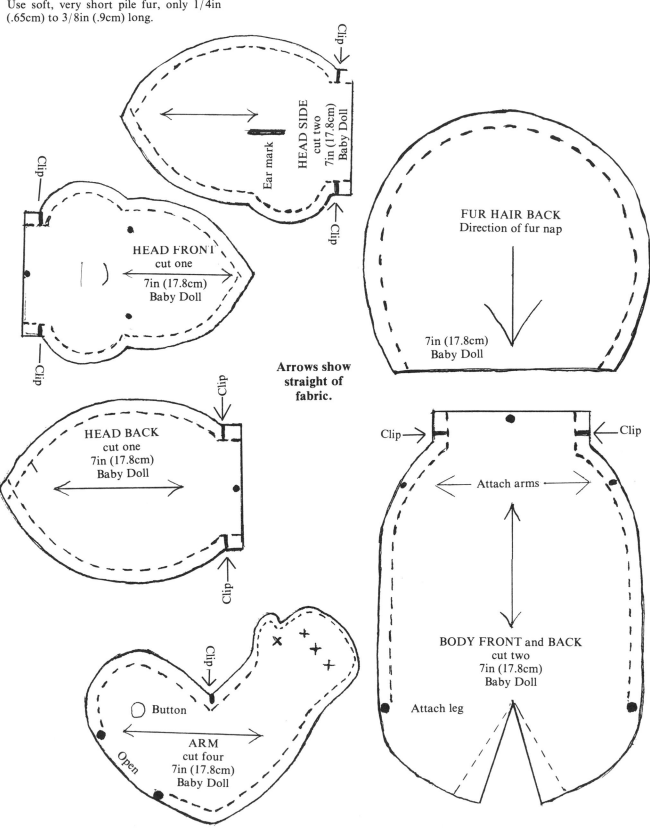

Clip

HEAD SIDE
cut two
7in (17.8cm)
Baby Doll

Ear mark

Clip

Clip

HEAD FRONT
cut one
7in (17.8cm)
Baby Doll

Clip

FUR HAIR BACK
Direction of fur nap

7in (17.8cm)
Baby Doll

Clip

**Arrows show
straight of
fabric.**

HEAD BACK
cut one
7in (17.8cm)
Baby Doll

Clip

Clip → ← Clip

Attach arms

BODY FRONT and BACK
cut two
7in (17.8cm)
Baby Doll

Attach leg

Clip

Button

ARM
cut four
7in (17.8cm)
Baby Doll

Open

155

**Arrows show
straight of
fabric.**

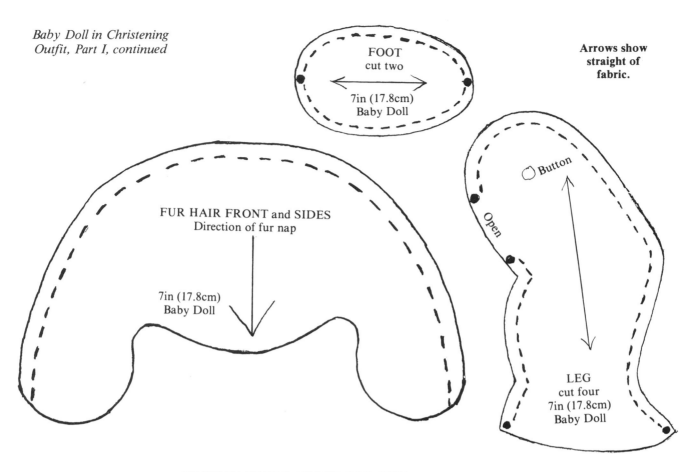

FOOT
cut two

7in (17.8cm)
Baby Doll

FUR HAIR FRONT and SIDES
Direction of fur nap

7in (17.8cm)
Baby Doll

Button

Open

LEG
cut four
7in (17.8cm)
Baby Doll

BODY FABRIC LAYOUT FOR TWO SMALL DOLLS

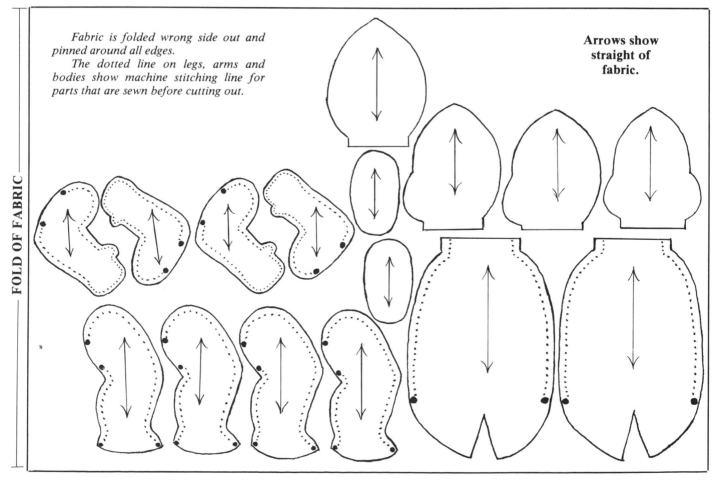

*Fabric is folded wrong side out and
pinned around all edges.*
*The dotted line on legs, arms and
bodies show machine stitching line for
parts that are sewn before cutting out.*

**Arrows show
straight of
fabric.**

FOLD OF FABRIC

Baby Doll in Christening Outfit, Part II

by **Mary Huber**

7in (17.8cm) Baby Doll by Mary Huber shown holding her petticoat and wearing her undershirt. Her footwear is in front.

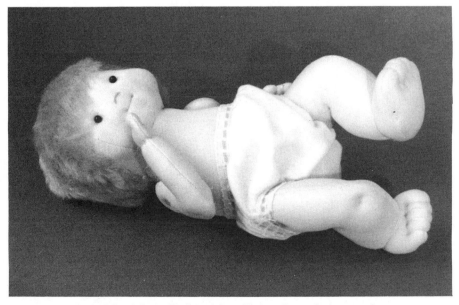

7in (17.8cm) Baby Doll by Mary Huber shown in her panties.

The first part of this article containing the pattern and instructions for making the 7in (17.8cm) soft-sculptured baby doll appears on page 148. The following pattern and instructions are for making the christening outfit for the baby doll. For a materials list, see Part I.

Doll Clothing

Trace pattern pieces on paper. To make the paper patterns for Skirt Parts and Bonnet Ruffle follow the measurements given on the Dress Fabric Layout. Before cutting out any patterns, apply wide transparent tape to the back side. Large pattern shapes could be taped around edges only. This taping enables one to trace around patterns more easily and accurately. It also strengthens the patterns for reuse. After taping, cut out the patterns.

Check the Fabric Layouts which are shown on pages 161 and 162. Lightly trace parts as shown.

Footwear

With right sides of sock and felt sole facing, pin at toe and heel, then hand-baste together. Stitch by machine, then turn right side out. To finish, add ties or applique.

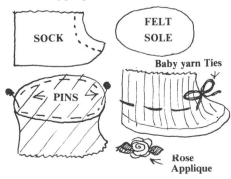

Illustration 22. Footwear for 7in (17.8cm) soft-sculptured baby doll.

Undershirt And Panty

With right sides facing, zigzag stitch Fronts to Back at shoulders. Since the ribbed knit fabric does not ravel and you do not want to add any bulky

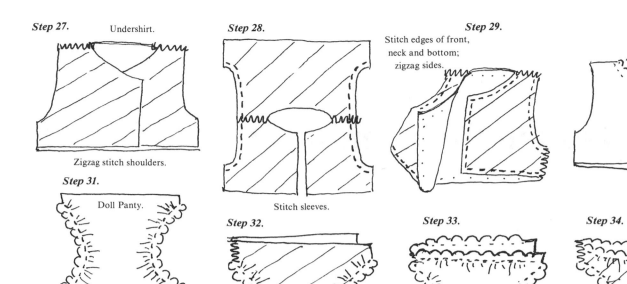

Step 27.

Undershirt.

Zigzag stitch shoulders.

Step 28.

Stitch sleeves.

Step 29.

Stitch edges of front, neck and bottom; zigzag sides.

Step 30.

Snaps

Step 31.

Doll Panty.

Elastic lace along leg edges.

Step 32.

Zigzag one side.

Step 33.

Elastic lace along waist.

Step 34.

Zigzag other side.

stitching to this little shirt, simply turn sleeve edges inside a bit and straight stitch in place. Do the same to Front and neck edges. Turn shirt wrong side out and narrow zigzag stitch each side seam. After this, turn shirt bottom inside 1/8in (.31cm) and straight stitch along edge. The shirt center overlaps and for closures, soft ties or two snaps can be added. Soft cotton 3/8in (.9cm) straight lace could be hand-stitched around shirt Front and neck if you wish.

Doll Panty

First, measure the lingerie elastic to fit around doll's legs, add 1/4in (.65cm) for seam and mark two lengths. Do not cut the elastic until each length is sewn on the panty. Also measure doll's waist, add 1/4in (.65cm) and mark this on the elastic.

Check steps 31 through 34. Sew elastic along leg parts, stretching elastic fully as you sew. Do this on the right side of panty. Make two rows of stitching 1/4in (.65cm) apart. Turn panty wrong side out and zigzag stitch one side of the panty, then add elastic along waist on the right side. To finish, turn panty wrong side out and zigzag stitch other side.

Petticoat And Bonnet

Check *Illustration 23* for the petticoat and steps 35 through 41 for the bonnet.

Only one pattern is needed for the petticoat. The only difference between center back and center front is that the front is placed on the fold while the back is cut. With right sides facing, narrow zigzag stitch front to back at sides. Turn back center edges to the inside and stitch, then turn them inside again, about 1/2in (1.3cm) and slip

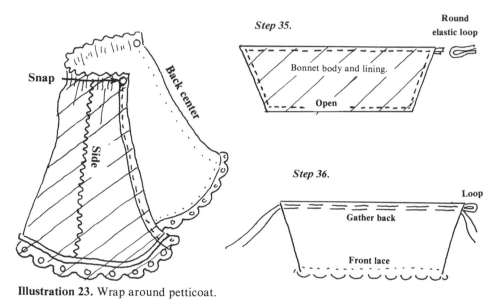

Snap

Side

Back center

Illustration 23. Wrap around petticoat.

Step 35.

Round elastic loop

Bonnet body and lining.

Open

Step 36.

Loop

Gather back

Front lace

Step 37.

Narrow zigzag edges

Step 38.

Step 39.

Step 40.

Ribbon ties

Step 41.

Back closing loop and button.

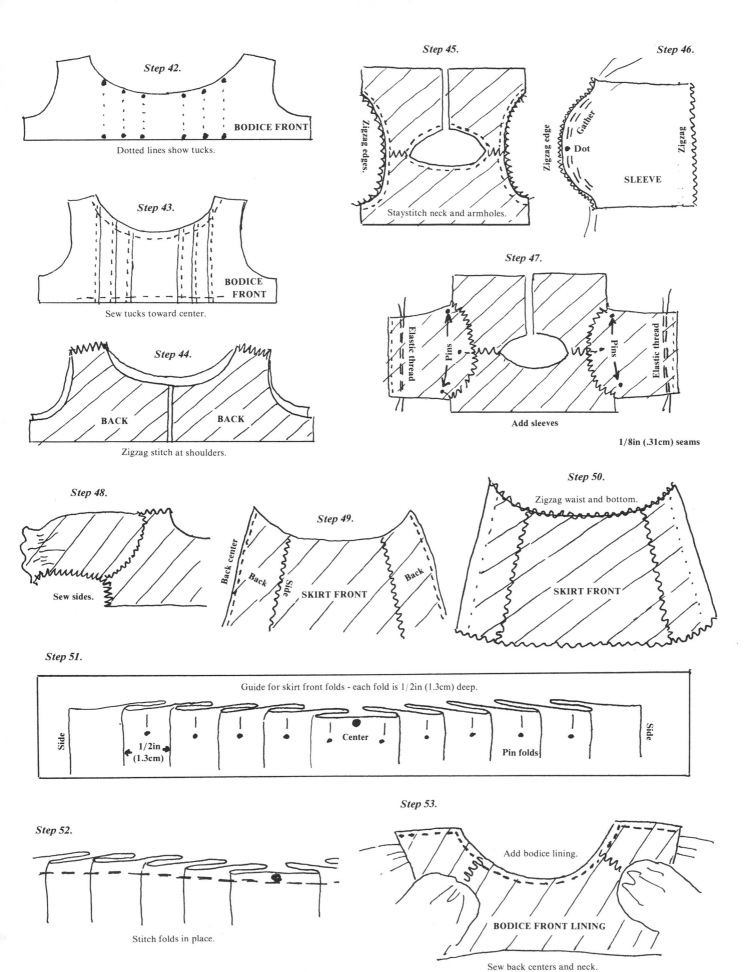

Step 42.

BODICE FRONT

Dotted lines show tucks.

Step 43.

BODICE FRONT

Sew tucks toward center.

Step 44.

BACK   BACK

Zigzag stitch at shoulders.

Step 45.

Zigzag edges.

Staystitch neck and armholes.

Step 46.

Zigzag edge

Gather

Dot

Zigzag

SLEEVE

Step 47.

Elastic thread

Pins

Elastic thread

Pins

Add sleeves

1/8in (.31cm) seams

Step 48.

Sew sides.

Step 49.

Back center

Back

Side

SKIRT FRONT

Back

Step 50.

Zigzag waist and bottom.

SKIRT FRONT

Step 51.

Guide for skirt front folds - each fold is 1/2in (1.3cm) deep.

Side

1/2in
(1.3cm)

Center

Pin folds

Side

Step 52.

Stitch folds in place.

Step 53.

Add bodice lining.

BODICE FRONT LINING

Sew back centers and neck.

159

stitch in place. Narrow zigzag stitch along waist, turn inside slightly and sew close to edges for narrow hem. Apply mesh elastic or lingerie elastic with two rows of stitches, stretching elastic fully as you sew. Add gathered eyelet along petticoat bottom; this should show a bit under dress. Sew snaps at waist of center back to finish.

For the doll bonnet, start by sewing bonnet body and lining together as shown in step 35. Right sides of fabric must be facing, a loop of round elastic must be inserted at back end and an opening is needed for turning. Turn right side out. Sew lace along front end and make two rows of gathers along back end. Pull gathers until back measures about 3in (7.6cm), then tie threads on each side.

Narrow zigzag stitch all sides of bonnet ruffle. Now turn each long end to the inside slightly and stitch close to the edges forming a narrow hem. Add two rows of gathers in the center as shown in step 38, then pull gathers to fit around front end of bonnet. Hand sew ruffle onto bonnet making sure the gathers are even around. Add ribbon ties and button at back closing.

Doll Dress

This is the most difficult part of the clothing and more care and skill will be needed. If the fabric is non-raveling it will make sewing much easier. If you use the tiny 1/2in (1.3cm) very fine sequin pins, time spent in hand basting can be saved. Use them whenever directions call for pinning, but make sure they are on top of fabric for sewing.

Start the dress by making the tiny tucks in Bodice Front. Check steps 42 through 47. Pinch the fabric where indicated by dotted line and sew tucks with no more than 1/16in (.15cm) stitching. Three tucks are on each side of Bodice center and when completed they are basted to face the center. Pin, then sew by machine.

With right sides facing, sew Bodice Front to Bodice Backs at shoulders using a zigzag stitch. To reinforce this little bodice, staystitch around neck and armholes, pulling back on the two machine threads as you do this. Zigzag stitch armhole edges. (Sew Bodice Front Lining to Bodice Back Linings and set aside for later use.)

Begin work on sleeves by first checking step 46 and zigzag stitch edges, make two rows of gathers and dot on sleeve as shown. After this, have right sides of Bodice armholes and sleeves facing as you sew them together.

Illustration 24. The completed christening dress.

Match dot on sleeve to shoulder seams, pin here and also at each end. Pull sleeve gathers and add a few more pins. Stitch sleeves, stretching fabric as you sew. Before sewing the sides of sleeves, first turn edges inside and straight stitch to form a narrow hem.

Also add two rows of elastic thread at wrist, making sure elastic thread is on the inside of sleeves. Tie the thread ends before sewing sides.

Have Bodice wrong side out as you zigzag stitch sides of sleeves and Bodice. Prepare to attach the skirt.

With right sides facing, zigzag stitch Skirt Front to Skirt Backs at the sides. Turn Back center edges inside slightly and stitch. To prevent raveling, zigzag stitch waist and bottom edges of Skirt, then turn Back centers to the inside 3/4in (2cm) and slip stitch in place from waist to bottom. Next, the Skirt is folded or pleated. Check the guide for folding of Skirt Front and note that five folds are made to each side of center and then pinned. Each fold is 1/2in (1.3cm) deep. Folds face away from center of Skirt. For the Skirt Backs, make two similar folds on each Back facing away from center Back. Pin these, then stitch all the folds in place.

Attach Bodice to Skirt. With right sides facing, pin center front of Bodice to center front of Skirt, sides of Bodice to sides of Skirt, Bodice Back centers to Skirt making sure these extend 1/8in (.31cm) beyond skirt. Stretch fabric as you add more tiny pins. Now, straight stitch Bodice to Skirt using 1/8in (.31cm) seam.

Before Bodice Lining is added, staystitch around neck and armholes. Stitch Lining front to backs at sides, then press the bottom edge to the inside 1/8in (.31cm). Now, add Bodice

Lining to the dress. Have right sides of Bodice and Bodice Lining facing, carefully pin at center front, shoulder seams, back centers, stretching fabric as you do this. Make sure the edges of Bodice and the Lining are even as you pin. Stitch the Lining to the Bodice along Back centers and around neck. Pull backwards on the two machine threads and gently stretch the fabric as you sew. After this, turn lining to the inside of the dress.

By hand, neatly sew around the Back center and neck edges, but try to do this so stitches will not show on the outside of the dress. The Bodice Lining bottom is slip stitched on the inside, at the waist. Push seam upwards, match lining and bodice front centers, side seams and back centers as you slip stitch. Use an overcast stitch as you hand sew lining around the armholes. Stretch armhole opening as you sew.

Adding The Skirt Ruffle

Narrow zigzag stitch all sides of the Ruffle. Turn each long side of Ruffle to the inside a bit and stitch, forming narrow hems. Fold the Ruffle in half and lightly mark the center. Make two rows of gathers, the first row is 1/2in (1.3cm) from top edge of Ruffle and the second row is just below this. Pull gather threads until Ruffle fits all around Skirt of dress, pin center of Ruffle to center of Skirt Front. Wrong side of Ruffle faces right side of Skirt and the pinning is done 3/8in (.9cm) above bottom edge of Skirt. Even the Ruffle gathers as you pin it along bottom of Skirt, then machine-stitch over the gather line. Stretch fabric as Ruffle is stitched in place. To finish dress, add snaps at Back centers for closing and, if you wish, soft cotton 3/8in (.9cm) lace can be hand-sewn around the neck of dress. □

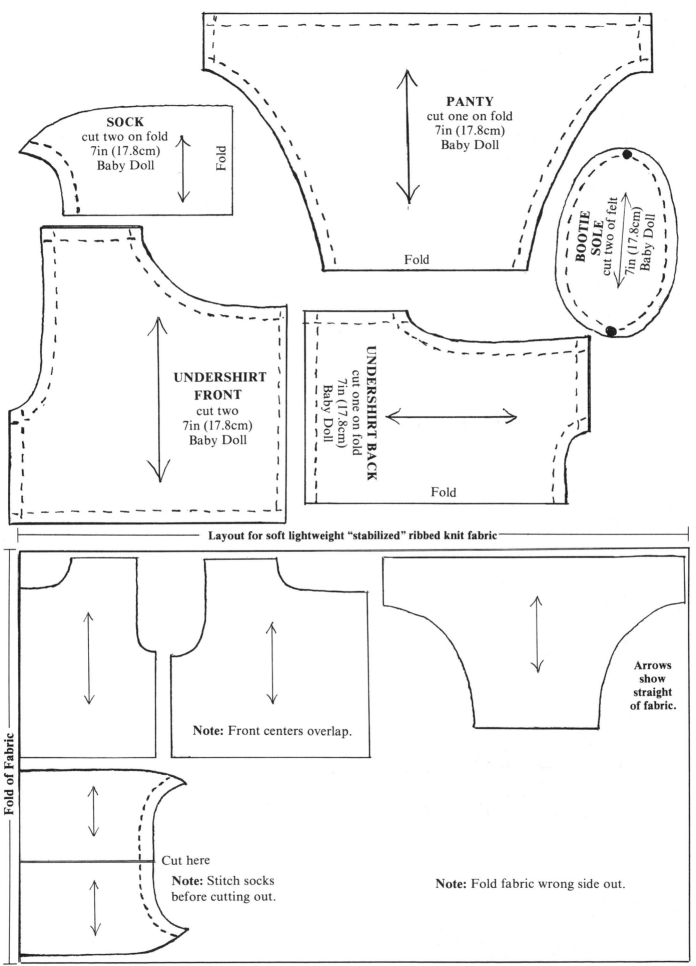

SOCK
cut two on fold
7in (17.8cm)
Baby Doll

Fold

PANTY
cut one on fold
7in (17.8cm)
Baby Doll

Fold

BOOTIE SOLE
cut two of felt
7in (17.8cm)
Baby Doll

UNDERSHIRT FRONT
cut two
7in (17.8cm)
Baby Doll

UNDERSHIRT BACK
cut one on fold
7in (17.8cm)
Baby Doll

Fold

Layout for soft lightweight "stabilized" ribbed knit fabric

Fold of Fabric

Note: Front centers overlap.

Arrows show straight of fabric.

Cut here

Note: Stitch socks before cutting out.

Note: Fold fabric wrong side out.

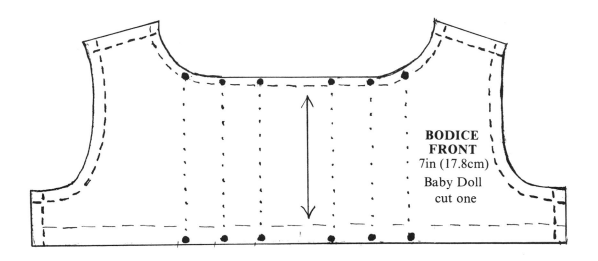

BODICE FRONT
7in (17.8cm)
Baby Doll
cut one

Make your own paper pattern pieces for A thru D.

3/4yd (.69m), 45in (114.3cm) Dress, bonnet and petticoat fabric layout

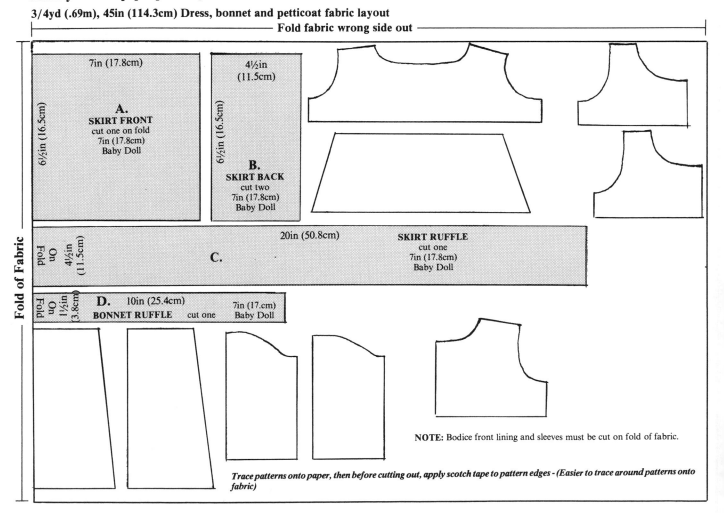

— Fold fabric wrong side out —

Fold of Fabric

7in (17.8cm)

6½in (16.5cm)

A.
SKIRT FRONT
cut one on fold
7in (17.8cm)
Baby Doll

4½in (11.5cm)

6½in (16.5cm)

B.
SKIRT BACK
cut two
7in (17.8cm)
Baby Doll

Fold on 4½in (11.5cm)

C.

20in (50.8cm)

SKIRT RUFFLE
cut one
7in (17.8cm)
Baby Doll

Fold On 1½in (3.8cm)

D. 10in (25.4cm)

BONNET RUFFLE cut one

7in (17.cm)
Baby Doll

NOTE: Bodice front lining and sleeves must be cut on fold of fabric.

Trace patterns onto paper, then before cutting out, apply scotch tape to pattern edges - (Easier to trace around patterns onto fabric)

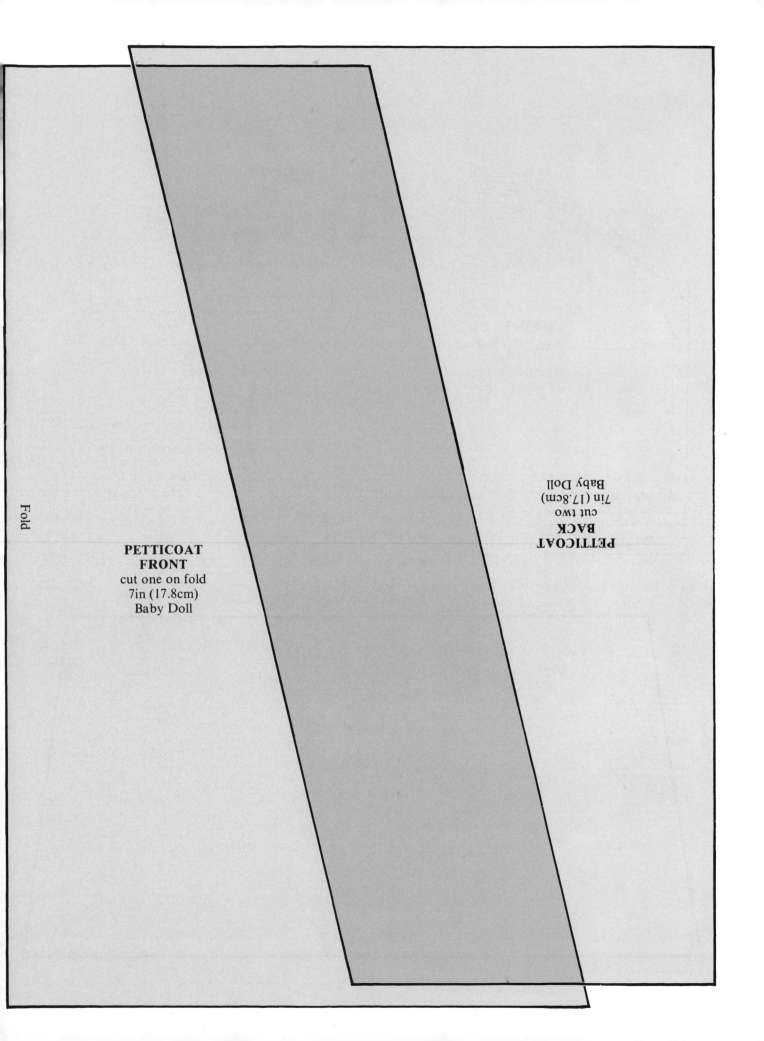

**PETTICOAT
FRONT**
cut one on fold
7in (17.8cm)
Baby Doll

Fold

**PETTICOAT
BACK**
cut two
7in (17.8cm)
Baby Doll

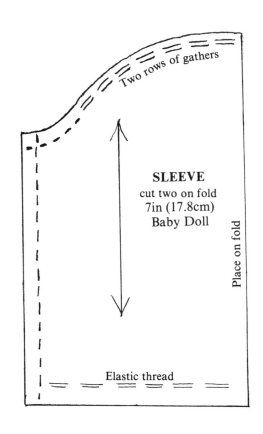

SLEEVE
cut two on fold
7in (17.8cm)
Baby Doll

Two rows of gathers

Place on fold

Elastic thread

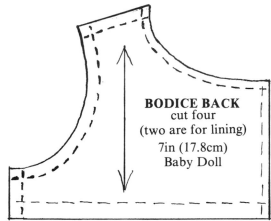

BODICE FRONT LINING
cut one on fold
7in (17.8cm)
Baby Doll

Fold

BODICE BACK
cut four
(two are for lining)
7in (17.8cm)
Baby Doll

Front

BONNET
cut two
(one is lining)
7in (17.8cm) Baby Doll

Back

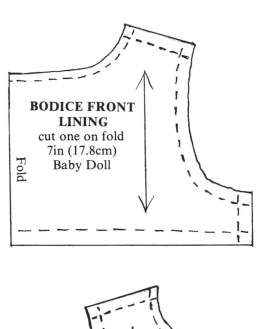

Sculpting Original Portrait Dolls

by **Lewis Goldstein, MFA**

This first article will list the necessary materials, take you through the process of sculpting the head and give you some direction on what to look for as you do each step. With these instructions as a reference, you can practice and play on your own and your proficiency will surely and quickly develop. Before long, you will have a porcelain portrait of someone you love standing before you.

MATERIALS:

1. One piece of 3/4in (2cm) plywood, 5in (13cm) by 5in (13cm).
2. One 3/8in (.9cm) dowel, 5in (13cm) long.
3. Moist modeling clay. Six pounds is plenty. I prefer a stoneware (cone 5 or above) clay, white or beige, without grog or sand.
4. Some small plastic or wooden modeling tools. One should have a narrow, spatula end and another round and blunt.
5. Small cat's tongue brush.
6. A plastic bag. Produce bags from the market are perfect.
7. A turntable. (This is desirable but optional.)
8. A spray atomizer.
9. Plastic Puppennagen eyes. Have sizes from 12mm to 22mm on hand. The size used will depend on the size head you sculpt.
10. Two photographs of your subject. It is best to have at least 5in (13cm) by 7in (18cm) photographs, one front view at eye level and one profile view, also at eye level, color or black and white.
11. A 6in (15cm) or 12in (30cm) ruler.
12. A small set of calipers (optional).

Step 1: Drill a 3/8in (.9cm) hole in the center of the 5in (13cm) square piece of plywood and glue in the dowel. This will be your sculpting stand.

Step 2: Make a round ball of clay about 3in (8cm) in diameter. Then elongate it a little to make an egg shape. Scratch a light line vertically down one surface to indicate the front.

SCULPTING A CHILD'S PORTRAIT

"Welcome!" I am pleased and honored to be writing this series of articles on how to sculpt portrait dolls. In my years as a doll sculpting teacher, the desire to sculpt a portrait doll of a loved one has been most often expressed. Therefore, I would like to share some step-by-step instructions that will help you to realize this desire. It is not difficult to sculpt a portrait, but it does take time, patience and persistence. It is not for those who expect instant perfection or for those who give up easily. It is like any other skill you have already learned. Take walking for example: What would have happened if, the first time you tried to walk and you fell down, you decided, "Walking just isn't for me. It's too hard and I don't have the talent for it. I'll just sit here and leave it for those who do it more easily?" So you must be willing to try and make mistakes. It may be easier for some, frustrating for others, but it is within the reach of anyone (that means you) who is willing to give it a go.

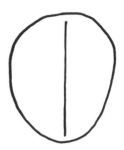

Illustration 1. Step 2.

Step 3: Make another ball of clay, this time 2in (5cm) in diameter. Flatten one side to make a giant gumdrop (you are going to learn so many wonderful skills besides doll sculpting). Join the gumdrop-shaped piece to the back of the egg shape towards the top. We are adding the back of the skull when we do this. We want the measurement from the chin to the top of the head to equal the measurement from front to back.

Illustration 2. 2in (5cm) diameter ball of clay flattened to look like a giant gumdrop.

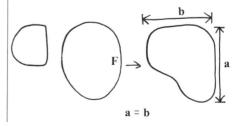

Illustration 3. Adding the back of the skull.

Step 4: Roll out a cylinder of clay 2in (5cm) in diameter and 2½in (6cm) long. Then flatten one end at an angle. This will be the neck. Join it as indicated in the diagrams. Once it is well joined, push the neck down over the dowel of the sculpting stand. Then make sure the vertical line down the front is still centered. Adjust if necessary.

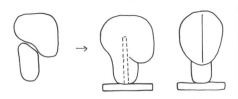

Illustration 4. Step 4.

Illustration 5. A photograph of the modeled clay.

Step 5: Now look down from above. The back of the head should be as wide (even a little wider) as the front. If your head is narrowed towards the back, add clay to both sides of the back of the head.

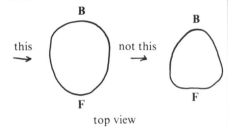

top view

Illustration 6. Step 5.

Step 6: Take out the photographs of your subject. Hold up the front view next to your head and look carefully for the widest point of the head and the general overall shape of the head. Add clay wherever necessary to create this overall shape. Keep referring continuously to the photograph. Turn the head sideways and refer to the profile view and shape the head all the way around.

Step 7: The following proportional measurements are for children about three or four years old. This is just a standard, a way to map out the features of the head. You must refer to your photograph for any deviations in this standard.

Measure from the chin to the top of the head and divide the head in half with a light horizontal line across the front of the face. Then divide the lower half in half again with another light

horizontal line. The top line is the eyebrow line, the second indicates the bottom of the nose. **Illustration 7** is for the child, **Illustration 8** is for adult demonstrations.

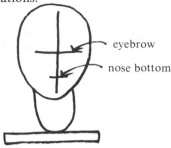

Illustration 7. Proportional measurements for the placement of the eyebrows and nose on the modeled piece.

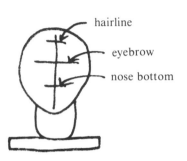

Illustration 8. Proportional measurements for the placement of the hairline, eyebrows and nose on the modeled piece.

Step 8: Carefully press in eye sockets just below the eyebrow line. Be sure to have enough space in the middle for the bridge of the nose. Children have rather shallow, wide nose bridges as the bones have not fully grown yet.

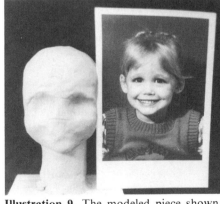

Illustration 9. The modeled piece shown next to the photograph of the child whose likeness is being sculpted.

Step 9: The Nose.

Press in and soften the space between the eyes and round out the indented bridge. Add a small round ball of clay just above the nose line. Smooth the top and sides into the nose bridge and eye sockets. Adjust from

front and profile views to match the width and turn of the nose in the illustrations.

Illustration 10. Adding a small round ball of clay just above the nose line.

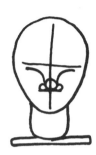

Illustration 11. Smooth the top and sides into the nose bridge and eye sockets and adjust from front and profile views.

Add two tiny nostril balls and join to the nose. Then gently press in two holes for the nostrils with a round-ended tool or end of a brush handle.

Step 10: Lips.

When placing the mouth you must look for the following:
1. How far down from the nose do the lips start?
2. How much does the upper lip protrude or recede? This will be apparent in your profile photograph.
3. How wide is the mouth? How far does the mouth extend beyond the nostrils?

All of the above factors are affected by the emotion expressed. Smiles and pouts, cries and laughs all change the shapes of the lips. In my study, the child has a big grin. This results in the lips being stretched across the jaws and the upper lip moving up over the gums, exposing the teeth. The space between nose and mouth is shortened, the width of mouth is widened and the protrusion is flattened. The corners go deeper into the cheeks.

I sculpt the upper lip first. I make a groove in the clay to correspond with the mouth opening, making sure that the corners of the mouth are deeper (further back on the face) than the center. The furthest point out on the mouth is at the center and not at the corners. This sounds obvious but you would be amazed at how many dolls are sculpted by beginners which end up with concave mouths. These poor dolls suffer greatly because when they kiss other dolls there is a space between their lips! I know that you all want well-adjusted dolls so please keep this in mind.

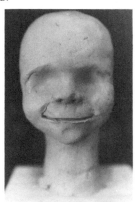

Illustration 12. The modeled piece as the face begins to take shape, especially the lips and mouth.

Then I push the lower lip area to get it out of the way. I add a small coil to the upper lip and work it up to the nose, checking in profile that it is not protruding.

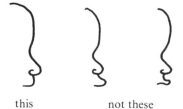

this   not these

Illustration 13. After adding a small coil to the upper lip and working it up to the nose, check in profile that it is not protruding.

Then I form three planes; the pooch just below the nose and the two side planes going back. Finally, I shape the lip portion by shaping it with my finger. Be careful not to push in and indent the lips as they need to be rounded and soft.

Illustration 14. Shaping the lips.

The lower lip is added as a coil stretching from corner to corner. Because she is smiling, the lower lip is also stretched flatter and placed with enough opening to add the teeth.

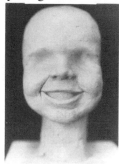

Illustration 15. The lower lip has been stretched flatter and placed with enough opening to add the teeth.

Step 11: Refer to your photograph now and sculpt the cheeks and the chin. Again, always work both sides and the front of your head continuously.

Step 12: To sculpt the teeth, I added a strip of clay into the mouth and curved it inward in the corners. The individual teeth are then carved with a sharp toothpick or dental tool and then smoothed with the cat's tongue brush.

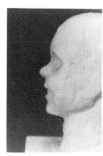

Illustration 16. Side view of the modeled piece as the teeth are being worked on.

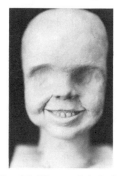

Illustration 17. The modeled piece with the teeth taking shape.

Step 13: The Eyes.

Prepare the eye sockets for the eyes by making sure they are both the same size and same depth. The Puppennagen plastic eyes should be popped in half; the back can be discarded. Choose the

size that fits comfortably into the socket. The right size will look bigger than they should be because once they are pushed into the sockets and covered with the eyelids, most of the eye is covered. Be sure both eyes are placed at the same level and then pushed in the same depth. From profile view, the tip of the eyeball should come to the inside of the nose bridge. If it sticks out too far it will look like a frog and you will know it!

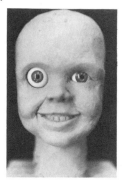

Illustration 18. Preparing the eye sockets and placing the eyes in.

For the lower eyelid, put a coil of clay that is fatter in the center and thinner at the ends over the bottom of the eyeball. It should cover the very bottom of the colored portion of the eyeball. Smooth this onto the face and add a pooch if your subject has one. Shape the bottom of the eye opening to match the photograph. Do both lower eyelids, then go on to the uppers.

For the uppers, add a coil that is fatter on the ouside and gets thinner toward the nose. Place this over the top edge of the iris and work onto the eyeball. The top of this coil forms the eyebrow ridge.

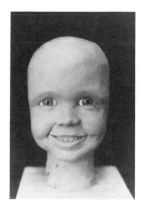

Illustration 19. The modeled piece after the eyes have been put in place.

There are a few reasons I recommend using these plastic eyes. 1. They enable you to start with two eyeballs the same size, with irises to use as placing guidelines for your eyelids. This makes it easier to get the eyes to match.

2. They are curved so that the eyelids will be properly curved when you cut the eyes out in the greenware and size them for fitting the glass eyes.

3. They give some life to the clay head and give a hint of how exciting your doll will look in the porcelain state.

Step 14: Now, once again, put your photographs next to the head; get up and look at it from a distance at eye level, and make adjustments. I like to stick the edge of the photograph into the side of the head and refer back and forth constantly.

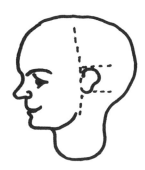

Illustration 20. The modeled piece shown with the photograph for referring purposes.

Step 15: Ears.

To place the ears, hold your head in profile. Measure from the front of the forehead to the back of the skull and find the halfway point. Draw a vertical line at this point. At the level of the eyebrows draw a horizontal line at a 90 degree angle to the vertical line. Draw another horizontal line at the level of the bottom of the nose. The ear will fit behind the vertical and between the two horizontals. Do this on both sides.

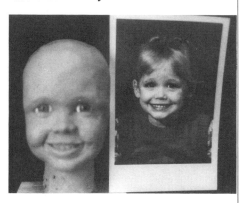

Illustration 21. Placement of the ears.

Make two coils of clay the same size and shape them into question mark shapes. Place one on each side of the head and be sure they fit within the guidelines. Look at the head at eye level and be sure they are not too high or too low.

Smooth the inside of the coil into the head and join the outside of the ear onto the head. Look at the head from front and side and shape to look like the photograph.

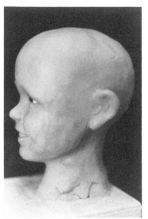

Illustration 22. The modeled piece showing the ear after it has been placed.

Keep the detail simple so that a two-piece mold can be made. Usually a wig will cover all or most of the ears so great detail is not necessary. If you want the ears to show and have more detail, study and model them accordingly and be prepared to make a four-piece mold or a separate ear mold.

Step 16: Next, and finally, cut the neck off 1/2in (1.3cm) below the chin and round into a ball at the end. This will fit into the socket of a composition body or of a shoulder plate. You can also choose to make a flange neck to put on a cloth body. This is often done with baby dolls. A third choice is to sculpt the shoulders right onto the doll head.

socket neck   flange neck   shoulder plate

Illustration 23. The neck can be made as a socket neck, a flange neck or as a shoulder plate.

If glass eyes are going to be used, then slice the back of the head off. A clay cone is then attached to the neck for the pour spout in the mold making process.

Conclusion: I hope this demonstration has proven useful for you. The next article will discuss the mold-making

Illustration 24. A view of the modeled piece nearing completion.

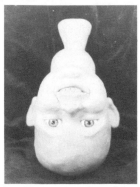

Illustration 25. Another view of the modeled piece nearing completion.

process and the process for refining your doll head. I recommend keeping your doll head covered in plastic and moist until the day before you make the mold. Then let it dry slightly overnight and make your mold. If you take time off between sculpting sessions, keep your doll head covered with a plastic bag and spray moisten it periodically. I wish you all lots of fun and success in your endeavors. □

ABOVE: Left: Illustration 26. 29in (74cm) porcelain portrait doll of Lionel Richie, of "We Are The World" fame, now owned by him, made by Lewis Goldstein. **Right: Illustration 27.** 37in (94cm) portrait doll of Steven Spielberg made by Lewis Goldstein.

Making the Mold of Your Portrait Head

by **Lewis Goldstein**

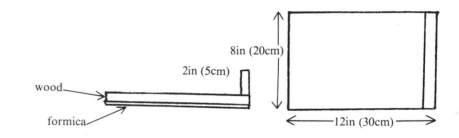

Illustration 1. Mold boards.

"Okay! Now I have a clay head. What am I supposed to do with a clay head?"

I will give you a multiple choice test. You remember, like the ones you used to have in school. Here are your choices to your question: (a) Use the head as a door stop; (b) Let it dry out, fire it and then glue the pieces together after it explodes; (c) Put it on a shelf until the next time you clean out unfinished projects; or (d) Make a plaster mold so that you can pour the head in porcelain and make an original doll.

Since answers a, b and c need no further instruction on my part, I will skip them and write this article on mold making.

MATERIALS:

An area large enough for a small table, with access to water. It must be a room that can be messed up.

A table that is level yet can be gently rocked back and forth. A formica top is best.

Casting Plaster. Use either a pottery plaster, casting plaster or molding plaster. Plaster of paris can be used but often costs more than the above because it is repackaged in small quantities. Buy your plaster in 100 pound sacks and keep it in a large plastic trash can.

Plastic buckets are needed for mixing plaster. The three gallon size used for household cleaning is fine. Any excess plaster should be left to harden in the bucket and then cracked out into the trash. **Never** pour plaster down a drain.

Tincture of green soap can be

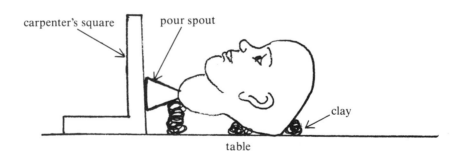

Illustration 2. Positioning the head.

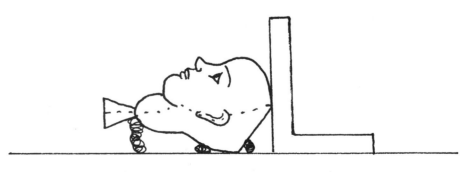

Illustration 3. Finding the parting line.

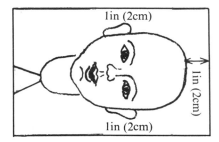

Illustration 4. Box drawn on the table to indicate outer edges of clay bed.

Illustration 5. Making the clay bed.

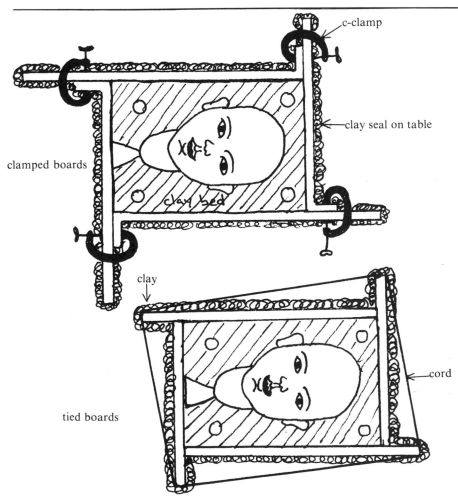

Illustration 6. Clamped and tied options for mold box.

bought at a pharmacy. It is used as a separating agent for the plaster. Mold soap can also be used and is available from ceramic supply stores.

Mold boards. You will need four boards for the mold box. I recommend 3/4in (2cm) thick sink cutouts with formica on one side. An exterior grade plywood with one smooth side can also be used. A good size is 8in (20cm) by 12in (30cm) for all four boards. For those of you who will be making molds regularly, I suggest the formica covered boards and I recommend you attach a 2in (5cm) by 8in (20cm) piece of wood to one outside end of each piece. Use carpenter's glue and screws to join the piece. See **Illustration 1.**

Four wide-mouthed and deep c-clamps for clamping the boards together are needed. Note: If you use boards without the added piece of wood, the c-clamps will not be needed. The boards will then be held together with clay and a cord tied around them.

Moist modeling clay is used for the clay bed and to seal the boards. You can use the same clay you used for the head.

Modeling tools are needed for smoothing the clay bed.

A small carpenter's square is used for finding the parting line.

Various sizes of eye-sizers are used for making the key marks in the clay bed.

A rubber mallet.

A cheap 1/2in (1.3cm) brush.

A stirring stick for the plaster and a scoop for taking plaster from the bag.

DIRECTIONS:
Step 1. Upon finishing the sculpting, leave the head uncovered to dry for about 15 hours. The head should not be dried completely nor should it be soft and wet. Place the head face up on the table top and put some little pieces of clay around it to hold it steady. The neck should be supported with clay so that the pour spout base is at right angles to the table top. See **Illustration 2.**

Step 2. Finding the parting line. We are making a two-piece mold. The parting line is that line which connects all the points that are furthest out on the doll head. It is found by placing one side of the square on the table top and sliding it up to the head. The vertical side will touch the head at the point furthest out. Make a mark at this spot and then move the square over 1/2in (1.3cm) and repeat the process all around the head. Then connect the marks and you have the parting line. See **Illustration 3.**

Step 3. On the table top, measure out 1in (2cm) from each ear and 1in (2cm) from the top of the head. Draw a box on the table top. The bottom line will be flush with the bottom of the pour spout. See **Illustration 4.**

Step 4. Build up a clay bed all around the bottom half of the head. Build the clay up to the parting line and be sure it is coming straight out from the parting line to the edge of the bed. The surface of the bed will undulate up and down but the surface will be parallel to the table top. The clay should not slope downward towards the table. See **Illustration 5.**

Step 5. Smooth the top of the clay bed out as much as possible and, with a flat modeling tool, work the clay bed right up to the parting line on the head. There should not be any spaces between the head and the bed. Also, be sure the bed is square.

Step 6. Soap the inside surface of the boards and place them up against the clay bed, forming a box. The boards will be staggered as in the diagram. The bottom board will be up against the end of the pour spout. The boards are then clamped together.

Illustration 7. Make sure outside edges of the bed are up against the inside of the boards.

Note: if no clamps are being used, the boards are clayed up all around the bottom and tied with a piece of cord to keep them from collapsing when the plaster is poured in.

After the boards are clamped, put a ribbon of clay around the bottom and seal them to the table top. Also seal the corners where the boards meet with

Illustration 8. Check to make sure outside edges of the bed are up against the inside of the boards.

some clay. Wherever there is a hole, plaster will find it and it is easier to use a little extra clay than to clean up a pool of plaster from the floor. See **Illustration 6.**

Step 7. Look inside and be sure the outside edges of the bed are up against the inside of the boards. Use an eye-sizer to press a shallow depression in each corner of the bed. See **Illustration 7 and 8.**

Step 8. Now we are ready to pour the first mold half. Estimate the total liquid volume of plaster you will need to cover 1in (2cm) over the tip of the nose. Put three-fourths of that amount of water into a bucket. For example, if you need one gallon of liquid plaster, put three quarts of water into the bucket. Scoop and pour plaster into the water until the water can hold no more plaster and some islands of plaster sit on the surface. Then let the plaster sit until the water soaks all the plaster down. Then you can stir the plaster till it is smooth and creamy. Note: Plaster can also be mixed by weight. Use three parts plaster to two parts water. Always add the plaster to the water.

Step 9. Pour the plaster into the mold box so that the plaster flows up and over the head. Fill until the nose is buried 1in (2cm). Shake the table gently back and forth to bring the air bubbles to the surface. Do this for about three minutes and then let the plaster set. If you see any leaks, plug them up quickly with clay. The plaster will set up, then heat up and then cool down. You can go on to the next step after the plaster starts to cool down. The approximate setting time is 45 minutes.

Step 10. Remove the mold boards and scrape away any sharp edges on the block of plaster. Turn the mold over and remove the clay bed from the back of the doll head. It will come off easily and you will now have a block of plaster with the back of the head sticking up. Engrave your name, date and copyright symbol on the back of the neck.

Step 11. Take a brush and the green soap and paint the top surface of the plaster. Be sure the plaster is well coated but without excess puddles or bubbles.

Step 12. Once again, put the boards around the block, clay and clamp (or tie) them as before. You do not have to re-soap the boards this time. See **Illustration 9.**

Step 13. Mix up another batch of plaster, pour and shake. Let it set up again.

Step 14. After the plaster cools down, remove the boards and bevel the edges of the mold. With the rubber mallet, knock the mold apart and remove the head from the mold. Sometimes it requires some firm whacks with the mallet so do not be timid. See **Illustration 10**.

Step 15. The inside of the mold can be washed with a sponge and a small amount of water. Band the mold together and place it in a warm, dry place for about a week. The first pour will pick up any debris and will act as a cleaner. It will have to be discarded.

Step 16. You now have a mold that can be used to pour porcelain dolls. The original clay head must be saved to use for measuring when we sculpt the hands.

Because the mold was made off an original clay model, the greenware you pour will require a lot of cleaning to produce a smooth porcelain finish. If you plan to make only a few dolls, this mold will be sufficient. If you wish to make a larger number of heads and want to cut the cleaning time, then read on to the next steps.

TO PERFECT YOUR MODEL AND MOLD:

Step 17. Pour a head in the mold you made with porcelain slip. Pour it thicker than you normally would for a finished doll head. When this head dries, clean it and make any fine alterations you want.

Step 18. Paint a coat of transparent glaze on the greenware. Use only **one** coat of glaze as too much glaze will fill in the details when it is fired. Fire the glazed head to cone 06. The head will come out satin smooth and will only have shrunk about four percent. If you fire the head to cone 6, it will shrink about 18 percent.

Step 19. Now take the perfected model and make a new mold using the same procedures already described. The new mold will be very smooth inside and heads poured in it will require little cleaning. Note: If your parting line is off a little, it is possible the fired head

will get stuck in one half of the mold. Rather than force the head out and chip the mold, it is easier to gently break the fired head and remove the pieces.

You have now learned the essentials of original doll making and can finish your original head and fit it to a commercial composition body. If you have no experience with pouring, firing and china painting porcelain, we will discuss that in future articles. Next time I want to teach you the techniques of sculpting hands so that you can move on to sculpting completely original dolls. □

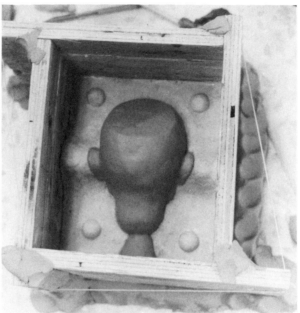

LEFT: **Illustration 9.** Put the boards around the block, clay and clamp them as before.

BELOW: **Illustraiton 10.** The mold with the head after the head was removed from the mold.

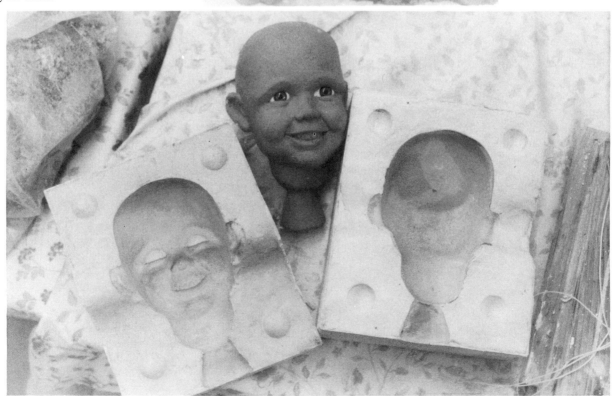

A WARNING to Doll Makers

by **Artie Seeley**

Photographs by **Bill Seeley**

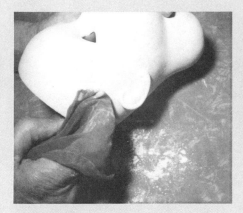

Illustration 1. What not to do! "Polishing" with nylon hose.

Illustration 2. Cleaning a wet-brush dampened seam.

Illustration 3. Smoothing seam with a wet sponge.

Young folks have an expression they use: "Get off my case!" That is exactly what many of you who are reading this are going to say. However, do read on and think about what I am trying to share with you which is for the good of your own health.

Just recently I heard of the second ceramic shop which was going out of business. The owner and teacher is being forced to close because of a white coating that the doctor found on her lungs. The other teacher I knew gave up about a year ago. She was "feeling poorly," could not get to feeling better and, in a final examination, the doctor found her lungs were also coated with a white paste.

By this time you may have guessed what has happened. They were both *dry cleaning* porcelain. One young lady has been at it for only four years. She worked in a classroom with possibly 20 students all scraping away at seam lines

and then picking up a piece of nylon hose to "polish" and blow away the dust.

In the first place, we all know that seam lines must be removed. I remove lines with the needle end of a cleaning tool. Just rub the needle sideways down the seam and the ridge is gone. If possible, do this when the head is still wet. Studios will tell you this cannot be done; but if you furnish your own wet plaster bat and a plastic bag, the head you are going to work on can be kept damp for days. If the head is dry, use the same method and let your downward scrapings fall onto a wet paper towel or a wet cloth towel; or wet the seam lines with a brush before scraping, the object being not to breathe any of the dust.

Your next tool is a very fine sponge and a pan of water. The only place you need to use this is where you have scraped. The damp sponge will smooth

and heal the clay where you have broken the original surface. There is no need to rub the face or any other part of the outer surface of the head. The natural surface of the clay on the head is smoother than anything you can achieve by rubbing. Rubbing destroys this surface and so you continue to rub, to breathe the dust, to fill your lungs, and, who knows -- you may be next! If you think I am trying to scare you, just remember, I am!

If you must work on a dry piece, *always* wear a mask, work over a wet towel and do not blow the dust on your neighbor or anywhere else.

Think about this: Think of the people working in clay who have already been breathing it. Once in the lungs, the clay settles and stays there. There is no cure. It does not just go away.

Now, I am "off your case." You are on your own. Good luck!! Most important, good health! □

Greenware Cleaning:
For a Finer Bisque — and Dustless!

by **Patti Chaddock**

Photographs by **B. J. & P. M. Chaddock**

Illustration 1. *The work area showing the placement of supplies and equipment.*

RIGHT: Illustration 2. *Place a facial tissue on the work area and keep it damp while working.*

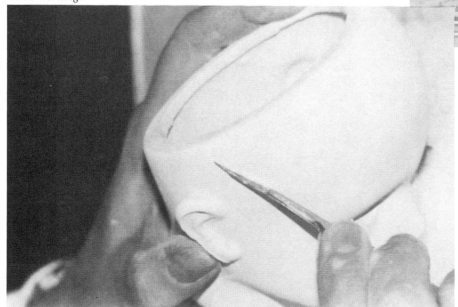

Illustration 3. *Remove the seams by shaving with a scalpel or similar knife.*

Upon opening a doll studio for the first time in the spring of 1986, the problem of greenware "dust" arose, not only in the studio but where the studio opened into the house. This was about the same time that the "health hazard" was receiving much notoriety. After working with methods which were not successful in controlling the dust, I began experimenting with other methods and came up with a workable technique.

With a little practice, one can shorten the time spent cleaning greenware WITHOUT altering the contours of the modeling (even being able to repair defects in the surface of greenware without alteration) and having a

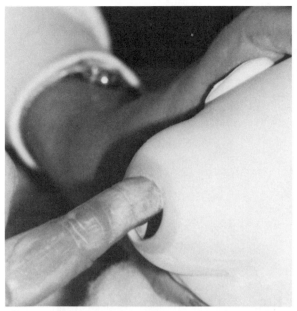

Illustration 4. *For rough edges, dip your finger into the solution cup and run the solution around the edges to smooth the roughness.*

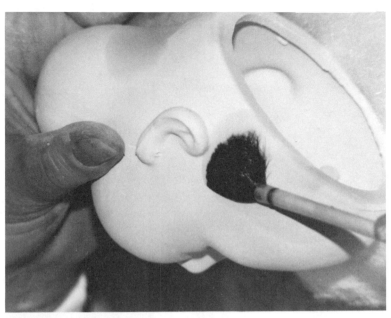

Illustration 5. *Dipping the china mop into the solution, place FLAT on the seam and, with a side-to-side movement, work down the seam.*

finer smoother finish to the fired bisque. Now, even a CRACKED head no longer need be considered a loss.

MATERIALS:
Spray bottle filled with water.
Facial tissues.
Ultra fine tulle.
Cleaning knife.
Lint free towel.
Two terry cloth hand towels.
Small plastic tray, approximately 4in (8cm) by 6in (15cm).
Distilled water.
Pure glycerin.
2oz disposable cup.
4oz or more disposable cup.
Eyedropper.
Small (number one or number two) china mop with very soft hair.
Small round soft hair brush.
Small spotter with soft hair.
Stylus.
Loop tool.
Head, poured in WHITE porcelain slip, dried one-third the normal drying time with eyes cut and all repairs made.*
8oz applicator bottle with a closable top filled with 7oz of porcelain white slip, the same as the head, and 1oz of glycerin, well shaken.

*Instructions for repairs are at the end of the article.

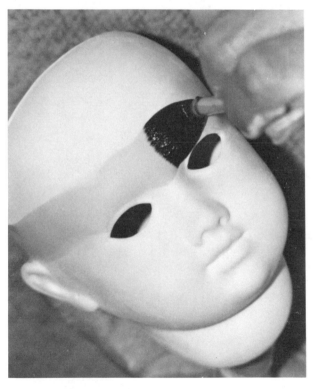

Illustration 6. *Starting above the ear, draw brush straight across the forehead, above the eyes, to above the other ear.*

It is very helpful, but not necessary, to have a fan of some description to cool dry the head as you work. I use an air cleaner, the kind that has a top surface grill through which the cool air blows.

INSTRUCTIONS:
SETUP: Start by placing one terry towel, folded once, under the lint free towel. This will be your work area. Fold the other towel to fit inside the plastic tray. This is your brush blotting cloth. Fill the 2oz cup with distilled water and add 1ml (approximately 20 drops) of pure glycerin. This is the solution cup. Fill the other larger cup with distilled water only. This is the rinse cup. (See Illustration 1.)

TECHNIQUE: Place a facial tissue on the work area, spray liberally with water and keep it damp while working. (See Illustration 2.) Remove seams

Illustration 7. *Starting at the bridge of the nose, draw over one side, drape over the tip of the nose down over the mouth and chin all the way to the spare hole.*

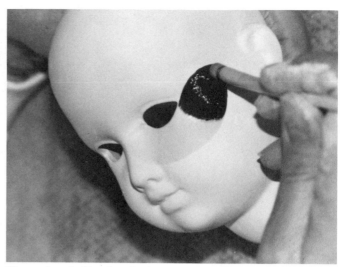

Illustration 8. *For the cheeks, move horizontally from the nose, under the eyes, up to the forehead to the rim.*

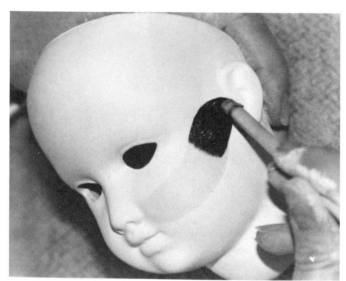

Illustration 9. *Again, move horizontally from the nose, under the eyes, up to the forehead to the rim.*

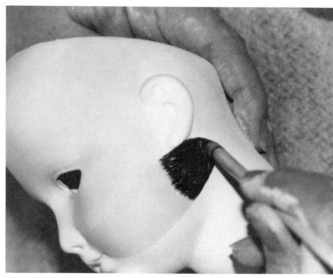

Illustration 10. *Move horizontally from the nose, up to the ear.*

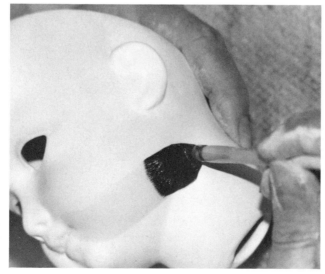

Illustration 11. *Move horizontally from the nose under the cheek up to the ear.*

using a scalpel or similar knife. Using only the side of the blade away from you, do not cut but shave the seam away. Use a motion that moves from you. Do not cut into the outer shell of the greenware, remove only the seam. (See *Illustration 3.*) If the greenware particles should dry while you are working, just respray the tissue and loose greenware.

The rim and spare hole should have been trimmed during the pouring process. If there are any rough edges, dip your finger into the solution cup and run the solution around the edges to smooth roughness. (See *Illustration 4.*) ALWAYS rinse in the rinse cup before returning to the solution cup after working on the head with your brushes or fingers. This keeps your solution

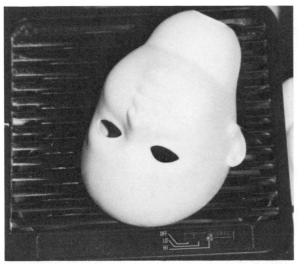

Illustration 12. *When the head is cleaned to your satisfaction, you can air dry the piece overnight or place over a cool dryer.*

Illustration 13. *Cut the eye shape with a knife.*

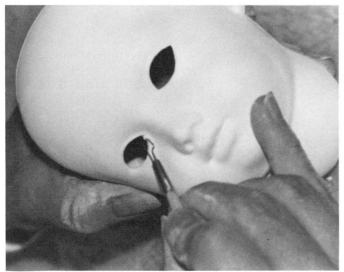

Illustration 14. *If you have to remove any outside edges after beveling, use a loop tool.*

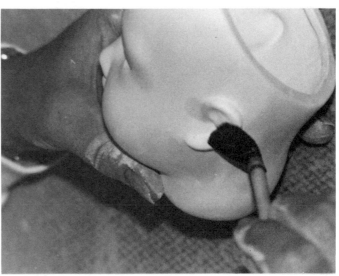

Illustration 15. *Clean the seam from the ear by using a china mop loaded with solution.*

clean. Before proceeding, spray the tissue and loose particles, roll it up and throw it all away.

Using the china mop, rinse and blot on the blotting cloth (do not drag it through the nap as you will break the hairs). Dip the mop into the solution, place FLAT on the seam and, with a side-to-side movement, work down the seam. (See *Illustration 5.*) To repeat, rinse, blot, load china mop with solution and continue with the side-to-side movement until the seam disappears. Note: The success of "the disappearing seam" rests in part on the quality of the mold and the slip used, but this technique will give it its best appearance. I must caution you here NOT to overwork any one area. If the solution saturates the greenware, it will "bubble"

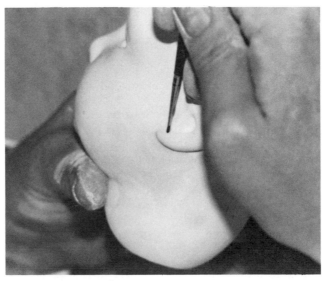

Illustration 16. *Load the smallest brush with solution and insert into the top hole.*

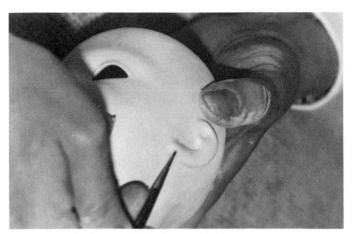

Illustration 17. *Insert the brush into the bottom hole.*

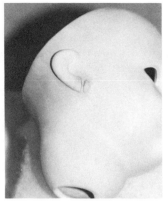

ABOVE LEFT: Illustration 18. *If you break the lobe, cut a channel where the hole should be.*

ABOVE RIGHT: Illustration 19. *Place a large corsage pin in the channel, moisten with solution, take the bottle filled with matching slip with glycerin added, shake it well and pour a dot onto the tissue. Use a small brush and cover the pin and channel with prepared slip.*

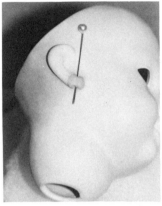

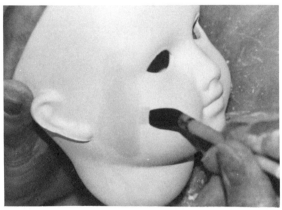

ABOVE LEFT: Illustration 20. *Repeat the addition of slip until the lobe is level and smooth.*

ABOVE RIGHT: Illustration 21. *Try to remove a hole with the side-to-side movement.*

and it is irreparable. Watch the inside of the head. If it appears wet, move on to another spot or place over a cool air dryer, not hot, such as an air cleaner, and work on another head. I usually work on three to four heads at a time.

The side-to-side movement is only used on areas to be evened, such as seams, or areas to be repaired, such as pock marks or slight growth marks. On all other areas, a very light pressured straight movement is desirable. The side-to-side movement picks up and fills in and the straight movement smoothens. The side-to-side movement requires more pressure than the straight movement.

After the seams are thoroughly cleaned, move next to the forehead. It is a good idea to remember to hold the head so that any drips that may occur will run onto an insignificant area. If you constantly have drips and runs, you may be overloading the solution into the brush. Try holding the brush on the rim of the cup for a moment to remove excess. Start above the ear and draw

the brush straight across the forehead, above the eyes, to above the other ear. (See *Illustration 6.*) Rinse, blot and reload the brush and move up to the next area parallel until the forehead area has been covered. Watch the areas behind the brush as you work. Here you will be able to detect defects in the greenware and cracks; in fact, they jump right out at you. If at any time you find a hole that the side-to-side movement will not remove or a crack, stop the cleaning technique to make repairs. See the instructions at the end of this article.

Next, go to the nose, mouth and chin area. Start at the bridge of the nose and draw over one side, drape over the tip of the nose down over the mouth and chin all the way to the spare hole. (See *Illustration 7.*) Rinse, blot, reload and do the other side, then the center. Keep your touch super light in this area. Note: If your head had yellow crust on the features, it will disappear with this technique.

Now for the cheeks. Move horizontally from the nose, under the eyes, up

to the forehead to the rim. Move in spoke fashion until you have covered the whole cheek area on both sides. (See *Illustrations 8, 9, 10* and *11.*) If you will try not to lift your brush before reaching an edge (that is, the rim, the back of the head or the spare hole), you will have a much finer finished product. You should be getting the hang of it by now.

Finish with the ears and the back of the head and sign your name and date. Then check the entire head for areas that may need more work. You may go over imperfect areas repeatedly until you get it smooth. Just remember not to saturate the greenware. Keep moving. Work on another area and come back to the trouble spot or use a cool dryer to speed things along. It is a good time to check your rinse water, especially if you have more work to do. If it is cloudy, change it now or at any other time it appears too cloudy. Incidentally, that cloudy water that you pour down the drain is the dust that would normally float through your air.

When you have it cleaned to your satisfaction, you can air dry it overnight or place it over a cool dryer. (See *Illustration 12.*) It must be dry to the touch and eye, but it is not necessary to dry it for days. While it is okay to soft fire, it is NOT necessary. Any crust has been removed with this method. The bisque is stronger through firing and the finished fired bisque appears whiter. You MUST fire slowly, to a true cone 6, at least two-and-a-half to three hours on low, three to four hours on medium and

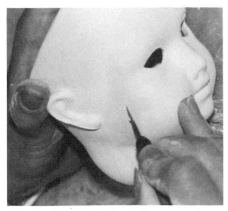

Illustration 22. *If the hole cannot be removed with the side-to-side movement, enlarge it with a stylus, making the hole irregular in depth and shape.*

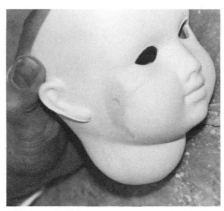

Illustration 23. *Moisten the hole with solution.*

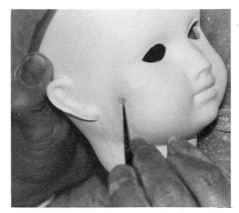

Illustration 24. *Using one of the smaller brushes, fill the hole with prepared slip. Repeat until the hole is full and level with the surface.*

one-half hour on high with your kiln ventilated and then closed on high until cone 6 is reached. It is also desirable to allow your kiln to cool, with the lid closed, the same amount of time as it takes to fire, before opening.

This technique has been developed on and for white porcelain. It can be used on tinted porcelain but some undergo a color change, so be warned!

Some porcelain slips are softer than others, so keep your brush strokes light as it is possible to leave brush marks in the greenware. If this occurs, use the side-to-side movement in a perpendicular manner. Then smooth with the straight movement, both ways if necessary. If this occurs repeatedly, try a softer brush.

Always remember to rinse, blot, reload with solution and apply with a light touch. This method takes a little practice, but you will find it worthwhile.

TIME, DRYING EXPLANATION: Start with a head that has been dried one-third the time usually needed to dry clean. In Arizona it is possible to dry clean within a few hours after pouring because of the extreme air dryness. In northern Illinois, on the other hand, greenware has to dry for more than three days. I now let a head dry up to 36 hours to cut the eyes and clean seams. The partially dried greenware FALLS instead of floating. If you work over a wetted facial tissue and keep it wet while you are working, it will not dry out and float. Then all you have to do is roll up the tissue and throw it out, dust and all.

Many of you have loads of DRY greenware in storage (as I do). Pouring

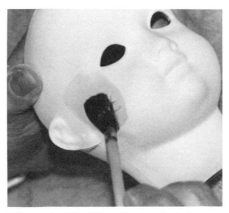

Illustration 25. *After allowing the hole to set up, with the solution on a china mop brush, use the side-to-side movement to even the area.*

is a tedious dirty job and I have done it ahead of time as I am sure you have. Do not worry, you can still use this technique with a little preparation.

TO PREPARE A BONE DRY HEAD: Prepare your work area as shown in *Illustration 2* with a wetted facial tissue. With distilled water, LIGHTLY spray the inside of the head. Hold the head so that any drips will run out the spare hole. WATCH to see how it absorbs. If it immediately turns back to white, it is super dry. WAIT two or three minutes and spray again. Continue to watch the inside of the head. When it holds a grayed down yellow color, it is wetted enough. Now WAIT until the outside begins to cool down. When it feels cold, you can begin eye cuts and do seams.

EYE CUTTING PROCEDURE: Prepare your work area as shown in *Illus-*

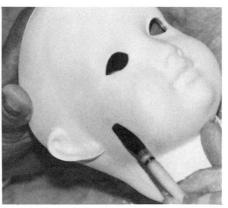

Illustration 26. *Use the straight movement to smooth the area.*

tration 2. Cut the eye shape with the knife as per usual. (See *Illustration 13.*) Cover the beveling tool with ultra fine tulle (net). When the tulle fills, swish it in the rinse cup and blot to remove as much moisture as possible. If you are using a wooden bevel tool, be sure to place it over a cool dryer to dry, when finished, as the wood might swell.

If you have to remove any outside edges after beveling, use a loop tool. (See *Illustration 14.*) DO NOT USE COARSE BRUSHES as they will scratch the surface. When finished to your satisfaction, load the china mop or a smaller brush (whichever is appropriate) with solution and run it over the eye area to smooth, using the cleaning technique described previously. You MUST by very careful to keep your touch light here as it is possible to alter the modeling. Spray the tissue, roll it up and discard it. Place the head over the cool dryer or air dry.

EARS: CLEANING, PIERCING, REPAIRING: If you are working on a head that does not require pierced ears, go on to repairs and clean ears during the cleaning process.

The very best way to pierce ears is to push a large needle through the lobe when the greenware is in the leather stage. If this has been done, clean the seam from the ear by using the china mop loaded with solution. There is no need to cut the seam away with a knife as the mop will smooth it sufficiently. (See *Illustration 15*.) Next, load the smallest brush with solution and insert it into the top hole and then the bottom. (See *Illustrations 16* and *17*.) Repeat, making the hole larger with each application until the brush hairs go completely through. Then, using the bigger brush, repeat the process until it will go through, also. Antique dolls had large ear holes, so make it large enough to see light through.

Prepare your work area as shown in *Illustration 2*.

If you do not have holes already punched for you, a small drill bit, the smallest you can find, will do the trick. HOWEVER, if you should break the lobe, cut a channel where the hole should be. (See *Illustration 18*.) Place a large corsage pin in the channel and moisten with solution. Take the bottle filled with matching slip with glycerin added, shake it well and pour a dot onto the tissue. Use a small brush and cover the pin and channel with prepared slip. Repeat until the lobe is level and smooth. (See *Illustrations 19* and *20*.) Rotate the pin as the slip sets up, then smooth it with a small brush and solution. Place over a cool dryer or air dry. Then use preceding ear hole procedure.

HOLE REPAIR: Prepare your work area as shown in *Illustration 2*.

When you encounter a hole that the side-to-side movement will not remove, ENLARGE it with a stylus (see *Illustrations 21* and *22*), making the hole irregular in depth and shape. Moisten it with solution (see *Illustration 23*), take the prepared slip, shake and pour a dot onto the tissue. Use one of the smaller brushes to fill the hole with prepared slip (see *Illustration 24*), repeat until the hole is full and level with the surface. Allow it to set up; then, with a solution-loaded china mop, use the side-to-side movement to even the area and then the straight movement to

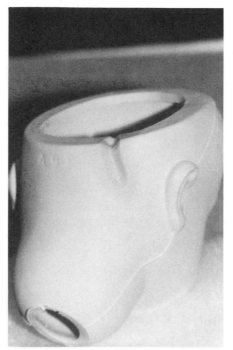

Illustration 27. In order to repair a crack, cut a 45 to 50 degree angle on one side of the crack and then on the other. Follow the line of the crack and extend slightly beyond the crack.

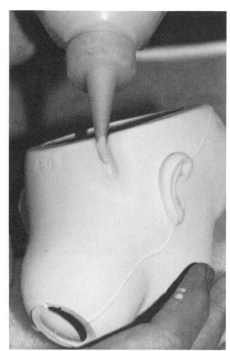

Illustration 28. Moisten the "V" with solution and pour slip into the "V," filling it completely.

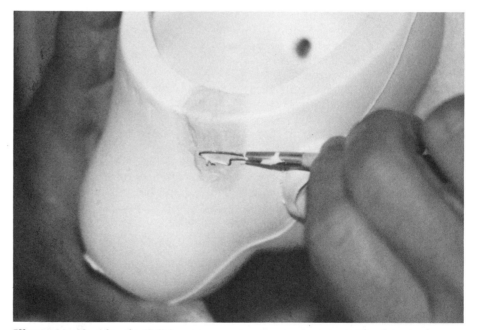

Illustration 29. After the "V" has set up, scrape away any excess with a loop tool.

smooth. (See *Illustrations 25* and *26*.) By using this technique, you remove no part of the modeling. You will have NO MORE FLAT CHEEKS!! The repair is virtually invisible in the dried greenware and fired bisque. Spray the tissue, roll it up and discard it.

CRACK REPAIR: Prepare your work area as shown in *Illustration 2*.

Moisten the crack with solution on the outside of the greenware so that you can see it clearly. You are going to cut a "V" into the greenware wall with the crack being the center of the "V." To do

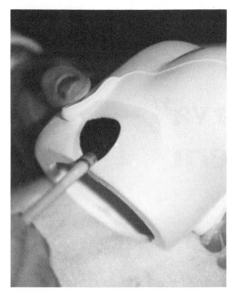

Illustration 30. *Use the side-to-side movement to even the surface.*

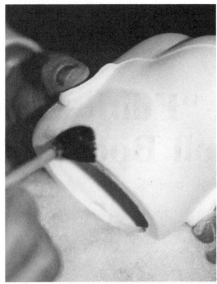

Illustration 31. *Use the straight movement to smooth the surface.*

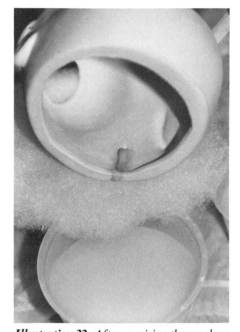

Illustration 32. *After repairing the crack on the inside of the head, allow it to set up.*

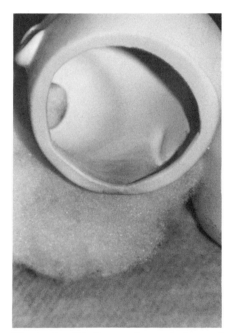

Illustration 33. *Even and smooth the crack on the inside of the head with the side-to-side and straight movements.*

this, cut a 45 to 50 degree angle on one side and then the other (see *Illustration 27*), follow the line of the crack and extend slightly beyond the crack. The lowest part of the "V" should penetrate 60 percent of the TOTAL THICKNESS of the greenware wall. The width of the "V" should be approximately 1/4in (.65cm). Moisten the "V" with solution and pour the prepared slip into the "V," filling it completely. (See *Illustration 28.*) Continue until the "V" is filled. Allow it to set up. Scrape away any excess with a loop tool. (See *Illus

tration 29.*) Use the side-to-side movement to even the surface, then the straight movement to smooth. (See *Illustrations 30* and *31.*)

Turn now to the inside of the head. You will be able to see the crack clearly as the moisture will have seeped through. Using a loop tool or a knife, cut a furrow into the crack. You will be able to see when you cut into the slip that you applied on the outside. BE SURE that you cut well into that slip, then moisten and widen the furrow. If necessary, moisten again and apply

prepared slip as on the outside. Allow it to set up, then even and smooth using the side-to-side and straight movements. (See *Illustration 33.*) You will see that you will completely cut away the crack and replace it with prepared slip. Place it over a COOL dryer, not HOT, to dry. Watch or work on something else, but continue to watch. If it dries without any evidence of separation, you have done it! If it does "recrack," it is probably because the moisture element was unstable. Allow it to dry to cool to the touch and repeat the process.

A FEW WORDS OF WISDOM ABOUT CRACKS: Some cracks are just not worth the effort! A crack in the essential modeling or eye area will depend on your proficiency. Until you feel comfortable with the technique, it probably is not worth it. However, you know that it can be done. It takes practice. Once in awhile, you will run across a crack that just cannot be fixed. Do not try this on any one cracked head more than two times, especially if you have another piece of greenware available. However, if you have paid $25.00 for a piece, or if it is an only piece or a limited edition piece of greenware, it is always worth another try. Even if you have to set it aside until you feel up to the challenge, believe me, it can be done! As you mature in the technique, you will repair as the norm and not the exception and be able to judge the repairable with a glance and discard the irreparable.

Speaking of irreparable, if you have a head that appears warped in the greenware stage, or a mold that continually puts out warped heads either in the greenware stage or during firing, it is not a good candidate for crack repair.

It is super important that you fire slowly, if you have a crack repair in the kiln. Every molecule must reach the same and maximum temperature of that heat level before the heat is elevated. Please practice good health precautions and always fire your kiln in a well ventilated area. All firings give off fumes.

One more thing — while I have been able to do extensive repairs without a cool dryer, the overall success rate was discouraging.

Good luck and happier, healthier, cleaner doll making! □

My Own "Edith Minerva" — A Doll Body Pattern

by **Beth Lincoln Beck**

Illustration 1. *16in (41cm) metal shoulder head doll by Buschow & Beck, with gray set glass eyes, upper and lower painted eyelashes, feathered eyebrows, an open mouth with five teeth and a dimpled chin. Her wig, of moth-eaten blonde mohair, is probably original. The shoulder plate has the Roman helmet and "MINERVA" on the front; on the back is an indistinct number, possibly a "3" or an "8."*

As a small child, I coveted my cousin's "Edith Minerva" tin head doll. I had to wait nearly 50 years for an "Edith" of my own.

"Edith" has an 8in (20cm) circumference metal shoulder head on a fully bendable cloth body and is 16in (41cm) tall. Her shoulder plate measures 4in (10cm) wide, at the back of the neck. The shoulder plate has a raised Roman Helmet and "MINERVA" on the front and what looks like a number "3" on the back.

"Edith's" gray eyes, once set to sleep, are now broken and stationary. She has painted upper and lower eyelashes, and feathered eyebrows. "Edith's" mouth is open, with five molded teeth showing and she has her original, somewhat moth-eaten blonde mohair wig. Her lower arms are quite detailed bisque, but with several chipped fingers.

Made by Buschow & Beck, this Minerva should date after "1904, (when) Sears Roebuck & Co. adver-

tised Minerva heads on pink silesia bodies, hair stuffed," as a new item, as stated in *The Collector's Encyclopedia of Dolls* by the Colemans. Silesia was a strong lightweight twilled cotton cloth. "Edith" was probably made after 1907, when a "new process combination celluloid washable enamel" was introduced, according to *German Dolls for Collectors* by the Ceisliks. This eliminated the chipping and flaking that left many earlier metal head dolls paintless. "Edith" has only minor chips.

Needing a body for another doll head, I made a pattern of "Edith's." It would make a nice body for that spare antique or reproduction head.

Any firm cotton material can be used, such as sateen or light twill. Unbleached muslin would also be suitable, but not knit fabric. The body can be stuffed with sawdust or any material that will make it very firm.

DIRECTIONS:

Trace pattern parts onto thin paper and cut from fabric. Pencil stitch line lightly on right side of front or use one of the "disappearing ink" pens. All seams are 1/4in (.65cm).

With right sides together and small machine-stitches, sew center fronts between Z's. Sew back upper leg to body back, matching O's. Start each leg at crotch and end at side seam. Sew body back/legs together between X's. Sew the body back and leg to body front at side seams. Leave the shoulder area between the V's open for stuffing. Sew the inner leg seam, starting at the crotch, and sewing to the bottom of each leg. Leave bottom of legs open for stuffing.

Turn right side out. Fold "seat" up toward waist and pin out of the way.

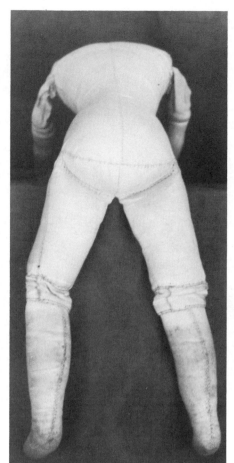
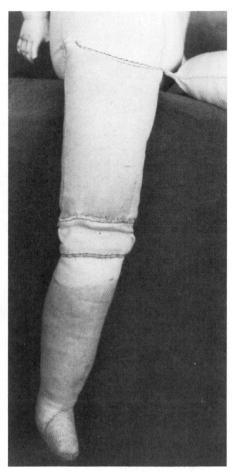

ABOVE LEFT: Illustration 2. Overall view of "Edith Minerva" showing her pink silesia body with knees and hips that bend easily. The body is stamped "HAIR STUFFED" and has a faint five-digit number under the shoulder plate. The lower arms are nicely molded bisque with some chipped fingers.

ABOVE CENTER: Illustration 3. Back view of "Edith Minerva" showing her seat and knee "joints."

ABOVE RIGHT: Illustration 4. Close-up of the knee detail of "Edith Minerva." Note the darker (red) stitching at the knee and thigh.

Sew across legs at stitch line twice (with red thread). Stuff legs very firmly with sawdust or other stuffing material and baste bottom edges together, flat, by hand. Do not turn in or otherwise finish cut edge.

Slash lower leg (foot area), just to the outer edge of O. Baste, then sew toe into lower leg, matching markings. Taper seam to point at back edge of O.

Sew back leg seam. Baste sole onto foot, matching X's. Machine sew. Turn, stuff very firmly, baste top edges together, flat, by hand. Overcast leg parts together, loosely, at knee. Be sure knee moves freely.

Fold in both long edges of knee bands 1/4in (.65cm) and topstitch (with red thread) near edge. By hand, slip stitch bands around knees to hide joining. Overlap ends at back of knee. Keep knee so that it bends.

Stuff body very firmly. Hand-stitch top opening. If using sawdust, a little fiberfill or cotton on top makes closing easier.

The upper arm pattern may need to be adjusted to fit doll's lower arms, also for desired length. Hands should fall just below crotch level. Sew arm seam, place bisque arm inside of cloth arm. Tie and/or glue arm in place. Turn, stuff very lightly, if at all. Fold raw edges of arm top to underside. Fold under corners to taper top of arm. Hand-sew arms to U area on body. Arms should swing freely. Sew and/or glue shoulder head to body. □

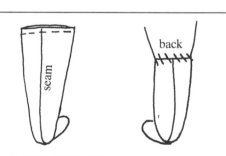

ABOVE LEFT: Illustration 6. Turn, stuff very firmly, baste top edges together, flat, by hand.

ABOVE RIGHT: Illustration 7. Overcast leg parts together, loosely, at knee.

Illustration 8. Tie and/or glue arm in place.

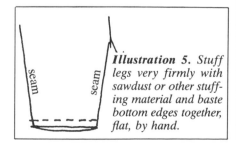

Illustration 5. Stuff legs very firmly with sawdust or other stuffing material and baste bottom edges together, flat, by hand.

My Own Edith Minerva

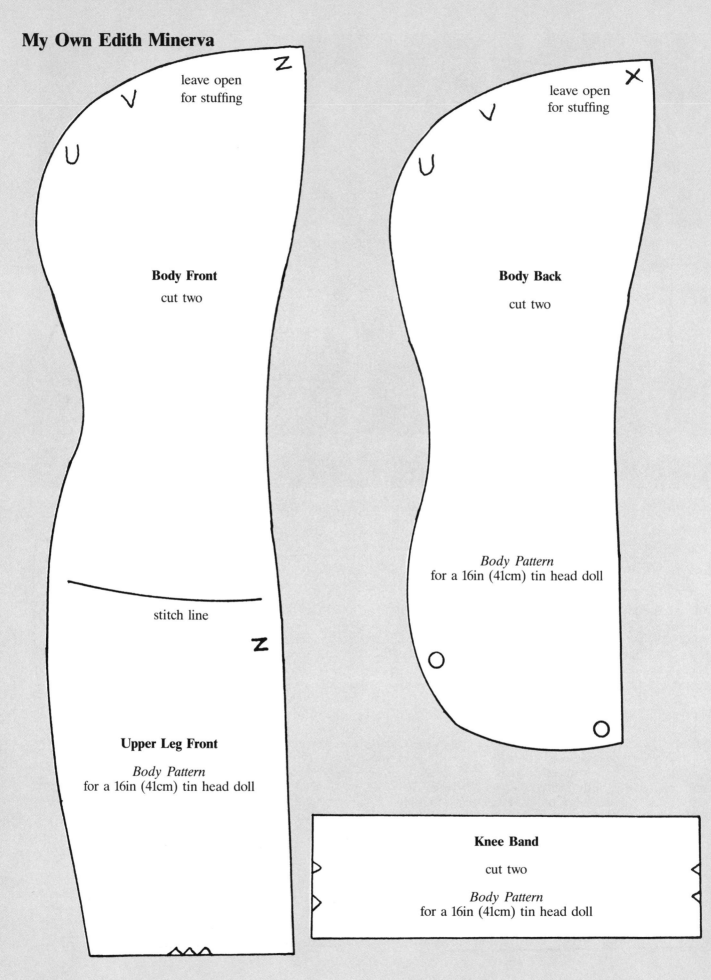

leave open
for stuffing

Body Front

cut two

stitch line

Upper Leg Front

Body Pattern
for a 16in (41cm) tin head doll

leave open
for stuffing

Body Back

cut two

Body Pattern
for a 16in (41cm) tin head doll

Knee Band

cut two

Body Pattern
for a 16in (41cm) tin head doll

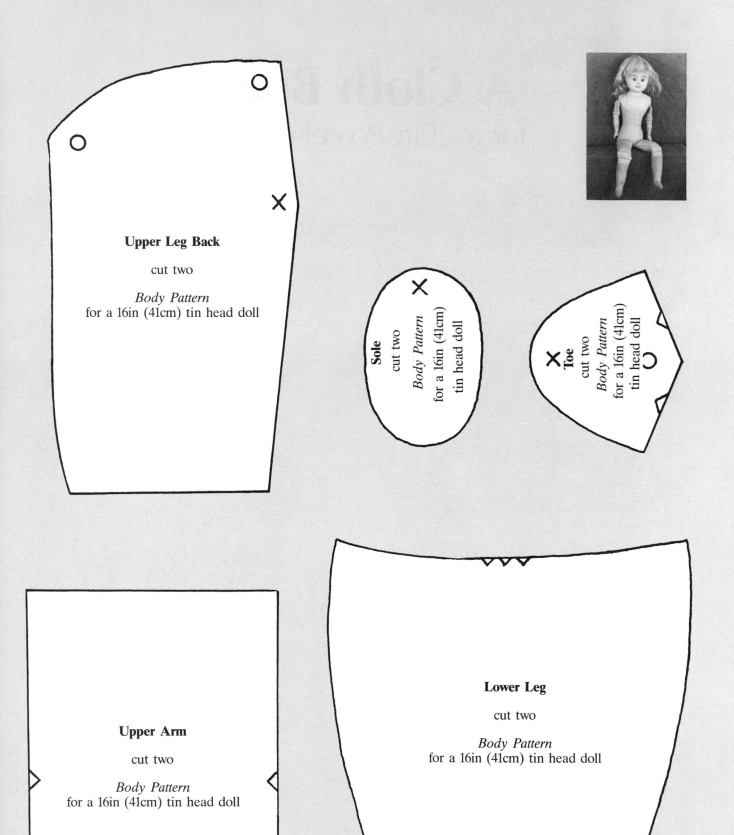

Upper Leg Back

cut two

Body Pattern
for a 16in (41cm) tin head doll

Sole

cut two

Body Pattern
for a 16in (41cm)
tin head doll

Toe

cut two

Body Pattern
for a 16in (41cm)
tin head doll

Upper Arm

cut two

Body Pattern
for a 16in (41cm) tin head doll

Lower Leg

cut two

Body Pattern
for a 16in (41cm) tin head doll

A Cloth Body
for a 20in Porcelain Doll

by **Ada McMickin**

1. Use cotton material.
2. Place the leg and arm patterns on fold of material. Cut out. Sew darts as indicated on pattern. Sew leg seams. Sew arm seams.
3. Now glue or sew the porcelain legs to the cloth legs and porcelain arms to the cloth arms.
4. Stuff with sawdust or cotton. Firmly pack the stuffing to within 1½in (3.8cm) of the top.
5. Sew legs to the bottom of the body after step 8.
6. Place body pattern on material lengthwise of the grain. Cut four pieces. The two notches indicate the front center seam and the back center seam.
7. Sew two pieces together, matching the center seams. Repeat. Press the seam open with a warm iron.
8. Match the sides with one notch and sew, being sure to sew with finished sides facing. This is the side seam.
9. Stuff the body up to 1½in (3.8cm) of the top. Firmly pack the stuffing and shape the body. Stuff extra fullness in the front for bosom.
10. Gather around the top with a strong thread. Pull tight and tie to keep sawdust from falling out.
11. Sew the cloth top of the arm to the shoulder of the body. The hand should come down to the hip line.
12. Glue or sew the head on the doll's shoulders. □

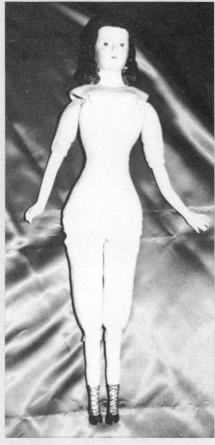

Illustration 1. 20in (50.8cm) porcelain doll showing the cloth body.

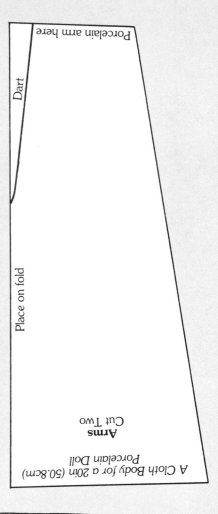

Porcelain arm here

Dart

Place on fold

Arms
Cut Two

A Cloth Body for a 20in (50.8cm)
Porcelain Doll

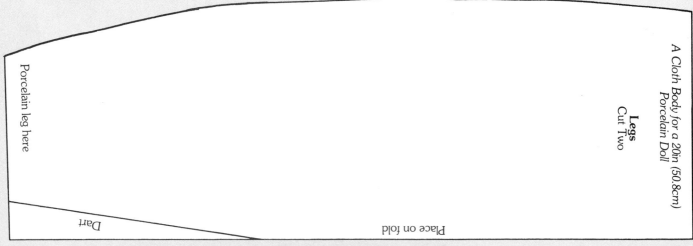

Porcelain leg here

Dart

Place on fold

A Cloth Body for a 20in (50.8cm)
Porcelain Doll

Legs
Cut Two

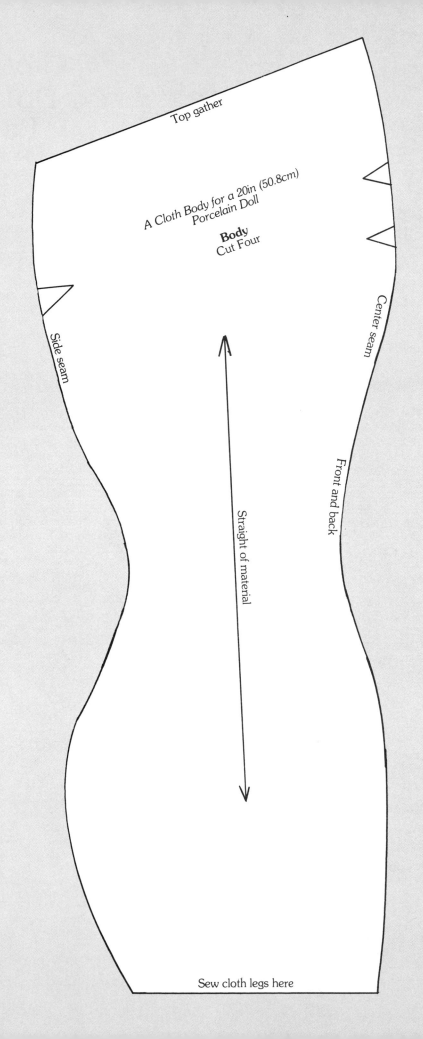

Top gather

A Cloth Body for a 20in (50.8cm)
Porcelain Doll

Body
Cut Four

Side seam

Center seam

Front and back

Straight of material

Sew cloth legs here

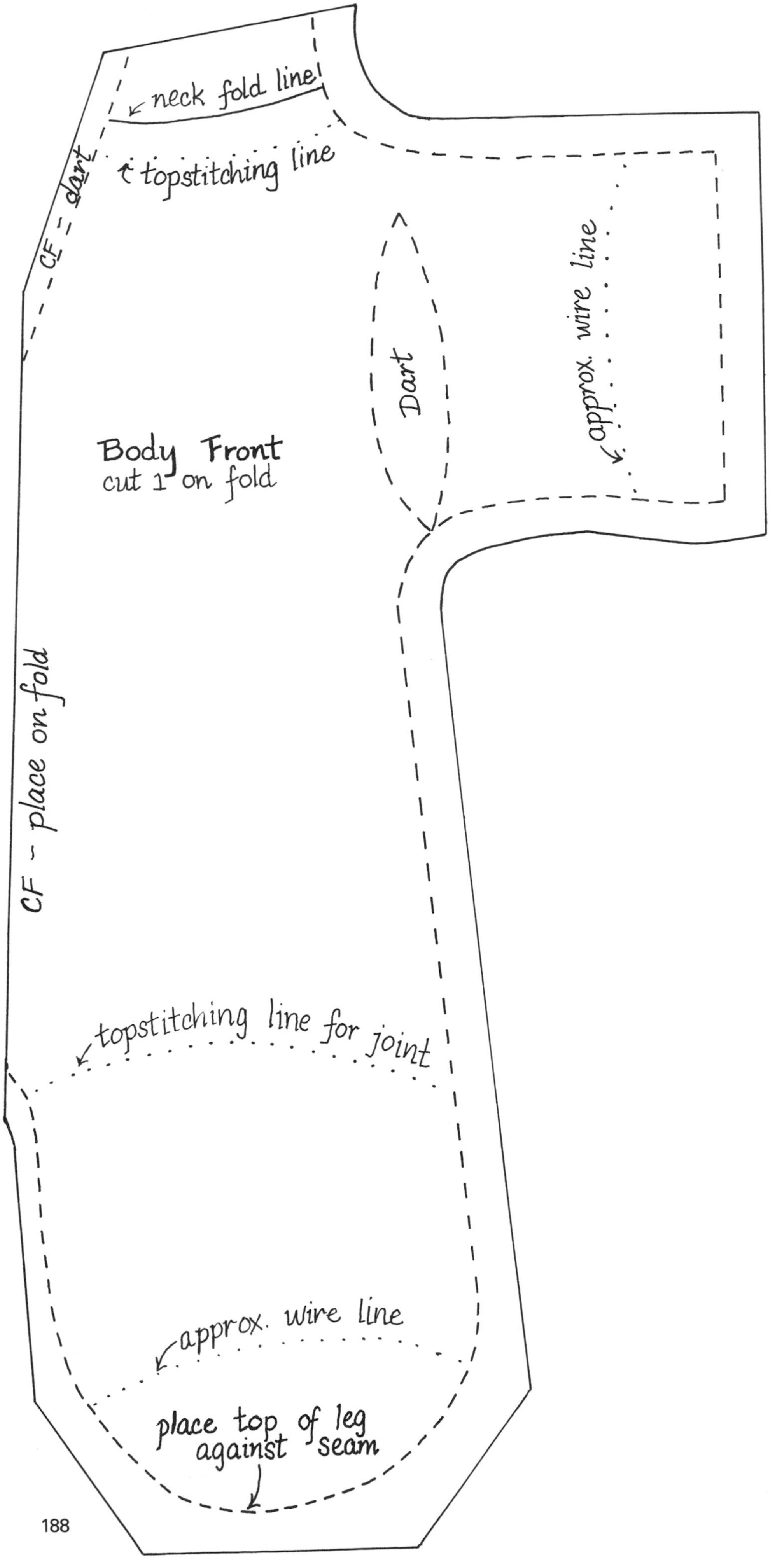

Cloth Baby Doll Body Pattern

by Sandy Williams

The original cloth body on this 15in (38.1cm) baby doll was badly soiled and torn. When I removed the cloth body and took the seams apart, I found that the body was once a medium pink broadcloth and not an unbleached muslin as I originally thought. The galvanized wire holding the body to the neck, arms and legs had almost rusted through to the body. She has a hard plastic head, blue sleep eyes; molded brown hair; red lips; delicately tinted pink cheeks; and vinyl legs and arms dimpled at her knees and elbows. She is marked at the nape of her neck: PB-25 //IDEAL DOLL//MADE IN U.S.A.

Use 1/4in. (0.65cm) seams except around the legs--trace these leg seams onto the broadcloth with the water-soluble pen. Also trace darts, neck fold line, wire guide lines and leg topstitching lines. Set your sewing machine for approximately ten stitches per inch.

Materials needed: 12in (30.5cm) medium pink broadcloth, matching thread, polyester fiberfill, #18 gauge copper wire, mama cryer, pinch nose pliers, water-soluble pen (found in fabric stores), two small rubber bands.

Sew the three darts on the body front. Sew center back seam of the two back bodies together except leave open between dots (this will be the center back opening). Pin rump to bottom of body back matching center back points, then pinning rump around bottom and up the sides of body back; sew together. Place body front on body back (with their right sides together); pin and sew body together except leave open at the neck; restitch crotch area for staystitching. Turn neck seam in on "neck fold line" and sew 1/4in (0.65cm) in from fold around neck to form a casing. Trim and clip curves and seams. Turn doll body right side out but not the legs. Insert one vinyl doll leg into a cloth body leg so that the center top of doll leg rests against bottom seam of cloth leg. Place a rubber band around doll leg flange using the "approx. wire guide line" as a guide--pull cloth leg down so that fabric is stretched tightly across top of doll leg. Repeat with other leg. Gently pull legs out to right side of body. Adjust doll legs so that they slightly "toe in" on the body. Push legs back into cloth body. Carefully remove rubber band from top of one doll legs. Place a length of wire around flange, twist ends so wire fits into flange snugly; cut twisted wire ends so they are about 1/4in (0.65cm) long; push sharp wire ends into flange so they will not cut the body fabric. Repeat with other leg. Pull legs right side out and lightly stuff legs to about 1/2in (1.3cm) of topstitching line; pin front body top stitching line to rump topstitching line; machine-stitch across topstitching line.

Push cloth arms back inside the doll body--insert one doll arm. Follow leg instructions except the two square points of fabric arm are *not* pulled down over arm flange--use the "approx. wire lines" as a guide in placing the rubber band around

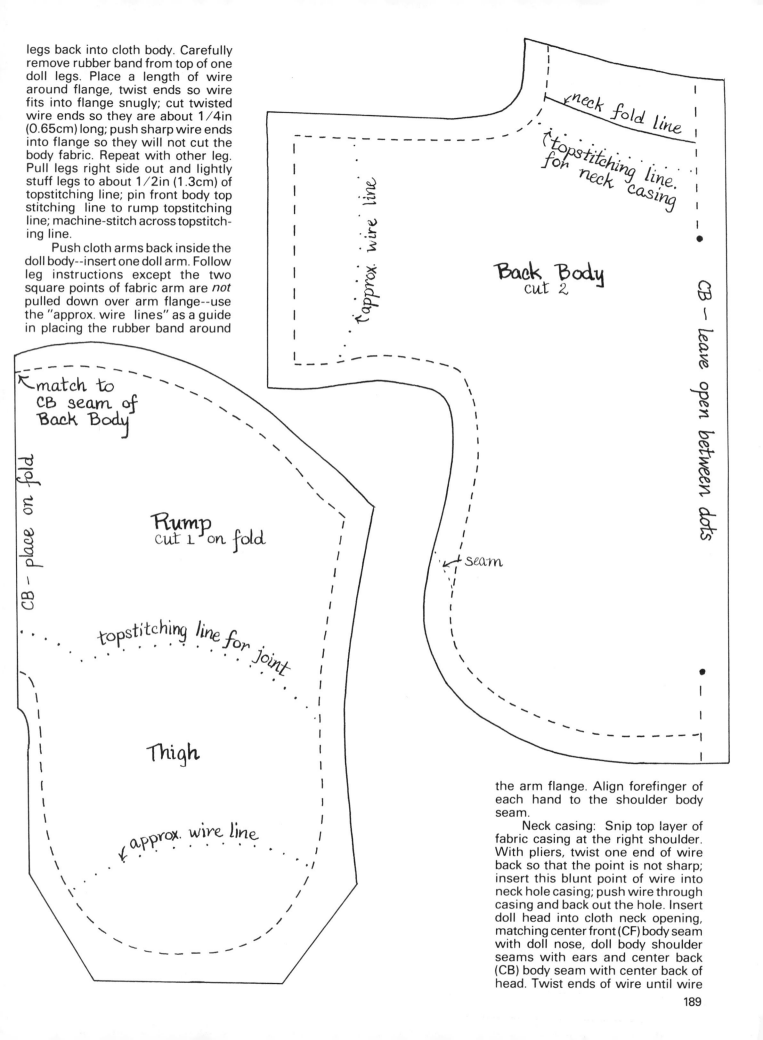

neck fold line

topstitching line for neck casing

approx. wire line

Back Body
cut 2

CB – leave open between dots

match to CB seam of Back Body

CB – place on fold

Rump
cut 1 on fold

topstitching line for joint

Thigh

approx. wire line

seam

the arm flange. Align forefinger of each hand to the shoulder body seam.

Neck casing: Snip top layer of fabric casing at the right shoulder. With pliers, twist one end of wire back so that the point is not sharp; insert this blunt point of wire into neck hole casing; push wire through casing and back out the hole. Insert doll head into cloth neck opening, matching center front (CF) body seam with doll nose, doll body shoulder seams with ears and center back (CB) body seam with center back of head. Twist ends of wire until wire

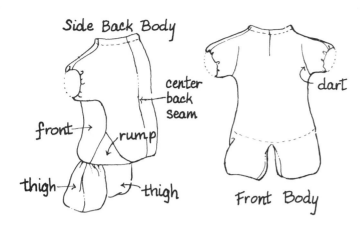

Side Back Body

center back seam

dart

front

rump

thigh — thigh

Front Body

rump

fits snugly in doll head flange; snip excess wire off; twist the remaining 1/4in (0.65cm) of twisted wire back into casing so wire lies flat against flange. Blindstitch casing opening closed.

Lightly stuff doll front body about 1in (2.5cm) deep. Stuff upper arms and rump area. Center the mama cryer about 1in (2.5cm) below the center back neck flange of doll head (holes on cryer will be facing you). Firmly stuff doll body--do not place any stuffing on top of cryer. Be sure doll can swing her arms forward easily and that her legs also swing freely. Blindstitch center back opening closed. Remove all tracing marks of the water-soluble pen by following package directions.

INDEX

SUBJECT

PATTERNS

AUTHORS